THE GREAT DEBATE

BETWEEN

JOHN W. RING

(Spiritualist)

AND

J. W. CHISM

(Christian Evangelist)

HEADRICK, OKLAHOMA
ERNST & TOLLESON
1908

PRESS OF
CHRISTIAN PUBLISHING COMPANY
ST. LOUIS, MO.

Reproduced and distributed
by
OLD PATHS BOOK CLUB
Box V, Rosemead, California
1956

John Allen Hudson, editor.

CONTENTS.

J. W. Chism.

J. W. CHISM was born April 1, 1865, in Comanche County, Texas, and was raised by Christian parents in Western Texas. He obeyed the Gospel at the age of 15 years. Early in life he desired to preach the gospel. He was a hard student of the Bible when a child, being conversant with the Revised Version the year it was published. Realizing the necessity of an education he began the study of grammar and mathematics at home. Later he began the study of Greek. About this time he began to preach, being about 26 years old. His wife was prepared to assist him some in the literary branches. He then devoted his entire time to preaching. After devoting much time to the study of Greek for six years, he began the study of Hebrew, which he keeps up, and is determined to master.

He has been preaching nineteen years and has baptized some 3,000 persons into Christ. Has engaged in more than 100 debates, some of them lasting 14 days. He has met almost every religious sect in the South, successfully. He has baptized two of his opponents in debate. He is now engaged exclusively in the evangelistic work, which he expects to continue through life. He is one of the finest artists in the State, and while he does not work at it, he keeps up with all the latest methods in photography. For six years he wrote life insurance.

His first wife, Fannie Campbell, died, leaving him six children, one of whom, Jack, followed the mother to the home of the blessed soon afterwards. His second wife, Burts Kemper, is a devoted Christian, and an ideal mother to the children of the first wife. She is also the mother of their one child. They live on the Kemper homestead, Lufkin, Texas.

J. W. Chism is one of the strongest men in Texas—a hard student..

A FOREWORD.

B ELIEVING that the debate herein published would be of vital interest to a vast number of people who were unable to attend, and knowing that both contestants desired a publication of same, we, the undersigned, had the debate stenographed and published. It is not for any motive of financial gain that prompted us to do so, and we ask the co-operation of both denominations in disposing of the books. Should we ever get back the actual money expended, we shall feel amply repaid.

Mr. J. W. Chism is one of the leading evangelists of the Church of Christ, a deep thinker, and logical debater, loved by his followers and highly respected by even his most sanguine opponents. Mr. J. W. Ring is probably the widest known expounder of Modern Spiritualism, a pleasant, affable and interesting speaker. His demeanor and flow of language when debating shows that he is a student of no little comment.

It might be well to state that the publishers do not belong to either of these denominations.

J. E. ERNST,
R. E. TOLLESON.

Ring-Chism Debate on Spiritualism.

4:15 P. M., August 20, 1907.

"RESOLVED, That the fundamental principles of Modern Spiritualism are identical with the spiritual basis of the religion of Jesus Christ."

JOHN W. RING Affirms,
J. W. CHISM Denies.

Moderators appointed are—
R. G. LEE, for J. W. Ring.
T. W. HEAD, for J. W. Chism.

Mr. Robert G. Lee, presiding moderator for and on behalf of the affirmative, now calls house to order, and after announcing program, introduces Honorable J. E. Ernst, of Headrick, O. T., who, by way of welcoming the debaters to Headrick, makes the following address of welcome:

"In behalf of the people of Headrick I wish to extend to you a hearty welcome. We have been looking forward to this occasion for some time, and have spared nothing that will bar the pleasure of this meeting. We give you free access to our city with all of its modern advantages, comforts and entertainments. Arrangements have been made with the street car promoters to carry all visitors about the city free of charge. Our natural springs and our famous parks are open to you, and I give you my personal assurance that you are welcome guests to all parts of the city. [After a careful investigation I was unable to discover any of the aforesaid street car railways, etc., and am willing to make oath that they do not at the present writing exist.—H. B. Hopps, reporter."]

—9—

"The occasion of this gathering is a religious discussion upon a very vital question, 'The Spiritual Gifts of the Christian Religion.'

"The two selected disputants, who shall cross swords on this occasion, are Reverend J. W. Ring, representing the one side, and Reverend J. W. Chism on the other. It is needless for me to say that they are both well-informed men of ability and national reputation.

"I bespeak for this assembly a great intellectual and spiritual feast. Mr. Ring is to affirm in behalf of Spiritualism, and Mr. Chism, who represents the Christian Church, appears as his opponent. We all believe that truth has nothing to fear by investigation; in fact, it is like gold, the more you rub it the brighter it shines. I hope that every one has come without prejudice and with unbiased minds to hear these distinguished gentlemen with candor and respect, after which you can render a verdict according to your own judgment.

"The people of to-day are making great strides along educational and religious lines. And as we advance in knowledge and power as a nation we are gradually coming in contact with new ideas and thoughts. Never in the history of the world has there been such a research in Bible study as in the past few years. Men are devoting their lives and their fortunes to this grand work. Cities are being excavated, after lying hidden for many centuries. Ancient literature and inscriptions on stones are being daily unearthed in Assyria, Babylonia and other countries, and turned over to the scientists for their inspection. This is indeed a grand work and a great help in procuring ancient history.

"It is a pleasure to know that in the same enterprising spirit we can meet each other on common ground and discuss our different ideas in a peaceable and pleasant manner. And it is pleasant to know that we are living in an age of enlightenment, where people are free and can enjoy their religious ideas without fear of molestation. And, my friends, if these meetings did nothing more than to give to all an opportunity to meet each other—to make new acquaintances, and renew old ones— I say, if nothing more than this, it were well worth the time to come. It lifts us up for a moment above the daily walks of life. It teaches us that there is something else in life besides work and money, and so again welcoming each and every one of you, I thank you."

Mr. Lee, presiding moderator, now introduces to the audience Rev. J. W. Ring, of Green Mountain Falls, Colo., to respond in behalf of the people, and he thereupon delivers the following:

"Gentlemen, Moderators, Ladies and Gentlemen: It is indeed refreshing that we can assemble here in this so-called new country to take a new view of these old ideas that have so long moved mankind with joy and pain, with light and darkness, with this wonderful mingling of hearts' emotions; and I trust only that we may have come in the sweet spirit of tolerance,—of Christ. You, as a body of people, are, in one sense of the word, a jury here to listen to the ideas which may be advanced upon these different propositions, and you are the ones to decide as to the impression which they may make upon you. I trust that you will have as unbiased minds as possible; we cannot be entirely unbiased, for we are religious just as our education has made us, and some of you will be Christians for thousands and thousands of years after you have shuffled off this garment of mortality, and some of you never could be Christians if you

—11—

were to live in the body for ten thousand years, because
your education will not admit. Those who know themselves to be spiritualists can distinguish themselves by
knowing a thing or two.

"Let us only say in the words of one who has spoken
wisely—

> "Truth crushed to earth will rise again,
> The eternal years are hers,
> But error, wounded, rises with pain,
> And dies amid her worshipers."

The Moderator, Mr. Head, here introduces Rev. J. W.
Chism, who thereupon responds to the address of welcome with the following:

"In behalf of my brethren and friends, I wish to state
that we appreciate duly the remarks that were made by
the first gentleman in welcoming us to the little town,
and I assure him that, for one, I shall use the courtesy
of the free transportation on the street cars to take in
the Park. I think about the first park that I shall take
in will be the Mountain Park; it may be farther than
it looks like to me, but I think I can walk there and back.

"Also, we are glad of the privilege of assembling with
this people for the purpose of investigating a subject of
vital importance—a subject that not only has to do with
man as he is, but a subject that has to do with man as he
will be hereafter; one upon which the eternal welfare
of man may depend. Hence we ask you to bear with us,
to study with us, to reason, read, criticise and examine
for yourselves, using your reasoning faculty, as you are
to be the jurors, to cast within your minds the decisive
votes as to where and what truth is. My sole desire is
that you may know the truth, for I am sure the truth
will make men free, and that he who is made free by the

truth is a free man, indeed. For my part, I shall strive to conduct myself through this series of discussions so the people of this little town, or who may come to hear the close of the discussion, may be glad of the privilege of having heard the discussion. Thank you."

By the Presiding Moderator, R. G. Lee:

"Now, ladies and gentlemen, we will read the proposition that will engage the attention of Mr. Ring and Mr. Chism for the next three days. The proposition is, 'Resolved, That the fundamental principles of Modern Spiritualism are identical with the spiritual basis of the religion of Jesus Christ." John W. Ring affirms; J. W. Chism denies. For thirty minutes you will have the privilege of listening to Mr. Ring affirm on this proposition.

Opening Invocation, by Rev. Ring.

"Supreme and eternal essence of life; in whom we live and move and have our beings, our souls reach up to thee, the source of sunshine and of life, of strength and of beauty; for an influx of spiritual understanding, divine life, energy and love. For an addition to all those virtues that make our lives expressive of the divinity that is implanted within. Basked here in the sunshine of this material beauty and exhilaration, our spirits crave for a similar spiritual baptism of thy love and the benediction of understanding. So have we assembled here in the spirit of seeking for truth, that we may be free; as individual spirits may we continue day by day to seek for that unfoldment of the soul that will bring us nearer to the greater oversoul. Nearer to the baptism that assumes us an eternal life. May the unfolding of each individual soul bring us nearer to each other, until through our respective creeds and doctrines we see the eternal light of truth—the magnitude of which man has not comprehended, the beauty and magnificence of which is sufficient for all the children of men. May our souls leap up and on to the great source of their being until, baptized with this spiritual strength, they shall live always in the light of that eternal spirit of life that men call God

> "May our each individual soul,
> A part of that stupendous whole,
> Be filled with that life-giving light,
> To guide our feet in paths aright;
> And touched by thy abiding grace,
> May each find and fill his own place."
>
> "Amen."

Reverend John Ring's Opening Address.

Spiritualism, the opposite of materialism, is the foundation upon which absolutely all religions have been established; and whether ancient or modern, Spiritualism is the soul of Religion. The rebinding of the individual soul to the eternal oversoul—the awakening of the Spiritual consciousness, to its relationship, as a part of the one eternal spirit. The pages of ancient history, both sacred and profane, are filled to overflowing with occurrences of psychic phenomena, all of which indicate the presence of the Eeternal Spirit with individual spirits. In the days called ancient, these phenomena were looked upon as revelations—special providences from the almighty Spirit to the Children of Earth. The fact of their being the result of natural law was not grasped by the majority of individuals at that time; hence, if there be any distinction between ancient and modern spiritualism, it lies not in the difference of phenomena, but in the difference of acceptation of the same. Even so might it be said of truth, of God, of Life, of all Things that tend to the well-being of individual man. They are eternally the same, but you and I differ in our comprehension of them. The fact that you and I were born in this country indicates that we are interested in the Religion of Jesus Christ. Had the fact been that we were born in Persia or India, we would have been interested in the Religion of India, we would have been interested in the Religion of Mohammed or of Buddha. Hence, we can say with confidence that the fundamental principles of Modern Spiritualism are identical with the Religion of Jesus Christ, because the Religion of Jesus Christ is but another stepping-stone of the unfoldment of that great essence of Religion that blossomed in the religion of Buddha—that spoke to us through the inspired lips of Confucius—that came to a portion of the World through Zoroaster. So in various climes and nations have these phenomena been presented—have these Messiahs and Christs made men to know the truth according to their capacity to receive. You and I discern the truth as our environment, our education, compels us, and only by careful and persistent investigation may we anticipate the possibility of enlarging or modifying our concept of truth. Spiritualism is as old as the aspiration of the human heart—as deeply seated as the emotions of human nature—as full of God as is this great universe that throbs and beats with His animation, until Pope has so wisely said :

"All are but parts of one stupendous whole,
Whose body Nature is, and God the Soul."

Through all ages of the past Spiritualism has made

its appearance and interested the people who were capable of Spiritual discernment, and has made hopeful the souls of the Children on Earth. March 31, 1848, in Hydesville, through the now famous Fox Sisters, then little girls, came that which has been declared the "Modern advent of Spiritualism." Not until less than fourteen years ago was there conceived any idea of organizing the forces of Spiritualism under an independent movement, for it was supposed that since Spiritualism is the foundation upon which all religions are formed, that the various sects, creeds and denominations would appreciate the modern advent of "the old-time Religion," and receive it warmly into their bosoms. Finding it otherwise, which you know, have you any of the history of the early manifestations of Spiritualism under its modern advent. (These little girls from Hydesville were carried through the streets of New York to the theatre where they might manifest this God-given power under police guard for fear the Christian gentlemen of the city might take their little lives, even as the selfsame gentlemen's grandfathers had dismembered the children of New England because they were possessed of "familiar spirits.")

In the City of Chicago, Spiritualism formally organized under its modern advent, and a National Spiritualists' Association was brought into existence. This National Spiritualists' Assocation, though but fourteen years old, has caused its influence to be felt in every civilized nation of the earth, and counts as its adherents many of the crowned heads of Europe—the scientists and thinkers of the entire World. Paralleling this, you will recall the fact that there was no Word written of the "Teacher of Galilee," the respected Mes-

I Am Always

John H. Ring

siah, Jesus, until at least seventy-five years after he had passed from this mundane sphere. After several years of activity in a general way it was found necessary to make some formal declaration that the World might know exactly where Spiritualism, in its modern advent, might stand, owing to the fact that the so-called Christian Church had divided and subdivided itself into almost a thousand creeds, sects, etc., and seemed not to know where they were. People began to ask, "What is your concept of Deity?" "What is your conclusion concerning the continuity of life?" "The possible continuation of the personal identity?" "The means and modes of life in the World to be?" So there were made formal declarations in this selfsame City of Chicago, which we shall endeavor to elucidate to you, and place parallel with them the utterances of our Elder Brother, Jesus of Nazareth, and which stands as the fundamental principles of Modern Spiritualism and identical with the spirit ual basis of the religion of this man whom we all respect, many love and not a few worship.

Our first declaration says, "We believe in Infinite intelligence." That does not say anything about God, does it? Not specifically, for had we said that we believe in God, then any one could have said, "Which God? Why there is but one God." Oh, yes, there are almost as many Gods as there are people, because we are finite beings, and we conceive the Infinite only by comparison. We do not grasp the Infinite because we are finite. "We believe that the phenomena of Nature, physical and spiritual, are the expression of infinite intelligence." The grain of sand upon the lapped shore of the sea—the blade of grass or clinging moss upon the mountain side—the flower that blooms in the dell or in rock crag—the stars that glisten in the heavens above us—the birds that move in the air—the beasts that rove the field—the men of the earth, red, black, yellow and white—are all expressions of Infinite Intelligence. Our third declaration says, "We affirm that a correct understanding of such expression and living in accordance therewith constitutes the true Religion." "We believe in Infinite intelligence." We believe, in other words, that a part of intelligence made its manifestation through Jehovah, the Jewish God, who said, "Thou shalt have no other Gods before me, for I, the Lord thy God, am a jealous God," indicating the nature of the people who made him. Yet we can see much of beauty, much of the necessary divine light for that especial age and people. So we can pick out and enumerate, specifically or collectively, the Gods, Messiahs, Christs and Saviors of the World, and see that each of them has in his time and place born unto the children of men a part of the eternal whole. In this vast arena of conception we can realize that all is divine—that each is necessary in his place—that every man, woman and child, every beast and bird, every grain of sand, every leaf of tree, every petal of flower, has its part in the great economy of nature.

I realize that many of you have formed in your mind already the idea that the Spiritualists are a Godless set, but if you can produce a bigger God than this—one that will weigh more in absolute pounds, and express more of the actualities of worth, I would like to have him put on exhibition. The infinite intelligence that moves the children of men to live their lives as their education and environment permits them—that bows at the shrine of truth as it appeals to them, and gives unto every other man the selfsame privilege, that says to every individual, "Live according to the laws of nature, and you are living the fullness of the true Religion." What is nature? Nature is triune in its expression— the body, soul, spirit—the physical laws under which we live now, the spiritual laws under which we live now, and the psychic laws to which we are tending. As you and I live under these laws of physical life to-day, so we live under the spiritual laws of life's exactitude. When you and I transgress a physical law, we suffer even as we are compelled to suffer when we transgress a spiritual law. You might say, these are simply at random statements—that they have no especial significance with any of the words of the "Teacher of Galilee," but if you can read this book, called the New Testament, and after having read all of the conditions attendant to its formation, realizing all of the interpolations, etc., and can find any passage that does not indicate the statements made, I would like to find it. For instance, let us look at the third chapter of John. This is the old story of Nicodemus, the man that slipped around in the night to visit the medium—just as they do to-day. I can see old Nicodemus—you know he was an old man— with his lantern and his crooked stick, creeping along to go and see the Medium, after night. I do not know whether he had an idea that spiritual manifestations came better in the dark than in the light, or whether he was kind of sneaking around. I believe he rather understood the law, and understood he had to go in the night, but Jesus said to him, "If I have told ye earthly things, and ye believe not, how shall ye believe, if I tell you of heavenly things? And no man hath ascended up to heaven, but he that came down from heaven, even the son of man which is in heaven." Not that he was in heaven—not that he was going to be in heaven, but that he is in heaven. A little further down in the 19th verse, "And this is the condemnation, that light is come into the World and men love darkness rather than light, because their deeds were evil. For every one that doeth evil hateth the light, neither cometh to the light, lest his deeds should be reproved. But he that doeth truth cometh to the light that his deeds may be made manifest, that they are wrought in God." You notice the frequent references made to the need of light, because my Honorable opponent is going to talk a great deal of this "dark seance business." I want you to notice that dark light business, it is very interesting—very necessary.

In the eighth chapter of this selfsame book of John, along toward the close, in the 58th verse, "Jesus said unto them, verily, verily, I say unto you, before Abraham was, I am." We believe in infinite intelligence. We can see that the Spirit of Truth was not first made manifest in Jesus, but had been made manifest in all of the Messiahs, Saviors and Christs that had lived previously. In the same chapter, "Verily, verily, I say unto you, if a man keep my sayings, he shall never see death," blotting out the idea of two worlds. Spiritualism is the one life Religion. We are living our spiritual life now—we are living the only life that we will ever live—our spiritual life—and we must discern these things spiritually—we can not discern them otherwise, for with our spirit eyes only can we see spiritual things. Turning to an early part of this selfsame book, in the first chapter, I wish you would take that chapter home and read it very carefully. You had best not read too far in this chapter unless you want to find some spiritualism *per se*. At the latter end of the chapter you will find one of the clairvoyant visions of Jesus, in which he not only had his clairvoyant vision, but promised to Nathaniel an even greater clairvoyant vision. In this third chapter I want you to especially remember that 13th verse concerning the fact that Christ is already in heaven, because we are not talking about a heaven that is away off somewhere—"the kingdom of heaven is within you." "A correct understanding and living in accordance with these phenomena constitutes the true Religion." If we are going to live the true Religion, we must live the religion of Jesus—in the 10th chapter of this same Epistle of John—of course, we don't know by whom this was written, but it was the Scripture, according to John—in the 35th verse of the 10th chapter, "If he called them God's, unto whom the Word of God came, and the scriptures can not be broken; say ye of him, whom the Father has sanctified, and sent unto the World, thou blasphemest; because I said, 'I am the Son of God'? If I do not the works of my Father, believe me not. But if I do, though ye believe not me, believe the works; that ye may know, and believe, that the Father is in me, and I in him." As to our right or privilege to judge the children of men, any of those with whom we associate—as I have heard people judge the Religion which I have the privilege and honor of representing—even since I came here some of the good people that have shaken my hand have said, "Oh, this Spiritualism; it is a terrible thing," and I expect it is—I expect it is—because it is the philosophy, combined and linked with these phenomena, that brings before the concept of the human race "the old-time Religion" when men walked and conversed with spirits and knew that it was a part of their daily life. In the 4th chapter of John is that famous story of the woman of Samaria, who met Jesus at the well, and the test that Jesus gave her. Is there not a beautiful lesson there conveyed of the power of spiritual discernment, of the faculty of acceptance, of delineating—of "divining," if you like the word? He could see these things, and in his conversation with her he said, "But the hour cometh, and now is, when the true worshipers shall worship the Father in spirit and in truth; for the Father seeketh such to worship him. God is a spirit; and they that worship him must worship in spirit and in truth." They had been talking about worshiping in the mountains or in the Temple at Jerusalem, but it must be in spirit and in truth. She went out and said, "Is not this the Christ?" In the 16th chapter of Luke I want to refer you to the 17th verse. "It is easier for heaven and earth to pass, than one tittle of the law to fail." "We believe in Infinite Intelligence." We believe that every atom in nature is a part of this Infinite Intelligence. It is, therefore, the expression of law, and the only means by which we can live the life and worship God in spirit and in truth is to live according to law. In this same book, in the 15th chapter, is the story of the Parable of the Lost Sheep. You are all familiar with that. However, I want to call your attention to the fact that the joy cometh from the one sinner that returns—not from the thousands that had not sinned. And I wish, also, to call your attention to the man Jesus' contempt of the law of equity by which he abolished all laws binding upon the children of men, save the law of service to mankind, of loving God and loving men, and the only means by which we can love God is

by serving men. In other words, the Religion of Spiritualism, in its modern advent, and the spiritual basis of
the Religion of Jesus Christ are identical in so far as that
they are a Religion of service to each other rather than
"service" to the Glory of God. We glorify God by our
service to mankind, by doing something to benefit the
World. As our Sister co-worker has said:

> "So many faiths, so many creeds,
> So many paths that wind and wind,
> When just the simple art of being kind,
> Is all this old World needs."
>
> —*Ella Wheeler Wilcox.*

It is not a religion that has this form or that form or
the other that belongs to the people of the community
in which that respective religion may exist, but the great
Universal Religion that is being ushered into this, the
morning of the twentieth century, under the guise of
Spiritualism, but under the names of various sciences—
christian, mental and spiritual, and otherwise—the Religion that is universal, that accepts all Christs and all
of the Gods, and makes mankind all into one unit—I
in you and the Father in me, and we are all one family;
we are all parts of the one stupendous whole.

———

Thereupon, Mr. T. W. Head, Moderator for and on
behalf of the representative of the Church of Christ,
Mr. J. W. Chism, introduces the gentleman to the audience, who thereupon delivers the following address:

Gentlemen, Moderators, Brethren, Friends:

I am most assuredly glad that, by the providence of a
loving Father, I am permitted to stand before you this
evening in the negative of the proposition which has been
read; and which my friend has undertaken to prove:

That the base of modern Spiritualism is identical with the spiritual base of the Religion of Jesus Christ.

It is one thing to affirm a proposition, but quite a different thing to *prove* that proposition.

I must confess, that, if *assertions* prove anything, the gentleman has proven his proposition. But where—Oh, where, is the proof? Where has he given us evidence that even looks like a hint at proof, that, The base of modern Spiritualism is identical with the spiritual basis of Christianity? What proof, sir, did you submit? [addressing his opponent] Yea, echo answers, what proof did he submit?

He read a few passages from the New Testament; he said a few words about the Fox girls in 1848, but in the name of common sense, and reason, where is his evidence upon which he purposes to prove that "the base of modern Spiritualism is identical with that of the Religion of Christ"? Evidence is in order, Mr. Ring; just a little evidence, please, and not so many assertions.

But I shall follow the gentleman closely, and show you some of the things that grow out of what he said. But I desire in this speech to impress upon him, that we need some evidence, we need the base of modern Spiritualism brought out—we desire to see it in its present teaching—in its practice. Jesus Christ, from whom the gentleman quotes, says, "You shall know a tree by its fruits." Says of prophets and teachers, "By their fruits ye shall know them." Then, I know no way to examine modern Spiritualism, but by its fruits; and I ask the gentleman to present us the teachings of modern Spiritualism. I submit, ladies and gentlemen, that there is no evidence in the universe to prove that the two are identical. Here is a flat denial of the gentleman's assertion. He asserts they are identical. This I deny emphatically. He is in the affirmative—the laboring oar is in his hand. I challenge him to submit the evidence. Bring it into court where it may examined—bring it into court.

You have listened to quite a nice address, so far as *flowery speech and pleasing sound* is concerned. I am not an orator, and especially when I get after false doctrine. And this time being after false doctrine, I shall not strive to be an orator, but shall strive to speak so that I may be understood.

He begins with a statement like this, "Spiritualism is the soul of religion." I deny it. You have asserted it. Bring your proof; I deny it emphatically. It may be the soul of *your* religion. But I am prepared to show you, ladies and gentlemen, that it is the soul of one of the most *corrupt* religions that God ever let live under the Sun. It is not the soul of the Religion of Jesus Christ, nor is it the soul of Christianity; it is not the soul of a Religion of *purity*. But *it* is the soul of a religion of LICENTIOUSNESS.

Did he not tell us in his speech that every man should serve the "Great Spirit" or the "Great All (or whatever he calls it) according as it is in him by his nature? If this be true, that black villain that takes the white girl by the roadside and follows his nature is serving his God—that is what he asserted. He asserted, "Let men follow according to that which was in them. In this arena of conception we realize that all is divine. That all things are an expression of that infinite goodness." Then let the black ravenous beast go free that outrages the white girl. I would like for the gentleman to *prove* his proposition if he can. I would like

— 25 —

for him to submit some evidence in proof of it. I am examining his reasoning, and what grows out of it? I deny that Spiritualism is the soul of truth, or of the true religion.

Ancient history is filled, we are told, with psychic phenomena which denote, or express, the presence of God with the human spirit; i. e., the presence of the great Eternal Spirit. I am willing to concede this. But ancient history is just as full of *phenomena* produced by impostors, striving to prove themselves "divine" by their sorceries.

But the gentleman quoted from Nicodemus. He said Nicodemus came to Jesus by night. He did not know why, but possibly (and he said he believed it), it was because he understood the law, that he had come by night. Ah, listen! It seems to me that a man who makes such an assertion as that would know what came almost in the next verse. "Men love darkness rather than light because their deeds are evil." Now he said that Nicodemus understood the law. That they had to come in the night, because the spirits would not come in the daytime. That is what he intimated. Most assuredly that intimation is in his statement. If Nicodemus had to go at night in order to get the benefit of the teaching, then the spirits work at night, but would not work in daytime, according to his statement. "He went at night because he understood the law." Then a man has to go at night, and Jesus Christ says himself that a man that loves night (darkness) rather than light—his deeds are evil [addressing his opponent]. You introduced it; I did not; it is your witness. According to the gentleman's own quotation, men love darkness rather than light because their deeds are evil. Is it possible that Jesus was looking down to this age of the World and, seeing what men would bring up, made this statement of them?

Much of the phenomena, and of that which excites the people most, that has been presented in time past by Spiritualists—modern Spiritualists—to prove their theories, I am prepared to perform in broad open daylight right on this rostrum. Get after me—get after me. I am prepared. You have heard of Spiritualists closing themselves up in a cabinet, being sewed up in a sack, head and foot, with men, sworn witnesses, to examine and see that they are closed up, and then cause their spirit to come out on the dimly lighted stage before the audience, go back into the cabinet and the witnesses find them still sewed up in the sack. I am prepared to be sewed up in the sack, and come back and talk to you; go back into the cabinet, and at the given signal the wit- nesses will find me in the sack sewed up just like you left me. That is not all. I just mention to you that one—it is up to you. I am ready to do this when you produce the other.

The gentleman's proposition is that modern Spiritual- ism is identical with the spiritual basis of the Religion of Jesus Christ. But, to follow him:

He said, "Spiritualism was the same anciently that it is now; only different in acceptation." Modern Spirit- ualism was not in existence then. Who ever heard in all the ancient records of their getting a table to answer by raps and knocks? Who ever heard of it? Who ever heard of it until the two little Fox girls heard some- thing knock—knock, about the house, and got scared at it? And when the Father could not find just what it was, the question was asked, "Are you a man?" No sound heard. "Are you a spirit?" Knock. The idea

— 27 —

of the Great Eternal God coming down to use tables to speak with and only using a *knock* for an answer which must be guessed at for its meaning. Say [addressing his opponent] can you use a varnished table? You tell the people whether you can answer questions with a table like this,—a varnished table. I am ready to answer questions with a table, too, whenever he undertakes the task. I am ready to show the people how it is done.

But he tells us again that "we who are born here in the United States are interested in Christianity, but if we had been born in India, it would have been in Buddha or some of those other heathen Gods." I am free to confess that man's environment has a great deal to do with him; that a man may be taught a falsehood, and believe it just as earnestly as if it had been the truth, and it has been so in every age of the World, but still, it does not prove what the gentleman asserted,—that the Religion of Jesus Christ was unfoldment of that of Buddha. Why did he not give some proof? Assertions are cheap articles, any man can deal in them.

Then he speaks about "these Christs" in the plural number, and about the Messiahs and Saviours of the World. I submit that, you should bring some of them to view,—bring us some evidence,—don't just *talk* about the Christs and Saviours of the World,—but bring the record of them. I challenge the gentleman to bring the record of them into court.

But he says, "Spiritualism is as old as the aspirations of the human heart." I deny it, and challenge again for proof. EVIDENCE, Reverend Ring, is in order to-day, *not assertions.* EVIDENCE is in order in this debate. We are not supposed to simply make *assertions,*—we want

In the Faith
J. W. Chism

them. You begin to see now where it started, its author and Father.

He turns us now to John, the third chapter, and cites the case of Nicodemus. We had noted Nicodemus' case, but there are some other things concerning it. He said of me, "He would be calling for the seance in the dark." Jesus Christ said, "Men love darkness rather than light, because their deeds are evil." Did he tell the truth? [addressing his opponent] Then why do you not show your seances in the light? Why is it that they always desire to run to the darkness to show these phenomena? I have promised that when they send the icy fingers of a Spirit around to touch my face, that I will show the people in the audience that Spirit. I have never found one yet who would undertake the job. They quit Mineral Wells, Texas, rather than undertake it. Again, our Savior says, "I have said nothing in secret" (John 18:20). Jesus Christ did not work in secret. Again, his miracles were public, open and abroad, in broad open daylight—*broad open daylight*. One morning, as he went into the little city Nain he met them bringing out a corpse, and in the presence of friend and foe he raised him from the dead. At Lazarus' tomb he stood and called, "Lazarus, come forth," in presence of friend and foe, and although Lazarus had been dead four days, he responded to the call and came out. Do the Spiritualists do anything like that?

Again, he cites us John 8:58, where Christ says, "Before Abraham was I am." And again, John 1:1, "In the beginning was the word and the Word was with God and the Word was God." Yes, and in the third verse John tells us that "all things were made by him,

But who was that word? The "Malak Elohim." The word "Malak," commonly translated "Angel," is the Hebrew word for "workman." Then the "workman God" was the one that *became* the CHRIST. The workman God was the one that was in the beginning, the one that is called *the word*. Christ said, "God is a Spirit." This is *Ruach Elohim,* Spirit of God. Then Jehovah God, Lord God, the ruler, then the Malak,—Workman. Again, he tells that we have a clairvoyant vision of Jesus Christ in the latter part of this chapter. I admit that it is clairvoyance. Clairvoyance means clear sight. I thought I would have to prove that it was clairvoyance. I have been laboring under the impression that Spiritualists claim that the spirits of the departed dead make known such things to men. But he admits it was clairvoyance, a clairvoyant vision. He says that Jesus Christ saw Nathaniel under the fig tree, and told him so. But does the gentleman tell us that it was the Spirit of some dead man that came and told him by the rapping of a table, that Nathaniel was over there? Such are the claims of Modern Spiritualism. Clairvoyants do not have to go to the place to see men; nor do they have to make everything dark. But they see in broad open daylight.

Again he quotes the passage that the kingdom of heaven is within you. The right rendering of that passage is, "The kingdom of heaven is among you." Again, he quotes John 10:38. Christ says, "If you do not believe me, believe the works that I do, for the works that I do bear witness who I am." GOOD! We would like to see the works you do. If the base of Modern Spiritualism is the same as the spiritual base of the religion of Christ, let us see the *works* that it does. Where are the men that you raised from the dead? Where are the works that you do? We will show you some of them before it is done, but in speaking of John 10—35, he says, "We do not know by whom it was written." You understand, ladies and gentlemen, that I am not responsible for the gentleman's ignorance. It was written by the Apostle John. I am in no way responsible for his ignorance. I plead, "Not guilty." But he tells us, "Christ says we must worship in spirit and in truth, for God is a Spirit." Truth! But to worship in spirit is to worship intelligently. David says, "Your heart shall live forever." A man reasons with his heart. But a man's spirit is his reasoning faculty. It is the reasoning man. His Spirit is the thinking man; it is the man that God Almighty commanded in the garden of Eden should rule over the lusts of the flesh. Then to worship in spirit is to worship in reason, and intelligently.

TIME EXPIRED.

J. W. RING'S SECOND ADDRESS.

Well, I guess it is just about as easy to make assertions as it is to holler, "Evidence—we want evidence!" I "reckon" we are going to have it, because our Brother has promised to give us a Spiritual seance before the series are over. So we will not need to hunt up the medium that we had anticipated—our good Brother can afford us these phenomena, *perhaps.*

Continuing, however, I want to refer briefly to his sarcastic reference to why these phenomena take place in the dark, referring to some few cases where Jesus gave his manifestations in the dark. I wish I had time to take the New Testament, and go over it seance by seance, manifestation by manifestation, and see the overwhelming majority of the cases which took place in the dark, and under especial conditions. I also would like to refer to the fact that our good old friend Saul, when he went to communicate with Samuel, sneaked around in the night, disguised himself, because he could get no manifestations from his own mediums. In those days they had a trust, a combine or a union—something like they have to-day—and unless you belonged to the union, and paid your license, you could not give any manifestations. Saul had licensed a few mediums, but they could not get what he desired, and he hunted up some one else—he hunted up the old woman that resided in Endor. "Witch of Endor," but the Bible does not call her a witch; it calls her a woman.

When Jesus went upon the Mount of Transfiguration he did not take the multitude with him; he took Peter, James and John, in order that he might form the necessary conditions to produce the special phenomena that he wished to produce—that of Moses and Elias talking with him. The spiritual manifestation of Gabriel coming to Mary, telling her of the fact that she was to bear the Christ child, came as a vision; in fact, if we were to be real strict, we would see the Christian Religion is based upon a vision—the spiritual vision that Mary had when the same angel or spirit of Gabriel (that is spoken of also in connection with Daniel) came to her. It also came to Zacharias, and told him of the fact that Elizabeth was going to bear him a son. We find that all the conditions attendant to a seance were there—he was inside of the cabinet—the people were all outside at prayer—the circle was completed—the seance was formed, and he then received the message from Gabriel of the advent into physical life of the trance medium John. When John came upon this stage of action he declared himself to come in the power and spirit of Elias, and we have the unquestioned testimony of Jesus, our "Great Teacher," that John the Baptist was the medium through whom the spirit of Elias manifested. The case of this spirit manifesting through the mediumship of John the Baptist is one of the parallel cases of the manifestation of hundreds of mediums in Modern Spiritualism to-day. One of the conclusive evidences that Modern Spiritualism is a continuation of the spiritualism of Jesus is the fact that Jesus was accused of being possessed of the Devil. My good Brother said that I was very rapidly showing my relationship. I am a brother of the same family as Jesus Christ because he was accused of being possessed of the Devil; so am I. They said he cast out Devils by the Prince of Devils, Beelzebub. The milennial dawn people, who are going to have the World come to an end not later than a year from next September—you had better get ready—say that Spiritualism is one of the absolute necessities for the end of the World. So I guess we are from God, if the Devil did bring us; if the Devil did bring us, God must have sent us. You know the old negro mamma that prayed for bread, and the boys who heard her chucked the bread down the chimney and ran away. She saw them, however, and says "I sees you, but I knows de Lawd sent it, if you little debils did bring it." The same thing was said about Jesus—that he was possessed of Devils. He said, furthermore—this man Jesus—that he would send us a comforter, the Spirit of Truth to lead us into all understanding; that these signs should follow them that believe—in his name would we be able to do all of these things, as you will find in the last chapter of Mark; in fact, in all of the gospels. Mark 16-17— "and these signs shall follow them that believe; in my name shall they cast out devils; they shall speak with new tongues; they shall take up serpents; and if they drink any deadly thing, it shall not hurt them; they shall lay hands on the sick and they shall recover." I believe that my good brother meant what he said when he promised us a seance. I am looking forward to that with great anxiety, because he is evidently going to do some of these things that Jesus promised his followers they would be able to do. According to the philosophy of its modern advent we realize that each medium is possessed of his explicit powers of mediumship, and that not each is possesed of all those various gifts, as we shall bring in later by Paul. Evidently our good brother is especially blessed of the Lord, and is going to give us a variety of phenomena. This same Jesus is recorded by John to have said that this spiritual comforter, whom he is going to send to us, is going to lead us into all understanding—is going to be a comforter. I want to know if my good brother can show us any evidence that the Religion of Jesus, as it has been interpreted by the churches of the past, can show wherein they have comforted the human race? To how many mothers that have grieved for their babies has this religion said, "your child lives because you can see its dimpled face, and feel its clinging embrace?" How many instances have we on record of where these church religions have taken the mourners into the seance room, dark or otherwise, and given tangible evidence of the continuity of life— the continuation of the personal identity? The silence

is broken only by the heart-rending sobs of the mother
as the Minister says, "God moves in strange, mysterious
ways his wonders to perform." The phenomena of Spiritualism—although our good Brother, as did the enemies
of the days of Jesus, accuse us of being of the Devil—
comfort the hearts of mothers; they come to the children bereaved. He will say these are only statements;
that there is no evidence. The World is full of them,
but my good Brother will never be able to see them;
neither will you nor I until our Spiritual eyes are opened.
Jesus was not able to do many wonders because of the
unbelief of the people, and he had to go to another town
because there was too much unbelief. Yet my opponent tells us that we should be able to present these
phenomena without any attendant conditions. Jesus
always had these attendant conditions, and was compelled to leave his own home because of the unbelief
of the community. Some time during these meetings
I have some slate writings I want to present to you,
and I want to show them to you in connection with the
thought of those received by Moses on Mount Sinai.
My good Brother says that he is going to judge the
World, that he has a right, and that he is going to
judge the people. I can not, because Jesus could not.
In John, the 9th chapter, beginning with the 24th verse—
"Then again called they the man that was blind and
said unto him, give God the praise, we know that this
man is a sinner," speaking to a man whom Jesus had
healed. "He answered and said, whether he be a sinner
or not, I know not; one thing I know, whereas I was
blind, now I see. Well, said they unto him, what did
he to thee? How opened he thine eyes? He answered
unto them, I have told you already, and ye did not hear;

wherefore would ye hear again? Will ye also be his disciples?"

If sufficient evidence were brought here to make every individual conscious of the truth of these phenomena, the dear good Christian Brethren, by faith, that have not yet brushed off the scales of faith, and put a little knowledge into their hearts and lives, would not be able to see anything whatsoever. My opponent said that we let people move along according to their own way of going, and that we should judge people, and tell them what is right. The church has always been doing that—they have changed their standards of right just as often as they have their statements. You know it was but a few years ago, comparatively speaking, that the Presbyterians sent all unbaptized infants to Hell. Not long ago they had a big Sunday-school picnic, and took all the infants up above. It was their standard of right—they were judging people, but Jesus does not judge people—he leaves it to the Word of God. I suppose my Brother can tell you about the Word of God. It is contained in these gospels; but if anybody wants to inform themselves about it, I have some little books in which you will find that there is no evidence whatever that it is the Word of God; that it is like any other book written by man.

In this same Book of John, in the 12th chapter and 47th verse, we find some words recorded as having been spoken by Jesus: "And if any man hear my words and believe not, I judge him not; for I came not to judge the World, but to save the World. He that rejecteth me, and receive not my words, hath one that judgeth him; the word that I have spoken, the same shall judge him in the last day." The word of God is written—

not in books, but in the vastness of nature everywhere. In Luke, 6:26, Jesus gives me some consolation: "Woe unto you, when all men shall speak well of you, for so did their fathers to the false prophets." I am glad they do not speak well of me. I am glad they have got it in for Spiritualism. My good Brother told me he was right after me—told me this morning he intended to pull out every feather I had, and sit on me good and heavy. [His opponent at this juncture said, "Amen."] "But I say unto you which hear, love your enemies, do good to them that hate you, bless them that curse you, pray for them which despitefully use you. Unto him that smiteth thee on the one cheek, offer also the other * * * * but love ye your enemies, and do good, and lend, hoping for nothing again; and your reward shall be great, and ye shall be the children of the Highest; for he is kind unto the unthankful and to the evil." My Brother's Elohim over there in the Old Testament was a certain god which belonged to certain tribes, and certain people; but, thank God, I am a child of the most high—the God that is "kind to the unthankful, and to the evil." Verse 36: "Be ye therefore merciful, as your father also is merciful. Judge not and ye shall not be judged; condemn not and ye shall not be condemned; forgive and ye shall be forgiven." And so the chapter goes on, speaking of the universality of the Supreme Spirit of the "Infinite Intelligence" that moves in nature everywhere. I rejoice that I can not judge; I can not say what is good and what is bad, save as it appeals to me, and since I am changing constantly in my concept of right, the same as you are if you are growing at all, I guess that "whatever is, is best," even if it does not appear right. My good

Brother went down south where I have lived, and where the negroes ravish the white women. I do not know whether it is any worse than it is in the North, where the white men do the ravishing; but it is said that here in Texas there was a man who committed murder—he was a white man, too; he was a criminal; he was proven so before the jury; he had religious counsel; the Minister went to him, and he said, "God knows I am sorry—God knows I wish I could give that man back to his wife and family. Will God forgive me?" "Yes, brother, God will forgive you." And the next morning the headline came out in the paper, "Jerked to Jesus." A criminal, his hands still stained with human blood, was "jerked to Jesus." Does this sound like the teachings of the "Man of Galilee" when he said, "According to his works shall man be justified?" or does the concept of Spiritualism sound as an echo of these teachings when Spiritualism says, "Every man lives according to the law of his being, and, in time or eternity, evolves to the status of expressing the fullness of his life?"

I rejoice that in the light of spiritual philosophy I can look through the sinner, and see the soul of God— that underneath all the corruption of each individual, whether it be the black, red, yellow or white man, that I can see the divine spark of life—the light of every man that cometh into the World, that can not be put out. I can see that divine spark climbing upward and upward and onward and onward to the expression of the divinity with which it is endowed, because God has made all things that were made. The World is beautiful because it is the incarnation of God's holy spirit— not limited, not bound by the confines of creed or doc-

trine. I can see the beauty in all religions and conceive that they are all tending toward the expression
of that which is beautiful and that which will express
the Godliness with which we are possessed.

In the seventh chapter of Luke is recorded the pathetic
story of the woman ministering to Jesus. He had gone
to eat with some publicans and sinners, and was severely
criticized for his action. "And behold a woman in the
city, which was a sinner, when she knew that Jesus
sat at meat in the Pharisee's house, brought an alabaster
box of ointment. And sat at his feet behind him weep-
ing, and began to wash his feet with tears and did wipe
them with the hairs of her head, and anointed them with
the ointment." "Now when the Pharisee which had
bidden him saw it, he spake within himself, saying, this
man if he were a prophet, would have known who
and what manner of woman that is that toucheth him: for
she is a sinner." The man had not spoken, he had
simply thought this. "And Jesus answering, said unto
him, Simon, I have somewhat to say unto thee. There
was a certain creditor which had two debtors: the one
owed five hundred pence, and the other fifty. And
when they had nothing to pay, he frankly forgave them
both. Tell me, therefore, which of them will love him
most? Simon answered and said, I suppose that he to
whom he forgave most. And he said unto him, thou
hast rightly judged. And he turned to the woman
and said unto Simon, seest thou this woman? I entered into thine house, thou gavest me no water for my
feet, but she hath washed my feet with tears, and wiped
them with the hairs of her head. Thou gavest me no
kiss; but this woman since the time I came in hath
not ceased to kiss my feet. My head with oil thou didst

not anoint; but this woman hath anointed my feet with ointment. * * * * And he said unto her, thy sins are forgiven. Thy faith hath saved thee; go in peace." Yet the presumed followers of this "Man of Nazareth" can take up the Religion of Spiritualism, and declare that it is entirely a work of his Satanic Majesty, after this man has thus forgiven the vilest. They have not been able to stop this ravishing for all of these hundreds of years.

I believe I referred you to the last chapter of Mark. It refers especially to the signs that are going to follow them that believe. My Brother said he would like some evidence. I wonder if he has attended any spiritual seances. [By his opponent: "They wouldn't let me."] He says he ran a medium out of Mineral Wells. Well, I guess he is just about like those people that compelled Jesus to desert his quarters. They were so hard he was afraid to attack them. Jesus said, "After all of these miracles, will ye not believe?" No, we are all from Missouri—we must be sighted.

I do not anticipate that my good Brother will know much about spirit phenomena until he has been in the spirit world about a hundred years and gets a few ideas of nature's laws, loses a few scales of faith, and sees that this universe is run by law and not by license. He is writing that down good and heavy—law, not license. In these phenomena of Spiritualism, with which we have to do in its modern advent, there are full parallels in the New Testament. He is going to ask me to parallel them. I presume I can, if he will give me time, plenty of it—it will take quite a while to get them all sorted out. They did not have spirit photography, because photography was unknown to them. Why, bless your

life, they did not know the World was round, and the
first man that said it was round, these self-same Christians said, "Cut out his tongue." So limited were they
as to believe the stars to be pieces of nothing left after
the Lord God had finished his job of making all things
from nothing, little knowing that they were Worlds re-
volving in space, peopled with individuals, perhaps as
brilliant as we. So we live in the highest unfolding
of these things, and we can anticipate that they will
impress all those who are possessed of spiritual discernment. You as individuals will never see the beauty of
spiritual phenomena in any of their unfoldment, or any
of their expressions until you are able to spiritually discern, until you are willing to knock that it may be opened
unto you, until you will go humbly as a little child and
say, "I am desirous of finding out concerning the phenomena." "Evidences of these spiritual phenomena are
to be found everywhere. We would not insult your intelligence by occupying the time to read, or to relate
the multiplicity of these occurrences as they have come
to the most noted people of the World. The fact that
the now risen Queen Victoria of England declared that
she found more comfort in the messages received through
the mediums of her court than through religion otherwise, is a certain evidence of the comfort afforded to
a remarkably intelligent woman. The fact that the
Prince Consort's place was left unoccupied, not only in
their private apartments, but on State occasions as well
because the Queen believed in his spiritual presence, indicates that one woman, who stands high in intellectual
qualities, as the World judges them, was comforted by
this beautiful religion. The fact that Flammarion of
France, Zollner of Germany, Sir William Crookes of

England, Hyslop, Hodgson, Minot Savage and a host of others of America say most emphatically concerning these phenomena, "If there is any evidence of the continuity of life, it is found in these phenomena." If my good Brother wants evidence, I will ask him to appeal to these gentlemen. Read their expressions. They are printed in book form, and can be had in many of the libraries; in fact, they are simply waiting for those who have the power of spiritual discernment to read them and be blessed, and no one, save those that are possessed of the spiritual discernment, can eat of this manna, drink of this living water, "but unto as many as will receive it shall be given."

———

J. W. CHISM'S SECOND REPLY.

Gentlemen, Moderators, Respected Friends:

I must confess that I am somewhat amused, and more surprised, at the turn events are taking. I did not understand that debating was man's *mere assertions*. I would like to have a little evidence along the line, but I am told that it is "just as easy to assert as it is to hollow evidence, please." Well, you understand, *evidence* is the thing that is needed in court. I confess, ladies and gentlemen, that I can not understand a thing unless I can have some *evidence* concerning it. Assertions are cheap articles—any man can deal in them.

But the gentleman has undertaken to *prove* a proposition, not merely to *assert* it, and let it be true because he asserts it, but he undertakes to prove it. Now I would like for the gentleman to submit some *evidence* that his proposition is true—that "Modern Spiritualism is identical with the spiritual basis of the Religion of

— 46 —

Jesus Christ." As yet, NO EVIDENCE has been submitted. He has submitted some statements from Christ —some of the things that Christ said, and that Christ did. But where! oh, where, is the evidence concerning Modern Spiritualism. The fact that he asserts that Modern Spiritualists do thus and so, does not establish his proposition. His assertion will not establish it, and we would like for the gentleman to bring us some evidence—we would like to see something along the line in the *form* of evidence. And when I call for evidence, I want logical evidence, I want evidence that would be acceptable in court. Of all the people to give illogical evidence, and things for evidence that is *not* evidence at all, Spiritualists cap the climax. I would like to know how he identifies the spirit? He does not see him. If he does not see him, may not the false spirit come and lie to you about it? Then, in the name of common sense, how do you know to whom you are talking? How do you know that his claim is right?

For the sake of truth, I would like for him to tell us how he knows that he is conversing with a certain spirit? A spirit that is a liar in this World, will he not lie in that one? A man that can impersonate another in this World, does he lose his power of impersonating in the other World? Tell the people how you know you are conversing with the spirit you claim to be conversing with. Your evidence, sir, would not be admitted in any court under the sun. Evidence must be something that man knows.

But, we are told about Saul and the witch of Endor. That is, the woman of Endor, possessed of a familiar spirit. We are told that she was a medium, and that Saul went to her because his mediums would not answer him. Will the gentleman examine the record in full, as he is in the lead, and show us, if he can, that the Bible says that Samuel came up? And will he show how they found out that it was Samuel who came up? When the woman said, "I see Gods ascending out of the earth," Saul said, "What form is he of?" and the woman said, "An old man cometh up; and he is covered with a mantle." The English version says, "And Saul perceived that it was Samuel." The Hebrew word for "perceived" is a word that has many meanings; it may have the meaning of perception through the sight, or feeling, hence Saul "felt" like it was Samuel. Yadang is the word (or as some would spell it "yada'"). And Saul FELT LIKE it was Samuel. Now, do not tell the people you can not read Hebrew—call up Samuel—he was a Hebrew, and if you can not call Samuel's spirit to tell you what the word means—your doctrine is false— is all there is to it. Now get after it. If his proposition is true, it is susceptible of demonstration. If he can not demonstrate his proposition, it is untrue, that is all there is to it. But the first thing that greets my eyes in the notes is where he quotes me saying, "I run a medium out of Mineral Wells." Something like twenty years ago they had a spiritual seance there, and a gentleman, one of whose children was dead, went into the dark room, into the seance, where they could see nothing; and they had the icy fingers of the dead child to touch his face. The next morning the man was almost crazed about it; they came to me; I was just a boy of twenty-two or twenty-three years, and I promised them if they would have another seance and let me in the ring I would show them the spirit that touched my face. But they decided it would not do. The medium said if they

T. W. HEAD, Bluff Dale, Texas,
Moderator for J. W. Chism.

ROBERT G. LEE, Headrick, Okla.,
Moderator for John W. Ring.

broke the circle, it would kill the medium. I told them
I would stand for that; but they would not give me
the chance. *He* said I could not tell until I saw a
demonstration of it in a seance. But *they* told me they
would not let me into the seance, until I promised not
to try to find the spirit. Would you let me in without
this pledge? Will you? Will you let me into it? Answer it before the people. Will you do it? Will you
do it? No, he would not. Why? Because he knows
when he does the fakery of the thing will be brought
to light. That is why.

Oh, but we are told about spiritual photographs. I
happen to be a photographer. I can make spirit pictures and pictures of ghosts. Yes, one time in my work
I made a photograph of some houses, and to my great surprise, when I developed the negative, there was the house
on the plate in its right position, and yonder on the cloud
was another just like it. It took me three weeks to
find out how it was done. But now I can make you
with your spirit by the side of you.

But he says, "I wish I had time to go through the
New Testament, and take up the cases that happened
at night, in the darkness, and examine them." In the
name of common sense what are you here for? What
did you come here for? Doesn't your proposition read
that, "The fundamental principles of Modern Spiritualism are identical with the spiritual basis of the Religion
of Jesus Christ?" Isn't the spiritual basis of the Religion of Jesus Christ written in the New Testament? In
the name of common sense what did you come here
for any way?

But he speaks of my sarcastic statements about darkness. No, it was Jesus Christ who said it, "Men love

darkness rather than light because their deeds are evil."
I did not say it.

Then he comes to the occurence on the Mount of
Transfiguration and says, "When Christ was transfigured, he carried nobody but the three apostles with him
—just three—he was not transfigured before the multitude." True; but it was not at *night,* was it? Neither
was it given for the World, but for the Disciples. But
what happened at the foot of the Mount, when he came
down? Right amid *friend* and *foe* he cast out a devil.

Then he tells us about the Angel to Mary, and says
it was in a vision. Well, what is a vision? He tells
us that a vision is something to be seen "in the dark."
A vision is something seen. Did you not know that?
Of course, Mary saw the angel which came into the room
where she was, and not only this, but she heard him
speak, and his address astonished her; and still more,
he told her the facts that would take place.

But again he tells us that, when Zacharias was told
of the birth of John, that he was in the cabinet. But
he was not. He was back in the Holy of Holies of the
Temple.

But he says he has one evidence that he is identical
with the spiritual basis of the Religion of Christ, and
that is, that "Christ was accused of being possessed of
the Devil," and he is accused of the same thing. Who
accused you of it? I did not. What I said was, that
the gentleman comes with the same *doctrine* that the Serpent did in the garden of Eden, "Thou shalt not surely
die." I said he was teaching the same doctrine that
the serpent taught in the garden of Eden; and again
I showed you that God Almighty intended that the *spirit-
man* should rule. But when man, in obedience to that

lie, allowed the flesh to rule, then it was that sin entered the World, and that man's sins separated him from his God. But he says, "Spiritualists are of God if the Devil did send them." Well, that is a pretty good admission. That looks more like it. Then he tells us an anecdote. Well, I confess I did not come to tell anecdotes; it may be necessary, however, before the discussion is through to show the gentleman's friends that I can tell an anecdote, because his friends may take that for evidence. Was that what you meant by that little anecdote about the negro?

But he says, "Jesus Christ says, 'I will send you a comforter.'" To whom was Jesus Christ talking when he said that? He was not talking to you. He was not talking to me. Jesus Christ was talking to his *apostles* when he made that statement. John, 16th chapter, beginning with the 7th verse, reads, "Nevertheless I tell you the truth; it is expedient for you that I go away; for if I go not away, the comforter will not come unto you; but if I depart, I will send him unto you." And again in the 13th verse, "How be it, when he, the spirit of truth, is come, he will guide you into all truth; for he shall not speak of himself; but whatsoever he shall hear, that shall he speak; and he will show you things to come." But does the gentleman mean to say these phenomena in this age of the World that he has been talking about are produced by that comforter that was to come? I thought you Spiritualists taught that it was the spirits of departed men who once lived on this earth, that are doing this work? Jesus says the comforter is the Holy Ghost. You seem a bit out of harmony with yourself just here.

Then he speaks of me as "my good Brother." Beg

pardon, sir, but I am not your brother. Do you claim it in flesh? I am in Christ, not in the flesh; you are not my brother at all. I deny the charge.

But he says of me, perhaps you will give them a seance. I did not come here to go on record on unequal but on equal terms. I am ready to go on record in a test when he is; I am ready when he produces his spiritual photograph to produce one, when he sends his spirit out of the cabinet when the man is sewed up in a sack—I am ready to walk out in person. Will he attempt it?

But he tells us that "the spirit came to lead us into all understanding." It does not read just that way. Christ says, "He shall teach you all things." The Holy Spirit was to guide the APOSTLES into all truth. The APOSTLES were to teach the people.

But again he speaks of the Religion of Christ as interpreted by the churches all along the ages. Is that his proposition? Is he here to talk about the Religion of Jesus Christ as interpreted by the churches? I am talking about the Religion of Jesus Christ as revealed in the book called the BIBLE. The Religion of Jesus Christ, as revealed in the BOOK. Again along this line he told us about the man that said the World was round and they cut out his tongue. Of course, that proves his proposition.

But he tells us that Jesus was unable to perform miracles in certain places because of the unbelief of the people. I knew of a doctor that could not cure a certain child because his parents did not believe. Does that make it true that if the parents had believed the medicine would have cured the child, that it took the faith to make the medicine effective? He seems to think so. What then? The parents did not believe and would not give the medicine to the child, that is all there is in it. So with Jesus. They wouldn't bring their sick to him, because they did not believe he could cure them, not that their lack of faith would make his effort ineffective.

But he says, "My good brother says he is going to judge the World." If you are speaking of me, excuse me, sir; I did not say that, there must be trouble with your understanding. The Apostle Paul says, "The Saints shall judge the World." Paul says it. I did not. Jesus Christ says, "These words that I speak unto you, they shall judge you at the last day." I did not say it. Nor did I say I was going to judge the World—excuse me, please.

But he tells us about the Bible—the time it was written and says, "I have some little books here; if you will just get one and read it, you will find that there is no evidence to prove that the Bible was inspired." Now if I just had a litle book with me to show it was inspired I could balance accounts. But you see my predicament (?). But, ladies and gentlemen, the thing that puzzles me is this; for several months I tried to arrange a proposition that this Book, the Bible, is of divine origin, and I could not get them to sign that proposition at all. And I am ready to affirm it yet, if I can get the gentleman to even dare take the negative. I am ready to show you by the best authority beneath the canopies of the high heaven, that they were written by the persons whose names they bear, and at the dates given.

But he says, "The Word of God is written—*not in the books,* but in nature." I am ready to confess that,

The heavens declare the glory of God, and the firmament showeth his handiwork." I am ready to confess that the broad universe that lies in the regions beyond, speak the Infinite wisdom of God, Jehovah. I am ready to show, if the gentleman will negative the proposition, that that Bible is a revelation from that God, Jehovah, the creator of the universe. But he says the Word of God is written not in books. How came you then to quote from the book? You quoted from the words of Jesus Christ and said it was the Word of God, and it is written in that book.

Luke 6:26, "Woe unto you when all men shall speak well of you." Said that was some consolation to him. Well, I confess I do not see it; there are other religious bodies men speak evil of besides him. I can see no special consolation in it to the gentleman. But he says, "Jesus says, 'Love your enemies.' " Amen. "Whatsoever you would that men should do unto you, do you also unto them." That is good. That is the very basic principles of Christianity—the base of Christian morality.

But he said, "The gentleman's Elowheems are but Gods of various Kings. I deny it, and challenge for proof. It is an easy matter to make assertions. So give us a bit of proof, please. Elohim is the God of the Bible, the God of the Jews, the God of the universe.

But, lest my time should run out before I am thinking of it, I have some rebuttal evidence to place against what the gentleman has asserted. He asserted that Modern Spiritualism, the fundamental principles of it, are identical with the spiritual basis of the Religion of Jesus Christ. Here are some of the teachings of the apostles of Jesus Christ, to whom the Christ said, "Whatsoever ye shall bind on earth shall be bound in heaven and whatsoever ye shall loose on earth shall be loosed in heaven" (Matt. 16:19; Matt. 18:18).

I submit, ladies and gentlemen, that Spiritualism is mentioned in the Divine Truth by these apostles, but not as the teachings of Jesus Christ. Paul in 2 Tim. 4:1-4 says, "I charge thee therefore before God, and the Lord Jesus Christ, who shall judge the quick and the dead at his appearing and his kingdom; Preach the word; be instant in season, out of season; reprove, rebuke, exhort with all long suffering and doctrine. For the time will come when they will not endure sound doctrine; but after their own lusts shall they heap to themselves teachers, having itching ears; and they shall turn away their ears from the truth, and shall be turned unto fables." The apostle, looking through the spirit of inspiration—the spirit of the Great and Eternal God; looking down in this age of the World, seeing that men would turn away from the faith of Christ, turn after their own lusts and follow these teachers that would teach them that they might walk in accordance with their lusts, warns us against them. The gentleman sitting before us to-day has been teaching you that it is best for man to walk after what he pleases—after his own lusts—that it is *best* to say the least of it. The apostle told you he was coming. Did he not tell us that just such as that would be taught? Listen! For the time will come when they will not endure sound doctrine; but after their own lusts shall they heap to themselves teachers, having itching ears; and they shall turn away their ears from the truth, and shall be turned unto fables." What are they turned unto? The fable of the Fox girls. But this is not the only place. Hear

— 55 —

Paul again as he gives a more full description of this, in 1 Tim. 4:1-3, "Now the Spirit speaketh expressly, in the latter times some shall depart from the faith, giving heed to seducing spirits, and doctrines of devils; speaking lies in hypocrisy; having their conscience seared with a hot iron; forbidding to marry, and commanding to abstain from meats, which God hath created to be received with thanksgiving of them which believe and know the truth." Here is a statement of the Apostle concerning Modern Spiritualism. Listen. Paul says, "The spirit speaks expressly that in the latter times." Did you get his qualifying word, "LATTER TIMES"? Paul was living in the time that then was, and through the spirit of the living God, seeing that after awhile time would be divided and subdivided, speaks of the very division of time as we now have it. Speaks of a time to come, as the latter times—speaking of it in the way in which we today speak of it. From the present we call *modern times.* From Paul's age, it would be *latter times.* History is divided thus—ancient, medieval and modern history. Modern history begins this side of the breaking up of the papal supremacy. And we are told that this new Religion, Modern Spiritualism, came up in 1848. Grant it. That is *modern times.* Came up the very time the Apostle declared that "the Spirit speaks expressly it would come up. "Depart from the Faith, giving heed to seducing spirits and doctrines of devils." Now I am prepared to show you, if the gentleman denies it, from quotations from his own writers, that the Spirits that talk to them many times are seducing spirits; that they admit many times that it is the spirits of devils—demons that are speaking to men. Hence we have these identified. In 1 John 4:1, John says, "Try the spirits." "Beloved, believe not every spirit, but try the spirits whether they are of God." How will you try them, gentlemen? By what rule will you know them? Listen to the 6th verse, "We are of God, he that knoweth God heareth us; he that is not of God heareth not us. Hereby know we the spirit of truth, and the spirit of error." The teachings of the Gospel are true, and if the spirits teach what this book teaches, they teach the truth.

Again, concerning the workings of miracles in modern times. Revelations 16:13-14 tells us, "And I saw three unclean spirits, like frogs, come out of the mouth of the dragon, and out of the mouth of the beast, and out of the mouth of the false prophet. For they are the spirits of devils, working miracles, which go forth unto the kings of the earth and of the whole world, to gather them to the battle of that great day of God Almighty. Again, in second Thessalonians 2:2, "That ye be not soon shaken in mind, or be troubled, neither by spirit, nor by word, nor by letter as from us, as that the day of Christ is at hand." Verse 9 tells us that the man of sin would come with all "power and signs and lying wonders. And with all deceivableness of unrighteousness in them that perish; because they received not the love of the truth, that they might be saved. And for this cause God shall send them strong delusion, that they shall believe a lie; That they all might be damned who believed not the truth, but had pleasure in unrighteousness." Here, then, we find the men that do not love the truth. But Paul says their professed miracles are but "lying wonders." But what is the truth? Christ says of God, "Thy word is truth." And again in Matthew 24:24, Jesus Christ tells us that false prophets would come and that they would show great signs and wonders in so much that they would deceive, were it possible, even the very elect. The apostles say that after a certain time the working of miracles would be lying wonders, and not true ones. That it would be unclean spirits that professed to work miracles. So I desire to look into the gentleman's wonders, and show the falseness of his claim.

TIME EXPIRED.

REV. J. W. RING'S THIRD AFFIRMATIVE.

Yesterday afternoon my opponent made special reference to the "modern advent of Spiritualism" through our now World-famous Fox Sisters as a fairy story. I wish there were more such Fairy stories. I wish there were more little children whose lives could be moved to utter these sacred truths whereby the prophecy of the great "Teacher of Galilee" might be fulfilled, when he said "a little child shall lead them." When we look upon these sweet little girls, only one of them yet bloomed into womanhood—the others yet mere children—receiving these phenomena that have aroused in the hearts of men and women throughout the entire World a realization of the Spirit of Truth and Life and Wisdom. It is indeed refreshing, and we can but wish with heart and spirit that there were more such sweet children—more such fairy stories. My opponent said that he considered I was a Son of Adam. I don't know that I can help it. I do not know exactly to which of the Fairy stories of Genesis he may have referred. You, who are familiar with the reading of the first chapter of Genesis, realize that there are two distinct Fairy stories as to the creation of mankind. In Genesis, chapter 1, verse 27, we read, "So God created man in his own image, in the image of God created he him; male and female created he them." In the second chapter, seventh verse, "And the Lord formed man of the dust of the ground, and breathed into his nostrils the breath of life; and man became a living soul;" continuing in the 21st verse is the wonderful surgical operation where the "Lord God" relieved Adam of one of his ribs and made therefrom a woman.

Verses 16 and 17, "And the 'Lord God' commanded ed the man, saying, of other trees of the garden thou mayest freely eat, but of the tree of knowledge of good and evil, thou shalt not eat of it; for in the day that thou eatest thereof thou shalt surely die." Twenty-fifth verse, "And they were both naked, the man and his wife, and were not ashamed." In the 3rd chapter is that wondrous, far-famed "Fall of Man." That is where he came to know good from evil—where he fell, or rather raised from a state of roaming in the field like the beasts thereof, to a reasoning, thinking human being. Chapter 3, verse 7, "—and they knew they were naked, and they sewed fig leaves together, and made themselves aprons." Does it not fill us with the spirit of rejoicing to know that according to this Fairy story our father and mother, who ate of the tree of knowledge, knew that they were naked? Continuing in this we read in the 21st verse, "Unto Adam also and to his wife did the Lord God make coats of skin, and clothe them. And the Lord God said, behold the man has become as one of us, to know good and evil; and now, lest he put forth his hand, and take also of the tree of life and eat, and live forever; * * * * so he drove out the man," for fear he should eat of the tree of life and live forever he drove him out of the garden—"because he has become as one of us and knoweth good from evil." I want to emphasize the fact that the day wherein Adam ate of the tree of knowledge he did not die, for in the 5th chapter and the 5th verse we read, "And all the days that Adam lived were 930 years; and he died." So he lived several days after he ate of the tree of knowledge—and he lived through days of wondrous fruition-days wherein he knew good from evil—days wherein he could buffet with the experiences of human life and bear its burdens and its sorrows, with its joys and its pleasures, and be "of all things a man." He lived long enough, as it is recorded in the 6th chapter and 6th verse—"And it repented the Lord that he had made man on the earth, and it grieved him at his heart." Image the Great God of this Universe, that Most High God, of whom you and I are the children, being grieved at heart because he had made man, and because man had learned to know good from evil! I have heard from advocates of the Christian Religion the statement that Adam died spiritually. Well, if he was going to die spiritually, why did not God say "thou shalt die spiritually"? Suppose he did die spiritually? Since in the sins of Adam all men died, then through Christ all men are made alive, as Paul stated. Referring directly to the words of Jesus in John 6:40 he said, "And this is the will of him that sent me, that every one which seeth the son, and believeth on him, may have everlasting life; and he will raise him up at the last day." I rejoice again in spirit to be a child of the Most High—the disciple of whom has said

"It is the will of the Most High that *every* child of earth shall be raised up in the last day." Although it grieved the "Lord God" at heart because man had been formed from the evolution of the ages, although it has become necessary to extend the Fairy story of six days' creation into six long periods, we are still living as children of the Most High, and Christ that has made himself manifest through Buddha and Mohammed and Confucius and Jesus, and Swedenborg and Andrew Jackson Davis giving us the power and strength by which we can evolve our ego until in the last day we shall find out at-one-ment with the Most High. Jesus is recorded to have said (John 6-63), "It is the spirit that quickeneth; the flesh profiteth nothing; the words that I speak unto you, they are spirit, and they are life." This is the echo of Moses and Aaron, and all of the prophets when they said, "It is the Word of God that quickeneth," and the Word of God is most conclusively proven to all intelligent spiritual students to be the message of the Spirit—the spirit that spoke to Moses in the burning bush—the spirit that wrote to Moses on the tablets of stone—the spirit that came and made itself manifest in divers forms and after various fashions to the children of Israel, and later to Jesus; and following him to his apostles, again to Swedenborg, and later to Andrew Jackson Davis, the Poughkeepsie seer whose "Nature's Divine Revelations" proclaims a harmonial philosophy to the multiplying intelligence of the human race. The spirit that has spoken through chosen media for time immemorial is the Word of God, so declared by all sacred writ, and so accepted by all spiritual teachers. Jesus realized this when he found that he was compelled to leave this mortal state of action, and he is recorded to have said in the 14th chapter of John, beginning with the 16th verse, "And I will pray the Father, and he shall give you another comforter that he may abide with you forever;" I want that "forever" underscored—we are going to need it. "Even the Spirit of Truth; whom the World can not receive, because it seeth him not, neither knoweth him; but ye know him; for he dwelleth with you, and shall be in you. At that day ye shall know that I am in thy father, and ye in me and I in you." It seems to me there can not be a clearer statement than the "presence of the comforter." The Holy Ghost, or mediumship, the power of the Spirit World making itself manifest in every clime and nation through the chosen media of the spirit world, has at all times brought to the children of men sufficient evidence of the Word of God—of the presence of "Infinite Intelligence." This "teacher of Galilee" conceived, by the general attitude of his followers, that there would come a time when the power of the Spirit—the Word of God—would not be held as altogether sacred —that there would be great trials and tribulations for those who declared themselves to be mediums as there has been in every age and clime. When Joan "The Maid of Orleans" went in the power and spirit of Almighty God to the Dauphin King of France and said to him, "I am here by the power of God to save thy nation;" when she went to the King, as he sat amid his courtiers disguised, that he might test her, and picked him out, and said, "Good Dauphin, I am sent here to save thy nations;" when she was in authority and placed upon her snow-white charger; went to the battle field and saved France—she changed the history of the entire World, and it was the Holy Church that made Joan a "human fagot." Jesus perceived these things, and in the 21st chapter of Matthew, the 43rd verse, he says, "Therefore I say unto you, the Kingdom of God shall be taken from you, and given to a nation bringing forth the fruits thereof. And whosoever shall fall on this stone shall be broken." He had been referring to the "rejected stone." Ah, the rejected stone is Spirit Communication—mediumship whereby the gates of high heaven are thrown open to the Children of Men, and the Angels of the Most High come to his incarnate children and breathe to them the Word of God.

The various denominations of churches. which stand in marked contradistinction to Christianity, can not fail to realize that this passage is written especially for their benefit. "Thy kingdom is taken away from thee and it is given unto another nation because ye have rejected the stone"—that of Spirit Communication. Lest you might think this was not especially considered by all of the writers concerning the life of this man, you will find the self-same story in the 20th chapter of Luke in the 17th verse. You will furthermore find in the 8th verse of the 20th chapter of Luke, "And Jesus said unto them, neither will I tell you by what authority I do these things." My respected ,opponent said yesterday "Why don't you show us something and tell us how it is done?" Jesus said, "Neither will I tell you by what authority I do these things. "You must ferret it out for yourself. If you want to find out concerning the spiritual gifts, you will have to become spiritual, but if you want to unite with churches rather than Christianity, you will find that "thy kingdom shall be taken away from thee and given into the hands of a nation" that recognizes the rejected stone—the best stone of all—Spirit Communication.

We were referred on yesterday to the 4th chapter of 1st Timothy, 4th chapter, 4th verse, "Now the Spirit speaketh expressly, that in the latter times some shall depart from the faith, giving heed to seducing Spirits, and doctrines of devils." Paul wrote the letter 1 Timothy to the people, realizing that there was going to be a great deal of trouble in distinguishing between the genuine and the false prophet, or the medium that we would to-day call genuine or fraudulent. So he wrote this letter to these people—called it his first Epistle to Timothy, one of his teachers, and warned them that in the latter days some would depart from the faith. Our opponent said he was talking about medium Spiritualism. Why in the name of common sense didn't he say, "In the year 1848 there will come the Devil in Modern Spiritualism?" He said "in the latter days." I want to here establish a fact in your mind that this man Jesus, in his normal condition, not possessed of the fullness of his inspirational condition, firmly believed that he was to establish upon earth a temporal kingdom. He anticipated that he was to be the King of the Jews— that he was to establish a temporal kingdom and that his twelve disciples should be the twelve Judges of Israel. He presumed that his followers would become the ruling people of the World. This is indicated in various instances in his life, especially in his crying that the cup might pass. When he was upon the Cross he groaned and said, "My God, my God, why hast thou forsaken me?" having hoped within his personality that he would become ·indeed and in truth the King of the Jews. He anticipated that he would unfold all of these spiritual gifts and powers, such as had been enjoyed in the previous days, the days of Moses. In the 12th chapter of Luke, in the 2nd and 3rd verses, he says, "For there is nothing covered, that shall not be revealed; neither hid, that shall not be known. Therefore whatsoever ye have spoken in darkness shall be heard in the light; and that which ye have spoken in the ear in the closets shall be proclaimed upon the housetops." All of the fruits of the spirit that we receive in our spiritual seances are simply messages which may be given to the World as it seems wise to dispense them. Jesus anticipated the establishment of such a condition. You realize, my friends, that whoever wrote the Book of Matthew was a Jew. He thoroughly anticipated that the Jews were to be the recipients of this Messiah, for they had long anticipated such an individual and that they would be the chosen people. In Matthew 10-8 he calls his twelve disciples, and gives to them their charge "Heal the sick, cleanse the lepers, raise the dead, cast out devils; freely ye have received freely give." If there is any organization in the World that has received the message of the "Teacher of Galilee," and endeavors to live thereby, it is the Spiritualists, who heal the sick, cast out the devils and minister to the requirements of mankind, regardless of whether they belong to the Church—simply because they are sons and daughters of the Most High. In the 25th verse "It is enough for the disciple that he should be as his Master, and the servant as his Lord. If they called the Master of the House Beelzebub, how much more shall they call them of his household? Fear them not therefore, for there is nothing covered, and hid that shall not be known. What I tell you in darkness, that speak ye in light; and what ye hear in the ear, that preach ye upon the housetops." Do you want anything more conclusive than that the followers of the Religion of Jesus Christ had a correct understanding of and were living in accordance with these phenomena, which constitutes the true Religion. In 2nd Thessalonians, 2nd chapter, beginning with the 9th verse "even him, whose coming is after the working of Satan with all powers and signs and lying wonders, and with all deceivableness of righteousness in them that perish; because they receive not the love of the Truth, that they might be saved. And for this cause God shall send them strong delusion that they shall believe a lie;" He says that that means Spiritualism. Well, I am very much afraid that it is on the other side of the house, for there are no strange delusions in Spiritualism. It is the simple, plain, every-day Religion that admonishes mankind to live according to the laws of their nature— to do unto their fellowmen as they would they should do unto them—to accept all mankind at their best, realizing that within each human life is encased the Spark of Divinity that cannot be extinguished. Since it is the "Will" of the Most High that every soul should be perfected, so does Spiritualism with its clean, pure, simple foundation say "All mankind shall gain an at-one-ment with the Most High, when all of the Children of Men shall know the Truth; the Truth shall make them free, and they shall live the fullness of the law of Love."

Thereupon, J. W. Chism, in the negative delivered the following:

Gentlemen Moderators, brethren, friends:

Again I am glad that by the providence of a loving Father I am permitted to stand before you to further discuss the question that my Friend has affirmed. It becomes necessary that I read the propositon that you may know what he is talking about. "*Resolved*—that,

The fundamental principles of modern Spiritualism are identical with the spiritual base of the Religion of Jesus Christ."

I asked the gentleman yesterday to please give us some evidence. His assertion that they are identical is not proof. A man can assert anything. I have long since learned that assertions do not prove anything. But I would like, if the gentleman has anything that even hints at evidence in the direction of his proposition, I would like for him to submit it that we may examine it.

In his last speech he began with the Fox girls and said I referred to them as a "Fairy story." Is it possible that the gentleman can not understand or hear what I say. I quoted the Apostle Paul, who said that men would turn away from the truth and be turned unto fables. Turn from the *truth* unto *Fables,* and I said it was a fable, and I say it yet. Has he proved it is not? Where is his evidence? He gives us a few utterances of flowery language and of "would to God that there were more of those beautiful fairy stories." "Oh, those beautiful, sweet, girls!" And he says it in such a sweet tone. If you would hear the gentleman in the soft, sweet language that he used, you would think that he was the sweetest thing under the Sun, and that Spiritualism was very sweet. But let me show you what God says about good words and fair speeches. Turn now to Rom. 16:17-18, "Now I beseech you, brethren, mark them which cause division and officers contrary to the doctrine which I have learned and avoid them, for they that are such serve not our Lord Jesus Christ, but their own belly, and by good words and fair speeches deceive the hearts of the simple." Did not the gentleman teach you yesterday that man to serve the Great God must serve according to his environments and his own inclinations? Is not this the one thing that the Apostle speaks of here when he said they serve not our Lord Jesus Christ but their own belly—their own lusts—their own propensities. He says that this very class of individuals are the ones who will with "good words and fair speeches deceive the hearts of the simple." Paul said it. You have heard the attempt made by the gentleman on this stand. There it is, and God's Word said it. I am not here to attempt by slick, soft, slimy language to get people to believe what I say. I am here to submit *stubborn* FACTS, and in that manner of speech that men may know that I KNOW they are facts when I present them.

But, again, he quotes in connection with the Fox girls, "A little child shall lead them." Shall lead whom? Tell these people, Sir, in your next speech, what the Prophet is talking about when he says "a little child shall lead them." Do not take up a scrap, or portion of the scripture in which the writer is talking about *one* thing and apply it to *another,* Sir. Tell the people what he was talking about. Ah, get your book and look it up. Again he tells you that I said He was the "son of Adam." Well, he says he could not help himself. I presume not. But I did say he was the Son of Adam. I do not deny it. He may deny it if he likes (laughter).

Again he says, that Fairy story in the book of Genesis. The record of Creation. He said there were two of them. I deny it. It is an easy matter to make assertions. I will show you there is but one, and I will show you from the very book he read. Gen. 1:26-29, "And God said, Let us make man in our image, after our likeness: and let them have dominion over the fish of the sea, and over the fowl of the air, and over the cattle, and over all the earth, and over every creeping thing that creepeth upon the earth. So God created man in his own image, in the image of God created he him; male and female created he them. And God blessed them, and God said unto them, Be fruitful, and multiply, and replenish the earth, and subdue it: and have dominion over the fish of the sea, and over the fowl of the air, and over every living thing that moveth upon the earth." That is the first chapter of Genesis. I read to the 29th verse. Now he says the 2nd chapter of Genesis gives a different account,—says God formed man of the dust of the ground. Well, let us see. Gen. 2:4-7. "These are the generations of the heavens and of the earth when they were created, in the day that the Lord God made the earth and the heavens. And every plant of the field before it was in the earth, and every herb of the field before it grew; for the Lord God had not caused it to rain upon the earth, and there was not a man to till the ground. But there went up a mist from the earth, and watered the whole face of the ground. And the Lord God formed man of the dust of the ground, and breathed into his nostrils the breath of life; and man became a living soul." Can you understand plain language? This second statement says, "These are the generations of them *in the day that they were created.*" It is not a different account; it is just a rehearsal of the same creation, giving additional facts. So it states itself, that it is an account of the *same things* mentioned before. But I want to know if I grant, for the sake of argument, that he was right about the creation of the world, does that prove his proposition? What does the gentleman mean by introducing this? Is it related to his proposition?

Again, he refers to Genesis 2:17, and tells us that Adam did not die in that day; that he lived 930 years. Show me where it says he would die in that day. There is the book open before him (lays a Hebrew Bible open before him)—the original language—show me where God Almighty said he would die in that day. There is the book—go after it. I knew what you were going to say. I came loaded for you. There is God's Word in the original Hebrew tongue—show it. It says, "That in the day you eat from it dying you shall die." I might render it in English: "If you eat of it in the day of your dying ye shalt surely die."

There was the tree of life to give him eternal life; there was the tree of knowledge for the purpose of giving him knowledge; but God's law forbade that he would partake of the tree of knowledge before he had partaken of the tree of life. But man yielded to his lusts and ate of the tree of knowledge before he had taken of the tree of life, and thus disobeyed God. Then he says that "God repented that he had made man upon the earth," and then poked a little fun at that. Of course, I was not expecting to meet an atheist or an infidel when I came here. I tried to get them on the proposition, but they refused to deny the proposition of the Divine origin of the Bible. I proposed to affirm it. [By Mr. Lee—"Yes, but you would not affirm."] Mr. Chism—"I have never and will never refuse to affirm." Mr. Lee—"You did refuse to affirm it." Mr. Chism—"Your statement, sir, is not true. I said in that letter I would not affirm that the Bible was inspired in *every word*, and you know it, sir. I said that I would affirm that it was an *inspired record,* and you know it. I know it hurts, Mr. Lee, but then the directions say 'take it.' "

But he says of Adam, "Some say that he died spiritually." The day he ate the fruit he died a *moral* death; he was *separated from God* by his actions. The word death means separation. Again, he attempts a quotation from Paul and misquotes it just a little. Paul says, "In Adam all die."

Then again he says, "They want to extend the fairy story of six days into six long periods." Tell what the Hebrew word *yowm* means? That is the Hebrew word. Tell us what it means. There lies a Hebrew lexicon, if you want to see it.

Again, he tells us that Christ operated through Buddha. I deny it, and challenge for proof. Why does the gentleman, in attempting to prove his proposition, just make assertions without submitting any evidence? Any man can *assert* things to be true. But where is the evidence that Christ came through Buddha? Where is the evidence? Only his assertion.

Then he comes to Swedenborg, and on down to Andrew Jackson Davis, and asserts that Christ manifested through them. (We will read some from Andrew Jackson Davis by and by.) John 6:63: "The Spirit quickens, the flesh profiteth nothing." He quoted this and said: "This is the echoing of Moses when he said 'Thy word would quicken.' " One time I must record the gentleman as stating it correctly—that is, the prophet so said. Then he speaks of the spirit manifesting through Moses, Swedenborg, and on down to Andrew Jackson Davis. Again, in another connection, he refers to the language of the Apostle Paul in 1 Tim. 4:1-3: "The Spirit speaketh expressly that in the latter times some shall depart from

— 71 —

the faith, giving heed to seducing spirits and doctrines of devils," and says: "If Paul meant Spiritualism, why didn't he say so?" He did not need to. He described the thing so clearly that if any man will read it and look at spiritualism he can see it.

First specification: *"Some shall depart from the faith."* I read from Scott's Handbook of Christian Evidences, Page 117, as quoted from A. J. Davis, who is the chief apostle of the system of spiritualism. He says: "Nor am I impressed to connect the Spiritual manifestations of this age with any occurrences of any analogous complexion and character which may have been developed in ages past." Phil. of Spiritual Intercourse, Page 14. Again, "The miracles and spiritual disclosures of this era flow *naturally* and *consequently* from the state of mental and moral development to which the Anglo-Saxon portion of the human race has generally attained." Ibid. Page 18. Dr. T. L. Nichols, a distinguished Spiritualist, when speaking of the mission of Spiritualism, says: "Spiritualism *meets, neutralizes and destroys Christianity.* A Spiritualist is no longer a Christian in any popular sense of the term. Advanced spirits do not teach * * * * the atonement of Christ; nothing of the kind."—*Nichols' Monthly Magazine of Social Science and Progressive Literature, for November,* 1854, *Page* 66. Again, "In the testimony of a spirit given in the *Banner of Light,* November 23, 1861, it is said: "Many times before we have said that we can not place implicit confidence in that which we find beneath the lids of the Bible." In the Educator, a book of 680 octavo pages, professing to come from the spirits of such men as Daniel Webster, John Quincy Adams, Martin Luther, etc., we find such stuff as this: "The being called God exists, organically, in the

form of the being called man."—Educator, page 303.
Says another Spirit: "Every one of you are gods manifest in the flesh." "The divine existence is one grand universal man." "Man is God's embodiment—his highest, divinest, outer elaboration. God, then, is man, and man is God."—Educator, page 526. I read from page 119 of Scott's Handbook. This is just enough to show us conclusively (although I have much more at hand I might read) that they have departed from the faith.

We have the evidence in that which went before us yesterday to show that they give heed to seducing spirits and doctrines of devils, to show that they are following after that which they know not. I asked him yesterday how he could identify the spirit. Has he answered me? I asked him if he could tell whether it was the right spirit or the wrong spirit. Hear his answer. "Oh," he says, "Jesus Christ on certain occasions refused to answer questions," and so he refused. Jesus Christ, in the passage referred to, said: "I will also ask you a question, and if you will answer me I will answer you. The baptism of John—was it of man or of God?" The question had been asked of him, "By what authority do ye these things?" So Jesus proposed to answer it if they would answer him. But they said, "If we say it was of God, he will say, why did you not obey him? If we say it was of man, the multitude will stone us." And they said, "We can not tell," and Jesus answered, "Neither will I answer you." Are you going to do me that way? Pop your question to me and see how quick I will answer you. No, that is only a dodge to try to evade the force of the arguments that I presented to you yesterday afternoon. That is all.

He comes next to the New Testament, John 4:15

where Christ says: "I will send you another comforter that He may abide with you forever," and says, "I want you to underscore that word *'forever.'*" Yes, the Hebrew law says that a man shall "serve his master forever." What of it? While Jonah was in the whale's belly it is said of him, "The bars of the earth were about me *forever.*" He uses the same word, while it was a period of only three days, and yet it says *forever*—uses the same word.

The word signifies an indefinite duration of time. It may be limited by surrounding circumstances that bring it down to a man's lifetime—to a short period of time— and it may be so limited as to make it express eternity. When the Greeks wanted a phrase to express absolute, endless duration they used the word twice, *forever and ever.* When the word is twice used, putting it in current English, it would be *"from age to age;"* but here he says "he shall abide with you *forever.*" With whom? Who was he talking to? If you will turn to your Bibles, in the chapter quoted, 14th chapter of John, you will find that our Saviour was talking to the twelve—talking to his Apostles—and he says that "The Spirit would abide with them forever." Through their age, their lifetime. He said, moreover, "Whom the world can not receive because it seeth him not neither knoweth him." What is it to know him? John says, "He that saith I know him and keepeth not his commandments is a liar, and the truth is not in him." 1 John 2:4. Then to know God you *must* keep his commandments, and Jesus commanded, "Go teach all nations, baptizing them." There is a commandment. Have you kept it? No? Then you do not know God. Hence he can not receive that comforter, his statement and argument to the contrary notwithstanding; for his witness says he could not receive it unless he knew God, and again he says, if he does not keep God's commandments he does not know him.

But, he says, "Jesus expected to establish a temporal kingdom on this earth." I deny the charge emphatically. I challenge him to show one passage in the life of Jesus Christ that gives any intimation that Jesus himself thought it would be a temporal kingdom. His disciples thought it, notwithstanding the fact that Jesus Christ continued to tell them that it would not be. Jesus says to Pilate, "My kingdom is not of this World," and before he was crucified, Mark 8:31, he began to teach his disciples how that the "Son of Man must go up to Jerusalem and be killed, and the third day arise again." What did he mean by that if he expected to establish a temporal kingdom? It seems that the gentleman will make any kind of a statement in his effort at proof. If he can get anything that he can make sound as if a spirit, or a medium, had anything to do with it, he kicks it up and gives it a twist.

But he says, Jesus says that "this book, this word would not always be held sacred, but that men would depart from it and that mediums would come up and suffer for it." If Jesus mentioned anything of the kind. it was to condemn it. And the apostles said that these men that called themselves mediums would be "giving heed to seducing spirits and doctrines of devils." Then he calls our attention to Joan of Arc, and says that it was the church that caused her to become a "fagot." Will you please give these people a little history of how the death of Joan of Arc was brought about? And be careful that you give it right?

But he says again, "thy kingdom shall be taken from

thee and given to another people." Who was Jesus talking to? Talking to the Jews. Why? Because they had rejected him. They had not rejected the ministration of Spirits. The majority of the Jews held to the ministration of Spirits. They had not rejected the Spirit that talked with their prophets,—they had not denied that at all. Everywhere in God's book it talks about the Spirit communication with men. But where does it speak about men communicating with *human spirits?* When he wants to take up the case of Saul and the woman of Endor, we are ready to take it up with him.

Then again he tells us that Jesus says, Luke 12:2-3, that, There is nothing secret but what it shall come abroad and nothing hidden but what it shall be made known, and he says "what I have spoken in darkness shall be known and come abroad." Who was Jesus Christ talking to? Why is it that the man will just take a part of a passage and cut off the context and make it appear that he was talking about something he did not have under consideration at all? Luke 12, and as he begins with the second, I will begin with the first verse. "In the meantime when there were gathered together an innumerable multitude of people, insomuch that they trod one upon the other, he began to say unto his disciples, Beware ye of the leaven of the Pharisees which is hypocrisy. For there is nothing covered, that shall not be revealed; neither hid, that shall not be known. Therefore whatsoever ye have spoken in darkness shall be heard in the light; and that which ye have spoken in the ear in the closets shall be proclaimed upon the housetops." Jesus here was talking in direct connection with the hypocrisy of men; that in their hypocritical ways they would get in dark places and try to keep their deeds hid from men. Paul says, speaking of the same thing, that, "every secret thought shall be brought into judgment." Therefore whatsoever I have spoken in darkness shall be heard in the light, and that which I have spoken in the ear in the closet shall be proclaimed upon the housetops, not what Christ spoke in darkness. "And I say unto you, my friends, be ye not afraid of them that kill the body and after that have no more that they can do.". Here Jesus Christ was giving his disciples instructions, showing them that they could not hide anything from God. I believe here I will call your attention to a statement of God Almighty which is recorded in the 45th chapter of the Book of Isaiah, concerning speaking in darkness. "I have not spoken in secret, in dark places of the earth. I said not unto the seed of Jacob 'Seek me in vain.' I declare the things which are of righteousness." What do the Spiritualists do? Go to the darkness. He told you yesterday that Nicodemus had to go in the darkness because he understood the law. God Almighty says, "I have not spoken in secret in any DARK PLACE of the earth." Listen again, Isa. 48:16, "Come ye near unto me, hear ye this; I have not spoken in secret from the beginning; from the time that it was there am I, and now the Lord God, and his Spirit has sent me." Here the Lord has emphatically declared that he did not speak in that dark corner of the earth; that he did not speak in secret.

Then he tells us that the disciples of Jesus were commanded to go and heal the sick, cast out devils, etc., and he says the Spiritualists do this. I will undertake the job of healing five to your one without medicine,— get after me. I will undertake the job of healing five to one without medicine,—I say, get after me. Again he quotes, "If they call the Master of the House Beelzebub, how much more they of the Household." Who has called you Beelzebub? I did not. No, I did not call him Beelzebub. I think he is a deluded man,—that is all. Again he says, "Then he refers to Thessalonians, 2:9, and says that means Spiritualism." Now the gentleman certainly misunderstood me. I did not think he was so badly rattled that he could not understand what I said. I was speaking on the subject of the power to work miracles after the Apostolic age, and I had just shown you that three unclean spirits like frogs were to come out of the mouth of the dragon and out of the mouth of the beast, and of the false prophet. That *these* had the power to work *miracles* and *deceive* people by the *miracles* they would work. And I called your attention to Christ, where he said that false prophets would arise, and would show great signs and wonders, so much that it would deceive were it possible the very elect. And then I called your attention to the fact that the Apostle Paul says "their wonders were lying wonders," and that when they were sounded down, they were not miracles at all, but only lying wonders.

TIME.

REV. J. W. RING replied for the affirmative:

I rejoice still that in my horizon of vision I see the beauteous light of spiritual truth shining through all manifestations of man's love. I rejoice to see the spirit of Christ manifest in the Messiah Buddha, because Buddha proclaimed the Golden Rule several hundred years before Jesus was born. I rejoice to see the spirit of Christ in Confucius because he too spoke the blessed

— 78 —

Golden Rule before Jesus was born. I rejoice that the horizon of my spiritual vision is not so limited that I can but see the personality of Jesus and lose sight of the broad limitless principles of Christ that were made manifest through his life.

My opponent seems to reject my statements. It is very easy to reject statements—very easy to say, "I declare this is not true." If I could afford to get down, I could say many such things. In the 24th chapter of Matthew, however, we read, "And Jesus went out and departed from the temple and his disciples came to him for to show him the building of the temple, and Jesus said unto them see ye not all these things, verily I say unto you there shall not be left here one stone upon the other.' Take heed that many do not deceive you, for many shall come in my name." "And false prophets shall arise and shall deceive them. And there shall arise false Christs and false prophets and shall show great signs and wonders, in so much as if it were possible, they would deceive the elect as the Sun cometh out of the West and shineth in the East. . . . Immediately after the tribulation of those days shall the sun be darkened and the moon shall not give her light, and the stars shall fall from heaven, and the powers of the heavens shall be shaken. . . . Verily I say unto you, This generation shall not pass, till all these things be fulfilled."

I suppose, according to the Greek, it means sometime else, but we are talking in English, if you please. If he did not mean "this generation" but this epoch, or this special dispensation, I want to ask my opponent again, "Why didn't he say so?"

He seems very anxious to know how we are going

to know the spirits. He must be wanting to visit a medium. (By Rev. Chism: I will if you will let me.) He read a little yesterday, but very evidently did not understand it. In the first epistle of John in the 4th chapter is given instructions of how to know whether they are genuine or not. "Believe not every spirit, but try the spirits whether they be of God, because many false prophets are gone out into the World. Hereby know ye the spirit of God; every spirit that confesseth that Jesus Christ is come in the flesh is of God." If Spiritualism does not declare that Jesus has come in the flesh and that Christ has made himself manifest (if it has not made itself manifest in every age and clime, as taught by the philosophy of Spiritualism), I am not able to see the light. Twelfth verse, "No man hath seen God at any time; if we love one another God dwelleth in us and his spirit is perfected in us. Hereby know ye that we dwell in him, and he in us because he hath given us his spirit." If this does not indicate an infinite intelligence, the indwelling of God's spirit, as the fundamental principles of Spiritualism declare, I am unable to see "common sense."

I was audacious enough yesterday to address my opponent as "Brother." He said. "I beg to be excused." (By Rev. Mr. Chism: "Amen.") 1 John 4:20, "If a man say I love God, and hateth his Brother, he is a liar, for he that loveth not his Brother, whom he hath seen, how can he love God whom he hath not seen, and this commandment have we from him that he who loveth God loveth his Brother also." And who is the Brother of Christ? The man that is looking up to the light of truth, beholding it as best his concept will admit, and permitting the same, glorious privilege to every other individual on earth. If I can not wear the "Christian Church goggles" to see the truth, am I at fault? If my Honorable opponent can not see the beauteous light of spiritual philosophy, is he at fault? In the Spirit of the Most High he is my brother, though I may not be his, because he refuses. In that broad humanity in which I live, the lowest, the meanest, even as with Christ, belongs to the great family of the all-seeing God, and I love them,—every one. According to all reasonable concept of thought my Honorable opponent,—perhaps myself,—has the same privilege of interpreting the religion of Jesus of Nazareth as had Paul or Peter or any other man. Paul was never acquainted with Jesus in the body, except to persecute him. He was never moved to receive the philosophy of Spiritualism as Jesus saw it until by clairvoyant vision he beheld the Spirit of Christ. Yet my opponent insists that we accept the interpretation of Paul. Considering the spiritual basis of the Religion of Jesus Christ, I concede him this privilege. He may invite in the conclusions of as many teachers of the Spiritual Philosophy of Jesus as he believes because it permits me the same privilege to refer to some of the concepts of this man Paul. As I told you, Paul conceived the fact that there would be many false prophets and anti-Christs arise. They met with them in their own midst. The fact that when they became Socialists on the day of Pentecost, stating that they were establishing a continuation of the Kingdom which Jesus had prophesied (stating that they would become thoroughly established in these spiritual gifts and own all things in common on the Socialistic principles), the treasurer tried to steal some of the money. With this insurrection in their own family they con-

cluded that of course outside there would be many
anti-Christs and he wrote to all the various churches
and told them that they must look out for these frauds,
and in the 19th chapter of Acts, 13th verse, "Then certain of the vagabond Jews, exorcists, took upon them
to call over them which had evil spirits the name of
the Lord Jesus, saying, We adjure you by Jesus whom
Paul preacheth." They were immediately called to account as to why they did this and Paul declared that
while they were fraudulent, for since the evil spirits recognized Jesus and Paul and did not know them, they
were fraudulent mediums. Continuing in this chapter
you will find that the Ephesians, some of the goldsmiths
who reconstructed the Gods, as the Catholics have to-
day in their accounts so much for repairs to this and
repairs to that. These people said, "Why, Paul is teaching some kind of a God—that we can not put on new
toes and new parts and our business is broken up, and
if you will read the continuation of this chapter you will
find that they went to the Town Clerk and they broke
up Paul's meeting, and Paul embraced the people who
had helped him through this disturbance without being
injured, and took his departure for another country.
Those people who were satisfied with the Spirit Com-
munications that they had received *perhaps* had the
same privilege to live thereby as Paul had to attempt
to impose his Religion upon them. In this same chapter, in the 8th verse, you will find that handkerchiefs
were brought to Paul that he might magnetize them,
and they were laid upon the sick and healed them. Our
physicians to-day perform the most wonderful cures by
magnetizing paper. Paper was scarce in those days
and the men sent their handkerchiefs—the women did

not carry handkerchiefs then—and they were magnetized by Paul and the sick were healed. I remember the case of my own Sister, who was declared to be possessed of an incurable disease by all of the physicians of the county (in fact, of that part of the State), and under treatment of Doctor Dobson, of California, in two weeks was restored to health by these magnetized herbs. These and many other psychic phenomena indicate that the fundamental principles of Spiritualism are identical with the Spiritual base of the Religion of Jesus Christ, if we can take Paul's testimony. This fraudulent element does not exist alone in Modern Spiritualism, but it existed in all the World of Spiritualism everywhere. We find, in fact, that this Jehovah was sometimes compelled to employ lying spirits in order to accomplish HIS ends. If you will read carefully the 22nd chapter of first Kings you will find there the experience of Jehoshaphat, the King of Judea, and Ahab, the King of Israel. They consulted one of the mediums of the Lord and he told them to go out against Ramoth-Gilead to battle and that they should succeed. Jehoshaphat was not satisfied and said, let us try another, and so they called together several hundreds of these mediums, and they all said, thou shalt certainly succeed: but still they were not satisfied. They wanted to try another, and they said there is another medium, "Micaiah." Ahab said, "I don't like him; he don't tell me good things." Isn't that just like Modern Spiritualists?

People go to mediums to-day and say, "I don't like They called this man and he said, "I saw all Israel scattered upon the hills as sheep that have not a shepherd; and the Lord God said, "These have no master: let it because I am not told the things I wanted to be told."

them return every man to his house in peace. And the king of Israel said unto Jehoshaphat, Did I not tell thee that he would prophesy no good concerning me, but evil?" Then they said unto this medium, "Look here— all of these mediums declare that we will certainly succeed; they said, "Why not?" "And the Lord said, Who shall persuade Ahab, that he may go up and fall at Ramoth-Gilead?" "And there came forth a spirit and stood before the Lord, and said, I will persuade him. And the Lord said unto him, Wherewith? And he said, I will go forth, and I will be a lying spirit in the mouth of all his prophets," and so on. So the Lord had employed a lying spirit to go and be a lying spirit in the mouth of all the prophets to the king of Israel to deceive him and get him up to Ramoth-Gilead, that he would fall, and you read the continuation of the chapter and find that he did fall. How are you going to tell who are the good spirits? By appealing to them with the best conditions possible. If Jehovah employed a liar to go and be in the mouth of all of the prophets of the king of Israel, I hardly believe that it is the mission of Modern Spiritualism to declare a trademark to put upon mediums. We can hardly afford so to do.

Returning, however, to the idea of the comparison of the fundamental principles of Modern Spiritualism and the spiritual basis of the Religion of Jesus Christ— bear with me while I read again the fundamental principles of Modern Spiritualism as accepted by millions of people all over the World. First, "We believe in Infinite Intelligence." Third, "We affirm that a correct understanding of such inspiration and living in accordance therewith constitutes the true religion." Acts 17:22 "Then Paul stood in the midst of Mars' hill, and said,

Ye men of Athens, I perceive that in all things ye are too superstitious. For as I passed by, and beheld your devotions, I found an altar with this inscription, TO THE UNKNOWN GOD. Whom therefore ye ignorantly worship, him declare I unto you. God that made the world and all things therein, seeing that he is Lord of heaven and earth, dwelleth not in temples made with hands. . . . For in him we live, and move and have our being." Do you have to stretch that very much, and the all-abiding presence of the Spirit of life and love as proclaimed by the fundamental principles of Modern Spiritualism? In 2nd Corinthians, we refer to Paul again, "We look not at the things which are seen, but at the things which are not seen; for the things which are seen are temporal, but the things which are not seen are eternal." The things which you and I do not see are the forces that are moving our lives. The spirits that overshadow us this evening, unseen to our physical sense of eye, are moving our lives—are influencing the unfoldment of our souls, and in that World of spiritual reality they move even as they move here; until they progress and attain a higher point of development. They are influencing us even as they would have done here because they retain their personal identity, as our fourth declaration states. Fourth, "We affirm that the existence and personal identity of the individual continue after the change called death." In referring yesterday to the fact that the Christian Religion is based upon a dream, my Honorable opponent felt moved to laugh to scorn the idea that it was a dream or that a dream had anything to do with mediumship or Spiritualism, but if you will read the first and second chapters of Matthew you will find that the Angel Gabriel, who had been associated with Daniel years and years before, retaining his personal identity, came to Joseph in dreams and at night and advised how this Christ child should be led that his life might be preserved—that he would become a great medium. You see the wise men, from the various directions, coming to worship at the shrine of this "teacher." We see them moved by this spiritual influence; and we can pick out scores of individuals among our Spiritualistic mediums to-day who have been likewise guarded, guided and protected by these unseen messages, even before their birth,—their names having been given exactly parallel to the case of this "man of Galilee."

I want you to especially read the experience of Saul with Samuel. I don't know whether Samuel talked to Saul or not—save as I read it from the Bible, I wasn't there. The Bible says that it is true, and since I have heard like spirit voices, I believe most emphatically that it is true. Not alone because that it is in here, but because my spiritual ears have heard similar voices. I want you to remember, too, that Samuel retained his personal identity and remembered the old grudge that he had against Saul. "Why disturbest thou me? You know that we are not on friendly terms." "Because the Lord answereth me not." Saul had gazed into the crystal as our mediums gaze into their crystal to-day, and it was blank; he could get no message, and he was compelled to go to some one whom he had declared illegitimate in giving spirit communication and he received the truth. So states the Bible, and I believe it because I have seen similar manifestations. His prophesy came true. Samuel spoke it through this medium from the spirit world, and through a medium that did not have the trademark of Saul, and yet it was true. I want to tell you of some other seances where they had crystal gazing. They had crystal gazing perhaps more than table rappings in those days because they were moving around constantly. The Israelites were a Bohemian set of people, moving from place to place, and their Holy of Holies was the Cabinet which the Spirit Jehovah had instructed them to build, and he made his manifestations there. Being a God of the Mountains, he was compelled to give most of his manifestations in the Mountains.

I need not refer you to chapter and verse of the fact that Jesus retained his personal identity when he returned. After he had ministered to the spirits in prison, after the graves had been opened and many of those that slept came up and appeared to those who were clairvoyants and able to discern spirits in the city, I would like to call your attention briefly to the fact that these apostles and disciples increased their numbers, by the signs and numbers which they gave, by the healing of the sick—by the casting out of devils and by the baptism of the Holy Ghost,—the development of mediumship When they found an individual who had not developed the power of mediumship, but could discern that therein was the latent property, they laid their hands upon him (as our developing mediums do to-day), and he was able to go forward and spread the gospel of Spiritualism as it had been taught by Jesus. Beginning with the day of Pentecost and going on from that time, we find one constant revelation of spiritual manifestations. The rush of winds,—the coming of the Holy Ghost,— certainly as the conditions attendant upon our spiritual seances to-day. In the second chapter of the Acts of the Apostles we find that they empowered some others that they found with this gift of mediumship, or the Holy Ghost, thus fulfilling the commandment of Jesus, to go and heal the sick and to show these signs. And had it not been for churchanity, Christianity would have gone on and on and its brightness would have illumined the ages even as it is illumining the ages to-day through the modern advent of Christianity called Spiritualism. These men, when they were reminded that they had not received the Holy Ghost, said, "What shall we do?" That is, "What shall we do to receive this?" And Peter said, "To receive this power of inspiration, repent and be baptized and ye shall receive the gift of the Holy Ghost, and so these signs and wonders went on." (By Reverend Chism: You did not read it right.) Well, you are good at reading, try it. (By Reverend Chism: I demand that you read it right, sir; Gentlemen Moderators, I demand that he shall read it right.) "Men and Brethren, what shall we do? And Peter said unto them, Repent and be baptized every one of you in the name of Jesus Christ, and ye shall receive the gift of the Holy Ghost." (By Reverend Chism: You skipped some— you can't run that over these people.) "Repent and be baptized every one of you for the remission of sins and ye shall receive the gift of the Holy Ghost." (By Reverend Chism: Good; that is correct.)

TIME.

J. W. CHISM, in the negative, said:
Gentlemen Moderators, Ladies and Gentlemen:

I am glad that I have the privilege of being before you again this evening, to examine the teachings of Modern Spiritualism. A man that will stand with the Book of God before his eyes and misread a passage to try to make out his case, dropping out an entire clause of that passage, and then when I call his attention he refuses to read it, and when I press him he still refuses, and finally had to call to the Moderators to make him read it, and again he read it wrong, and when I pressed him, he finally read it very lightly,—such is the advocate of Spiritualism. Ah! No wonder the Apostle said that men would "wrest the Scriptures" when we see the Word of God handled so deceitfully. What do you call that kind of handling of the Word of God? dropping a clause to make out his case. Paul said they would give heed to seducing spirits and doctrines of devils, referring to this very teaching. No wonder then that they handle the Word of God deceitfully. Right here, while we are on this point, I want to speak plainly again. The gentleman has been telling you from time to time about the spiritual mediums back in Bible times. I wish he would show me in that Bible a thing that looks like a spiritual medium. It seems that he realizes that in reading the Word of Divine Truth, he *can not* make out his case. So he has to *assert* that they *were* spiritual *mediums* to make it fit,—injecting here, and yonder, the explanation that, it was a *medium;* as though he were reading it in the passage itself. Ladies and gentlemen, the Bible mentions nothing of these *mediums* you have heard him talking about.

Again, he speaks about the indwelling of the "Holy Spirit" in them, and of their being guided thereby, as if they believed it. Spiritualists believe that the spirits which guide them are the spirits of departed or dead men, sir, and you know it. Why do you try to leave the impression on these people that it is the Holy Spirit talking to you when you know you teach otherwise? Why does he stand before these people and attempt to make them believe that the Spirit, which he claims is talking to them, is the Spirit of God,—The Holy Ghost, when he knows he claims it is human spirits? There is the man (pointing to his opponent) that will come thus, with his good words and fair speech.

He now presents the case of Saul and the woman of En-dor. The language of Saul is conclusive that Saul did not expect Samuel, nor his spirit to come up, in order to divine to him. Saul says, "Divine unto me by the familiar spirit." He did not say, call up some spirit be-ing and let them come and tell me so and so, but he said, "Divine unto me by the familiar spirit, and bring me up whom I shall name." But how "call up" Samuel? By the familiar spirit. But how by this spirit,—like a man would present Hamlet on the stage; i. e., impersonate him. But when the woman divined by the familiar spirit, she said, "I see Gods coming up." And Saul said, "What form is he of?" And she said, "I see an old man cov-ered with a mantle." And Saul *"perceived"* that it was Samuel. I called his attention yesterday to the Hebrew word, "yadang,"—perceived, which signifies to perceive either by *sight* or by *feeling,* and Saul FELT like it was Samuel. There lies the dictionary with the word in it,—you may turn to it, and read it. Don't tell me you can't read Hebrew! Call up the spirit of Samuel and let him read it for you. This shows us that Saul "FELT" like it was Samuel. Another thing, To grant for the sake of the argument that it was Samuel who came up in spirit would prove too much for him, for there was a Spiritual mantle on him. He was dressed just like he used to be. Say, Do men's clothes have spirits? That one had clothes on him. You tell these people whether or not your clothes have spirits. If it

—90—

was the spirit of Samuel, it was the spirit of his *clothes.*

But he tells us that Jesus Christ commanded the disciples to heal the sick and such like. But that was not the final, or great commission he gave them, when he said, "Go not into the way of the Gentiles, neither unto any City of the Samaritans, but go rather to the lost sheep of Israel. This was when he sent out the twelve, during his personal ministry. But the final commission says, "Go ye therefore and teach all nations, baptizing them in the name of the Father, and of the Son, and of the Holy Ghost: teaching them to observe all things whatsoever I have commanded you: and lo, I am with you alway, even unto the end of the world." Matt. 28:19-20, and in Mark 16-17 it says, "They shall take up my serpents." If I had one of these old rattlers I could run him out of the country with it. You give the snake to me in a split stick, and put just about eight inches of the biting end of him above the end of it, and see if I don't run him out of the country. He claims that they do the things that the apostles did. When Paul picked up the bundle of wood and the viper clung to his hand he shook it off into the fire, and received no harm. Will you do that? Try it, and see if the spirits will heal you. This would be a pretty good test of it.

Again he says, They asked the question, "What shall we do to receive the Holy Ghost?" Where did you learn that? *Where* did you learn it? I reckon it was some of his spirits that told him. He did not learn it in THAT Book (pointing to the Bible). I know what is in that. Peter had reached this conclusion, "Therefore let all the house of Israel know assuredly that God has made that same Jesus, whom ye have crucified, both Lord and Christ. Now when they heard this, they were pricked

— 91 —

in their heart, and said unto Peter and to the rest of the apostles, Men and brethren, what shall we do?" What was the cause of that question? The history of the case shows conclusively that they were made to realize that they had crucified the Lord of Glory; hence, "What shall we do." "What shall we do" for what? What did Peter tell them? He told them to "repent, and be baptized every one of you in the Name of Jesus Christ for the remission of sins, and ye shall receive the gift of the Holy Ghost." What shall they do? *Repent and be baptized. What for? For the remission of sins.* Then, what was the import of the question, "Men and brethren, what shall we do?" This import is found in the answer. The answer of the question shows it was FOR THE REMISSION OF SINS. "And ye shall receive the gift of the Holy Ghost," is a parenthetical clause, explaining a side issue. It being a parenthetical clause, to read the answer, "Repent and be baptized, every one of you in the name of Jesus Christ for the remission of sins, for the promise is to you and to your children, makes complete sense, and does no violence to the text. Then, they were NOT asking how they should receive the Holy Ghost, but how receive the remission of sins again. This could not mean Modern Spiritualism, for it rejects *baptism in the name of Christ.* And yet the gentleman says, "The fundamental principles of Modern Spiritualism are the self-same thing with this." But they are not. They reject baptism for the remission of sins, and he did not want to even read it. I had to *press* him, and PRESS him to get him to read it at all.

But to begin at the first of the gentleman's speech. He tells us that Buddha and Confucius proclaimed the Golden Rule. I deny it. They did not. I challenge you to quote in your next speech the language of Buddha, and Confucius. No, they did not. Their language was, "Whatsoever ye would that men should not do to you, do not you to them." That is Buddha and Confucius. Jesus Christ puts the affirmative, "Whatsoever ye would that men should do to you, do you even so to them." Confucius and Buddha only include the half of what Jesus Christ said.

But he says that I reject his statements, and say, "I deny it." And again, he says, "It is just as easy to assert, as it is to say, "I deny it." But you understand, my dear sir, that YOU are in the AFFIRMATIVE. The *laboring oar* is in YOUR hand. It is for you to submit *evidence,* not *assert.* When you *assert* a thing, all I have to do is, to deny it, and ask for proof. And when you do not produce the proof, you *admit* the denial. You have admitted it, in almost every instance, for you have never submitted the proof, on a thing I denied.

Then he reads from Matthew 24, "This generation shall not pass away until all these things be fulfilled." And says, "I suppose in Greek it means something else." How long will confessed ignorance attempt to teach the people! Ladies and gentlemen, if I did not know the subject-matter under consideration, or have a *fair* knowledge of it, I would not stand before you to debate. It is nothing for a man to plead his ignorance. That does not advance him before the people, nor prove his proposition. If he does not know the Greek and Hebrew, why does he make fun of it? Why does he not call on Samuel for the Hebrew, and I will say Themistocles for the Greek? You know you can get their spirits and talk to them. You say you can. Why do you not do it?

— 93 —

But "this generation." What generation? The one
he was speaking about. What one is he speaking about?
He is speaking about one in a certain day of the World.
He had spoken about one in which he was living. He
brought them down the stream of time to another generation, and says, *"This* generation." When *this* generation comes, it shall not pass until all is fulfilled. But
he quotes me, "I want to know how to try the spirits."
And he says he will show me how. Well! Possibly the
gentleman is getting wiser than his men used to be; for his
men have gone to record in instance after instance,
asserting that the spirits could deceive them. They
have left on record a number of statements of that kind.
But he says, "John tells you how to try them." All
right, I am ready to try it. In 1 John, the 4th chapter,
John tells us how to try the Spirits, and I am going to
try one now. "We are of God." (That is, the Apostles of
Jesus Christ.) "He that knoweth God heareth us; he
that is not of God heareth not us. Hereby know we
the spirit of truth, and the spirit of error." "He that
is of God hears us,"—hears the Apostles. All right,
what did the apostles say? The Apostle Peter said, "Repent and be baptized every one of you in the name of
Jesus Christ for the remission of sins." Have you done
it? Have you heard it? If not, you are not of God.
John says, "He that sayeth I know him and keepeth
not his commandments, is a liar, and the truth is not
in him" (1 John 2:4). Have you kept that command
of Jesus Christ? If not, you are not of God. The spirit
that he is following, rejects baptism. Hence, rejecting
the teaching of the apostles in this passage, so John
declares that "he is not of God." There it is. The
Apostle John said it, I did not. But I have tried his

spirits, all right, and have found that they are not of God.

But he said he had the "audacity to call me brother, and I denied it." Said, "I was not his brother." I still deny that I am his brother in any sense of the word. My mother taught me to call people Brother that were born of the same *parentage,* and not call people brother that were born of a different parentage. The greatest relationship I could have to him at all would be "tribal," and a long way off at that. But he says, * * * in Adam? * * * * Excuse me, I have put off the old man with his deeds. Old things have passed away, and all things have become new. But he read, "If a man says he loves God and hates his brother, he is a liar." I have not said that I hate my brother; I love my brother; I love my enemies. I have been trying to teach *this* man the way of truth. If I did not love him I would not try to teach him the truth. I am not his enemy because I tell him the truth, though I tell him in terse language. Jesus Christ said unto the Pharisees, "Woe unto you, scribes and Pharisees, hypocrites." Yet he was not their enemy. He was their friend, and he would have turned them from their hypocrisy if they would have heard him.

But he said, "We have the same privilege to interpret the Religion of Jesus Christ that the Apostles Peter and Paul had. I deny it, and challenge for proof. That has been one great trouble with this old world, and is still the trouble with it today. Every man claiming the *right* to *interpret* the Religion of Jesus Christ, and not willing to allow *God Almighty* to *interpret* it for himself. But he says, "Paul saw Jesus Christ by clairvoyant vision." I deny it. Paul says, "At midday, oh king, I saw in the way light from heaven above the brightness of the sun shining round about me and them which journeyed with me; and when we were all fallen to the earth,"—what made the others fall down if Paul was a clairvoyant and saw the vision? Paul says they "stood speechless" and "heard a voice," and "saw indeed the light" before they fell down, but heard not the voice that spoke to him, which was after they had fallen down. Jesus Christ appeared to him in person, in his glory and splendor.

Again he says, "Paul conceived the fact that false mediums would arise." Yes, sir, and he told us they would in his writings to Timothy. He described those fellows that departed from the faith, giving heed to seducing spirits and doctrines of devils forbidding to marry. We will hear from some of that marry business to-morrow.

But, he says: "In a socialist meeting at Jerusalem the treasurer attempted to get off with some of the proceeds." Say, did you never read the New Testament in your life? Where did you learn that the "treasurer" tried to get off with some of the proceeds? The apostles were the treasurers. Where did you learn that the treasurer tried to get off with the proceeds? The record of the Book of God shows that Ananias and Sapphira, his wife, sold their possessions and *kept back part of it,* and brought the balance and laid it at the feet of the apostles and said, "that is all." I just leave it for him to explain whether it is his ignorance of the truth or his willful perversion of it. I do not know which. I am willing to allow the gentleman to make his own explanation. He said it was the treasurer, when it was no such thing. Then he turns to Acts 19:13, and mentions a case there of certain vagabond Jews that tried to cast out devils by calling on Jesus whom Paul preached. But the devils said: "I know Jesus, I know Paul, but who are you?" Like they would of him if he undertook such a job.

Then he refers to Paul at Ephesus. Did you people understand the allusion he was making there? If there was anything at all in what he said, it was a thrust at the preacher. That these men had a craft and were making images of the gods, and hence they cried out against Paul because our craft is in danger. The intimation is that preachers were crying against Spiritualists, because our craft is in danger. I have been told that "a man who lives in a glass house should not throw stones." His intimation is that preachers have never traveled nor preached except for money. I presume you do yours gratis, do you? Never receive money for lecturing? But because this Demetrius, this silversmith, got his craftsmen together and raised an uproar in the town and kept it up for about two hours, therefore the fundamental principles of Modern Spiritualism is identical with the spiritual base of the religion of Jesus Christ. Is that your proposition? And is this your way of proving it? Then he tells us that handkerchiefs were brought to Paul and he magnetized them. Chapter and verse, please. I deny it. It is not taught in the Book, and he has not one particle of evidence but his *ipse dixit*. That is all he has. I deny that he magnetized them and demand the proof. Proof is in demand just now. I challenged for it. But reverting again to that Ephesus business. He said these men "carried the matter to the town clerk." Where did you learn that? Say, it says, when they raised that uproar in the city, "great is Diana of the Ephesians," the town clerk came in and with a good deal of difficulty quieted them down. The town clerk came to them; they did not come to the town clerk. Then the town clerk rebuked them, saying that they had nothing which they could report to the higher authorities, and might be called in question on account of this uproar. He ought either to read the Bible so he can learn to tell the facts in the case, or keep the Book in front of him and then be careful to keep two pairs of specs in reach of him, because he might leave out two paragraphs or a whole sentence.

But he tells us that Jehovah used lying spirits. Yes; why? The Apostle Paul said because men did not receive the love of truth God would send them strong delusions that they might believe a lie Ezekiel says that God will "answer a man according to his idol." Why? Because you reject his word. You show yourselves that you do not love the truth, and hence he sends a delusion, for they love unrighteousness. Unrighteousness is the falling short of God's commands. Then if men will not obey God's commands, the delusion comes.

But he says that I raise an exception to his statement that the Christian religion was based on a dream. I certainly did. I call your attention to note how he has shifted the tables on me. Yesterday he had up the case of Mary and the conception of Jesus. To-day he dodges out under Joseph in the dream, telling him to go to Egypt. Ah, when you turn to Luke, the first chapter, and read the record concerning Mary—the one that I told him yesterday was not a dream—he can not find his evidence. So he has to shift his evidence to try something else. Listen: "And in the sixth month the angel Gabriel was sent from God unto the city of Galilee, named Nazareth, to a Virgin espoused to a man whose name was Joseph and the Virgin's name was Mary, and the angel came in and said, 'Hail, thou that art highly favored; the Lord is with thee; blessed art thou among women.' " And when she saw him she was troubled at his saying, and cast in her mind what manner of salutation it should be, and the angel said unto her, "fear not, Mary." * "He shall be great and shall be called the Son of the Highest, and the Lord God shall give unto him the throne of his Father David, and he shall reign over the house of Jacob forever, and of his kingdom there shall be no end." I read to verse 33. This shows conclusively that the gentleman was mistaken about his dream in that which he brought up yesterday. That Joseph was warned to go into Egypt by a vision he saw in a dream I deny not, but the one he had yesterday in evidence was not that case.

Having completed the review, I will now begin with some work to which I want to call your attention in the first speech to-morrow. *A proposition that is susceptible of demonstration is not debatable.* I illustrated this yesterday. But I will illustrate again. If I make the statement that five times five equals twenty-seven, the proposition is not a debatable one. Why? Because it is a proposition susceptible of demonstration. If I can take five times five, in as many units, and put them together, and it counts out twenty-seven, I have proven the proposition. But when I attempt it and fall short by two, it proves the proposition is false. The gentleman comes with a proposition that is susceptible of demonstration. He says that the spirit is in them, that these wonders may be done by them, and that they do them to-day. Let him demonstrate. He says the same things that were done as recorded in the New Testament that they can parallel to-day—that it is identical. Then he can do the identical things, the self-same things. Let him take a man that has been dead four days and call him to life again, and do it amid friend and foe. He can not do it. He knows he can not. Hence, the proposition shows itself to be false in the very failure to demonstrate.

TIME EXPIRED.

(4:00 p. m. August 12, 1907.)

J. W. RING for affirmative.

This afternoon, in beginning our evidence, as we are placing it. before you from hour to hour, I have two special cases of spiritual phenomena which I am desirous of placing before you for your consideration, realizing that you, as a people, are to judge as to their significance, as to their import, as to how they shall impress you as individuals.

You are familiar with the fact that Saul went to visit this woman of Endor to communicate with Samuel, because he was not able to receive any communication through his prophets, or "men of God," or, as we use the term to-day, mediums. The term varies, but the principles are identical. He had received no answer through Urim. We find connected with Urim was Thummim and the Ephod (these were bright stones, similar to the crystals used by mediums to-day, in which these seers, prophets, necromancers, mediums gazed that they might concentrate their minds and receive the impression, or the spirit message, as it might be called). After Saul had failed to receive this communication through these other means of communication, we find that David, in a following chapter, calls upon the priest to bring him the Ephod, and he evidently gazed into this, or at least he inquired of the Lord, saying, "Shall I pursue after this troop, and shall I overtake them?" And in the following verse he was answered in the affirmative, followed, and succeeded. As to the use of articles as instruments for receiving communication, we find they varied in the days of old as they do at the present time. Some of our mediums use tables, some ouija-boards; some of them look into a glass of clear water; some of them close the eyes and some remain with eyes open; some of necessity asking for darkened places, others for the light; some before a large audience, others to an individual. To show you the similarity between the mediumship of to-day and the mediumship of the days of old, we refer you to the sixth chapter and 36th verse of Judges. It is useless to further elaborate upon the attendant conditions and these manifestations. If your intelligence is not sufficient to accept these things as evidence, it is beyond the power of presentation because of the lack of capacity to receive. Gideon asked for evidence from the Lord and is recorded to have said, "If thou wilt save Israel by mine hand, as thou hast said, behold, I will put a fleece of wool in the floor; and if the dew be on the fleece only, and it be dry upon all the earth beside, then shall I know that thou wilt save Israel by mine hand, as thou hast said." There is considerable complaint to-day as to the conditions attendant upon the reception of the various phenomena, yet we find that Gideon was compelled to appeal to the Lord Jehovah, to not only produce dew upon this fleece and leave all the rest of the world dry one time, but still another and still another time, to satisfy him, as a test, that he was receiving a message from the Lord. These evidences are given to you in the outset this afternoon that we may have an array of phenomena that have occurred in days gone by, recorded and largely accepted by thoughtful people, to place parallel with similar phenomena that occur to-day under the modern advent of Spiritualism. The thoughtful are asked to decide for themselves whether or not the similarity indicates that the law of those days is the law of to-day, and that these phenomena are a continuation of the existence of the self-same law.

In Second Kings, chapter 6, verses 5 and 6, we read, "But as one was felling a beam, the ax head fell into the water; and he cried and said, Alas, master! for it was borrowed. And the 'man of God' said, Where fell it? And he shewed him the place. And he cut down a stick, and cast it in thither; and the iron did swim." This is accepted as the result of the law of levitation, and when the self-same law is applied by our modern media we observe tables move and ponderous objects moved about the room—substances transported through substance—matter through matter. These phenomena to-day I proclaim to be identical with the phenomena as recorded in the Old Testament. Passing from the presentation of these phenomena, for surely in these various sessions we have had enough to convince those that are going to be convinced, and it remains for you to decide whether it is evidence or not. (You are the jury, as a body of people gathered together.) I want to especially emphasize the statement made on a previous occasion that we might say "the religion of Jesus is based upon Spiritual phenomena," since in Matthew and Luke we find that the Angel Gabriel, representing a band of spirits, communicated the advent of the individual that was to become the Christ-child.

On one occasion I quoted the visitation of this angel, spirit, or man Gabriel to Mary in the vision—her peculiar phase of mediumship—that of clairvoyance. On another occasion of the receipt of the self-same message by Joseph in a dream—his peculiar phase of mediumship—and surely I am not turning the tables upon you as a jury, nor upon my honorable opponent, because I quote from a certain portion of the Scripture one day and another portion another day. Surely this evidence is as good at one time as at another. I explained to you thoroughly the conditions attendant upon the reception of this message by Zacharias in the Holy of Holies, which is understood as the cabinet in which to receive the manifestation of Jehovah, the tutelary God, through all the days of the Israelites. I can not do more. It is evidence placed in your charge and you are to determine its worth. The fact that these two gospels refer to this proposition is sufficient, yet it is opportune that we call your attention to the fact that Mark, which was probably the first written gospel, wisely omits any mention of the immaculate conception or of the miraculous birth of Jesus (for similar conditions are reported to have attended the birth of the various Messiahs who have come into the World). Matthew writes from a Jewish standpoint. Luke writes rather from a Gentile standpoint, but the genealogies do not agree, and in the book of Luke we are told the Angel Gabriel promised the birth of the Christ-child. He also said that he would occupy the throne of *his Father* David; that he should reign over the House of Jacob. Has he ever done either? Are not the Jews as much of a nation to-day as they ever were? Because they have no specific land does not indicate that they do not enjoy their religion. It does not mean that they are not a nation unto themselves, and that they have never yet accepted Jesus as the Christ. They evidently claim for themselves the privilege to interpret the religion by which they shall live; and have not you and I the same privilege to interpret the religion which appeals to our heart? I remember the time when a minister of the Christian denomination, and another of the Methodist denomination spent an entire week determining the interpretation of baptism. They still disagreed as widely at the end as at the beginning, and they both claimed the privilege to interpret religion as it appealed to them. How are we all to decide upon the matter of religion? Do we all agree upon the matter of religion? Do not the individual members of various sects, creeds and denominations vary in their concept and acceptation of details? The Christian Scientists purport to be devout followers of Jesus Christ, yet they vary in their interpretation. That they are doing a great good in the world can not be denied. Our brethren, the Adventists, hold conclusions peculiar to themselves yet are good people, and among them are some individuals filled with the grace of God, if charitable deeds indicate anything. This attempt to interpret religion and compel other individuals to live by our individual interpretation has existed through all the history of Christendom; aye, through the history of all religious presentation. Peter, in his interpretation of the religion of the "teacher of Galilee," as recorded in the third chapter of the Acts of the Apostles, calls to memory the fact that Moses said to his congregation, "A prophet shall the Lord, your God, raise up unto you of your brethren like unto me. Him shall ye hear in all things whatsoever. He shall say unto you; and it shall come to pass that every soul which will not hear that prophet shall be destroyed from among the people." Here is the mandate of some one endeavoring to interpret the Religion and compel other people to live thereby—feel the thumb-screws, feel the various means of torture that have been inflicted upon the children of men to compel them to believe a specific religion. Peter turns this, which was spoken by Moses, to apply to the prophets that would follow him, that would be selected from his Brethren, and that would minister unto them, and said this meant Jesus. Did he frighten the Jews to whom he spoke? Did the House of Israel tremble? Well, not so far but that they still retain their religious conclusions. Nor has this admonition of Peter prevented the followers of the Apostles from falling away from spiritual gifts, until in the organic body of Christendom to-day we find not a single religion that emphasizes the gifts of the spirit, and give the demonstrations that have been afforded you by reference from this book, which gives us the history of this great teacher, and his promise that these signs should follow as many as believe.

A most elegant grand-stand play was afforded to those who were present yesterday afternoon when the Jury and one of the speakers were presented with a Hebrew Bible—with a book of Greek to tell whether or not the translation which we were studying meant what it said or meant something else. Fortunately, or unfortunately, we are compelled to accept the translation which is made to us. If this translation is erroneous, if these translators are at fault, and the salvation of Jehovah's Children depend thereupon, would it not seem that it would be wise for Jehovah to be attending to this translation and seeing that the proper translation is made? If you and I are being judged, and you are being sent to heaven and I am being sent to hell because the translation is wrong, it seems about time for Jehovah to be doing something, does it not? I appeal to you as a Jury.

Taking up the mediumship of the "Teacher of Galilee" to emphasize the necessary conditions attendant on the phenomena which he received on the Mount of Transfiguration, you will kindly remember that he not only selected the members of the circle to receive this phenomenon, but that they were surrounded by a bright cloud—the cloud that is known to have followed the prophets, the men of God, the seers, the mediums, if you please, of all the phenomena that are recorded in the Old Testament. If there is one medium that stands out in relief as a specific trance medium, it is that of John the Baptist. I dwelt upon this rather extensively on several occasions, and while there has been no attempt by my opponent to show any evidence that it was not trance mediumship, I want to present it again as evidence, referring you to Luke, the first chapter and the 17th verse, where the Angel Gabriel prophesied that John the Baptist, even before he was conceived, would go before him in the power and spirit of Elias. Matthew, chapter 11, verse 14, where the disciples were asking Jesus concerning Elias, and it is recorded that Jesus said, "And if ye will receive it, this is Elias which was to come." In the 17th chapter, the 12th and 13th verses, "But I say unto you that Elias is come already. Then the disciples understood that they spake unto them of John the Baptist." If the fact that John the Baptist was influenced by the Spirit of Elias, is a spiritual manifestation which was accepted as the forerunner of this Great Teacher of whom we are studying to-day, and if this same teacher promised that like signs would follow them that would believe, are not the adherents of the Modern Advent of

Spiritualism receiving the fruits of the Spirit? I beg of you to answer in the name of reason. If this was not the Spirit of Elias manifesting through John the Baptist, as a trance medium, is it to indicate the truthfulness of reincarnation—that it was not John the Baptist but that it was the reincarnation of Elias? Can we find any other plausible explanation of this condition which is brought about?

I feel confident, my beloved brothers and sisters of the Most High in the Spirit of Christ, that these evidences that have been given to you upon these several occasions have been sufficient to occupy your thought along this line of mediumship specifically, and if you are un-prejudiced, and if you are desirous of knowing the truth (and there is no shadow over your ability to consider, reason and logic), you will be able to see the relation-ship between the phenomena which took place in the days of Moses and the prophets, and these phenomena which took place in the days of Jesus and his apostles, and following (leading up through sacred and profane history), to the manifestations of spiritualism under its modern advent, when it brings to the World the self-same message of kindliness, of love, and of doing for our fel-low-man. We can learn concerning the spiritual basis of the Religion of Jesus Christ only as we search these gospels. We have presented to you chapter and verse, explained and elucidated the attendant condition of these phenomena. If you have given yourself any trouble at all in this age of enlightenment, you have seen similar phe-nomena; for it is abroad in the world everywhere. We have given to you the declaration of principles of the National Spiritualists' Association of the United States of America and Dominion of Canada, which is the authority concerning the fundamental principles of this great organization that is bringing light and freedom to the world, and it remains for you to decide whether or not there is a similarity, whether or not they are identical.

Our first declaration, "We believe in infinite intelligence." Second, "We believe that the phenomena of nature, physical and spiritual, are the expressions of infinite intelligence." Third, "We affirm that a correct understanding of such expression, and living in accordance therewith, constitutes the true religion." Sounds very familiar to Paul's, when he is recorded to have said in his letter to the Ephesians, 4th chapter and 6th verse, "One God and Father of all, who is above all, and through all, and in you all." Again, in first Corinthians, 3rd chapter and 16th verse, "Know ye not that ye are the temple of God and the Spirit of God dwelleth in you." Again in Acts, 17th chapter, 22nd to 28th verses, as I referred you yesterday to the unknown God which he proclaimed to the people, and declared that that which they worshiped ignorantly proclaimed he unto them. Again, in Romans, chapter 13, verses 8 to 10, in his admonition to the church, "Owe no man anything, but to love one another, for he that loveth another hath fulfilled the law. For this thou shalt not commit adultery, Thou shalt not kill, Thou shalt not steal, Thou shalt not bear false witness, Thou shalt not covet; and if there be any other commandment, it is briefly comprehended in this saying, namely, Thou shalt love thy neighbor as thyself. Love worketh no ill to his neighbor; therefore love is the fulfilling of the law." In the following chapter, the 14th, from the 7th to 17th verses, "For none of us liveth to himself, and no man dieth to himself, for whether we live, we live unto the Lord, or whether we die, we die unto the Lord; whether we live, therefore, or die, we are the Lord's. For to this end Christ both died and rose and revived that he might be Lord both of the dead and living; but why dost thou judge thy brother? or why dost thou set at naught thy brother? for we shall all stand before the judgment seat of Christ, for it is written, as I live, saith the Lord, every knee shall bow to me, and every tongue shall confess to God, so then every one of us shall give account of himself to God. Let us not, therefore, judge one another any more, but judge this rather, that no man put a stumbling block or an occasion to fall in his brother's way. I know and am persuaded by the Lord Jesus that there is nothing unclean of itself, but to him that esteemeth anything to be unclean, to him is it unclean, but if thy brother be grieved with thy meat, now walkest thou not charitably. Destroy not him with thy meat for whom Christ died. Let not then your good be evil spoken of, for the kingdom of God is not meat and drink but righteousness and peace and joy in the Holy Ghost."

J. W. CHISM, in behalf of negative.

Gentlemen Moderators, Brethren and Friends:

I am most assuredly glad that I am permitted, once again, by our loving Father to appear before you to further continue the investigations.

If the gentleman had commenced the first day of the debate, like he has this afternoon, to try to present a line of thought containing some argument, we might have had some debating. He has, I must confess, at least one time made an attempt toward making an argument. He has at last attempted to establish his proposition.

But I have a double task this time, as this is my last

speech in which I have the privilege of introducing new matter. I will, first, introduce some new thoughts, and then I will examine what this gentleman has said. There are one or two things, however, in the gentleman's last speech that I wish to examine before I take up the new matter.

He spoke about John the Baptist coming in the "spirit and power of Elias," and tells us this is transmediumship. Where did you learn that? But, he says, "You prove it was not." Well, sir, *The moon is made of green cheese;* you prove it is not. Am I here to prove a negative? *You* are here to *prove* your proposition. You being in the affirmative, the burden is on you. What does your *bare assertion* amount to? You simply *asserted* that it is transmediumship. The Bible does not say so! There is no writing of divine origin that *does* say so. Why did he not submit some *reasoning* to *show* that it was transmediumship? "But he shall go in the Spirit and Power of Elias." A man goes as ambassador from the United States in the Spirit and Power of this Government. I presume this Government has a Spirit that is transferred to that man, has it? In the name of common sense! "Spirit and power of Elias." That is under the same *authority* Elias was under. That is all. A man may be sent by this Government to England, and go in the spirit and power of this government. Does it make him a transmedium? What does he go in? Why, he goes *in* the *authority of that which is back of the government*— in the authority of the government, if you please. In the spirit, the teaching of that government. Then, what did John do? Go in the spirit and power of Elias. He was *sent* by the spirit that was back of, or that sent, Elias. That is, Elias was sent by the Spirit of Jehovah, and John came in the power and spirit of Jehovah. John came in the same *spirit*—teaching of Elias. Turning the hearts of the fathers to the children, as Malachi said. So we find what is to be done by John in the teaching of Elias. Elias was a reformer, reforming the hearts of the people. turning them back to their God. John was doing the same thing, hence, "In the spirit and power of Elias." Not transmediumship at all.

But he told you we had a grand-stand display last evening when a Greek Bible and a Hebrew Bible were laid before him on the table. Ladies and gentlemen, I must confess that I feel ashamed of an opponent that will make such statements as that. When, oh, when will *confessed ignorance* cease trying to teach the people? Does he not know Hebrew? Say "No?" Is it possible that Samuel did not know Hebrew? He was a Hebrew himself. Let him call up the Spirit of Samuel, and let him tell what these Hebrew words mean. Why don't he do that? Simply because *he knows* he *can't,* and he *knows,* too, that there is *not* a man in the *world* that *can* do it. Neither does he know anybody that knows anybody that can. They *have not* a man in America that will *undertake* it. I *challenge* them to the contest; let him try it; *let him try it.*

Oh, but he tells us, if we are being sent to hell because translations are wrong. Who said a translation was wrong? I did not. I simply called him to the Hebrew word *"yowm"* that was translated into English. The question came up on the word "day," and I simply called him to the Hebrew word for "day." I told him that I had a dictionary here. Not that it is wrongfully translated into English; but what is the meaning of the word "day." Let us get at the root of the word. I am not standing before this people just to kill time. I realize that I will stand in judgment before God. Now, I will give you that word "*yowm,*" the Hebrew word for "day." Gesenius gives us this definition of it: "*Yowm,*" day; "so called from the diurnal heat." Do you get the meaning of the word? Do you catch the idea? A period in which the sun passes over us from East to West is a period of heat, and hence is called "*yowm,*" because it means heat. That is the root idea of the word—"heat." Then God made the world in six successive heats. Again, the word is used to represent our day as distinguished from night. Again, the word is used to represent an "*indefinite period of time,*" as the "*day of Jehovah.*" Gesenius gives about three pages in the definition of the word. Here is the word; there are definitions in English. (Showing pages in lexicon to audience). No, it is not the translation that is wrong. It is not the translation that is leading men to destruction. It is men trying to deceive the people from translations. Men that are trying to twist it so as to prove something that is not in the translations. But I cited the Hebrew word for "day," and its root idea, to show the *meaning* of the English word "day."

But he wants to know if God had ever fulfilled either one of these prophecies as to Christ sitting on David's throne? Most assuredly. The Apostle Peter said that God had raised up Christ to sit on David's throne, and the Book of Chronicles says that David was "*on the throne of the Lord.*" But Christ is on the throne of God now, But the throne of God was the throne David was on, hence Christ is now on David's throne.

But he gives us two cases of Mediumship. One of these is Saul, King of Israel, with the woman of Endor; and the other one, I believe, he gave me was Gideon.

He said that Saul got "no answer from Urim and Thummim, the two stones, and the Ephod that was peeped into." And he tells us that David calls for the Ephod. Well, I reckon so! Say, what does Ephod mean? You should know what Ephod means before you make such a break as that. (Reading from Hebrew dictionary): "An ephod, a garment of the high priest, worn over the tunic and outer garment or pallium; without sleeves and divided below the arm pits into two parts or halves, of which one was in front, covering the breast and belly, and the other behind, covering the back. These were joined above on the shoulders by clasps or buckles of gold and precious stones, and reached down to the middle of the thighs; they were also made fast by a belt around the body." That is the Ephod. That is the stone David called for to get his revelations. Oh, in the name of common sense! Say, don't expose your ignorance like that. I don't want these people to know I am debating with a man like that.

Then he tells us about Gideon, and *says* he has the *parallel* in this country to the fleece and the water or dew on it. I wonder when the Spiritualists present such a case as that before the people.

Then he mentions the ax-head that floated. Where is the Spiritualist that did such? By the same law, he says, "ponderous objects are now moved about." When did you do that? Do you do that in the daylight or in the dark? I saw one of those *ponderous objects* moved about at Dallas last fall. The room was made dark and a man came in and *professed* to hypnotize a girl. Everything was dark in the room—we could scarcely see the girl. After a while he suggested that she move upward in the air, and she rose up, and then she moved upwards

8

and backwards and sideways, as he suggested that she move. And he then walked right around behind her, to show that there was nothing touching her, and at his suggestion up she went again and back and down to the ground again. He then suggested "wake up," and she ran straight forward off of the stage. But I happened to be close to the stage, and as she would go up and down I heard the little electric machine go "click, click, click, click." If they had struck a match in the room they would have seen the lever that was moving her up and down. "Ponderous objects raised?" Well, yes!

But he tells us that the Holiest of Holies was a cabinet that they had to go into. I wonder if he knows anything about that Holy of Holies? Say, are you not aware of the fact that from the time that that Holy of Holies was first instituted in the tabernacle out in the Wilderness that the *cloud* was upon it? The Shekinah of Glory? Are you not aware of the fact that there was a pillar or *cloud* by day and a pillar of *fire* by night over that Holy of Holies? Are you not aware of the fact that when Solomon prayed at the dedication of the Temple that the Glory of the Lord filled the Temple—the cloud filled it? That it rested over it until the destruction of the Temple in Jerusalem by the Babylonians? If he will give us something like this, that everybody may see, standing continuously in the sight of the people, they might have some confidence in the revelation that comes from that cabinet. But do you remember the challenge I made? He has not attempted to cause his Spirit to walk out across the floor.

Then he gave us a dissertation on Peter, and on what Peter should have said at Pentecost, and that Peter was making it a *mandate,* to *compel* people to obey his ideas of that doctrine. I told you the other day that he did not believe in the Bible. Here he comes in his *argument,* and even *denies* that the Apostle Peter, of whom Jesus says, "I will give you the keys of the Kingdom of heaven," had any right or power to explain the religion of Christ. The very one to whom Jesus Christ said, "I *give* you the *power to do* it." Spiritualism is just a late form of infidelity. That is all.

I now have a counter affirmation that I desire to introduce and I ask that the gentleman note it carefully. From first Timothy 4:1-3, "The Spirit speaketh expressly that in the latter times some shall depart from the faith, giving heed to seducing spirits and doctrines of devils, having their conscience seared with a hot iron, speaking lies in hypocrisy, forbidding to marry and commanding to abstain from meats." I maintain that this is a prophecy, by the Apostle Paul, of "Modern Spiritualism." Now I propose to take it up, item by item. First specification: *"In the latter times."* We call your attention to the fact that our common history divides time into *"modern,"* and *"ancient"* times. We speak of the time of the present, as, "modern times." Back yonder, is the "ancient time." The Apostle Paul, looking down the ages, seems to have gathered the idea that men would thus divide time. Speaking from his *view point,* instead of saying modern times, he says, "In the latter times." We are *today* in *that day* that Paul spoke of,—"the latter times." Even in the midst of us has come up a people calling themselves "The *Latter* day Saints," showing that everybody regards this time as *"the latter times."* But I read again, to show you that spiritualism did come up in *modern times.* Scott's Handbook of Christian Evidences, p. 117. I quote from Andrew Jackson Davis, to whom you have heard the gentleman refer a number of times, as one of the apostles of Modern Spiritualism —A. Jack Davis, if you will have it. But I read:

"Nor am I impressed to connect the spiritual manifestations of this age with any occurrences of an analogous complexion and character which may have been developed in ages past."

"The miracles and spiritual disclosures of this era flow naturally and consequently from the state of mental and moral development to which the Anglo-Saxon portion of the human race has generally attained." This gives us our first specification, that it had its rise in "*modern* times." The gentleman himself tells us that it rose in 1848, and said it has been organized only about fourteen years. Grant it; that makes it, then, the *latter* times. Our claim stands on the first point established.

Second specification: *"Shall depart from the faith."* Turn to the same volume, Scott's Handbook, page 118. I read from E. V. Wilson, one of their shining lights, who published a book in favor of Spiritualism, who says: "Truly, our religion is a religion of knowledge, and NOT a religion of faith." (Small caps mine. Speaker.)— Truths of Spiritualism, page 158. The gentleman himself, my opponent, has said as much from this rostrum, "that they were not acting from faith, but from knowledge." Hence, *"Have departed from the faith."*

But again, on the same point, same volume on page 116, he denies the *authenticity* of the *Bible,* and says that *"Christ* was a disembodied Spirit, controlling *Jesus* as a medium." My opponent again has said as much when he said it was the same as Buddha and Confucius. These statements show that they have *"departed from the Faith."* But again on same page, Scott's Handbook,

— 116 —

page 142, he exclaims: "Thanks to the All-Father and the dear old Mother God." On the same page, "Mary to our home returned, we to the work of the gods." Again, he offered to affirm the following proposition: "That the Christian religion, as taught, had its conception and birth in evil, and that the serpent of Genesis is really the founder of your Christianity, he foreseeing the necessity for a Redeemer."—Truths of Spiritualism, page 321. But again we find, on page 119 of Scott's Handbook, from Dr .T. L. Nichols, a distinguished Spiritualist, when speaking of the mission of Spiritualism, says:

"Spiritualism *meets, neutralizes and destroys Christianity.* A Spiritualist is no longer a Christian, in any popular sense of the term. Advanced spirits do not teach * * * the atonement of Christ; nothing of the kind."—*Nichols' Monthly Magazine of Social Science and Progressive Literature, for November,* 1854, *p.* 66. Again, on the same page of Scott's handbook, "Many times before we have said that we can not place implicit confidence in that which we find beneath the lids of the Bible." *Banner of Light, November* 23, 1861. Again, "The being called God exists, organically, in the form of the being called man." *Educator, page* 303. Says another spirit: "Every one of you are Gods manifest in the flesh." "The divine existence is one great universal man." "Man is God's embodiment, his highest, divinest, outer elaboration. God, then, is man, and man is God." *Educator, page* 526. Mr. T .L. Harris, a leading man among them, preached a sermon in London on the teachings of Spiritualists, in which, in summing up their general belief, he said:

"Fifth, That our Lord's theological and psychical teachings were but the reproduction of false mytholo-

gies." Again, in another series, "Fifth, that there is
no retrogression, through moral disorders, either of the
individual or of the species." "Sixth, that vice is virtue
in its unprogressive or germinal condition; that sin is an
impossible chimera." Or again, turn to another series:
"First, that the Scriptures are not the word of God, and
that the Divine Spirit never vouchsafed utterance to man.
Second, that the Messiah, our Redeemer, is not, in any
sense, a Savior of the soul from sin, death and hell.
Third, that he never met in combat our spiritual foe;
that he never overcame or cast out destroying spirits
from their human slaves; that he never made an atonement or expiation for sin; that he never rose in his re-
assumed humanity from the grave; that he never ascended glorified to heaven; that he never communicated the
Holy Ghost." Such are the teachings, if you please,
from the leading lights of Spiritualism. Hence, what
I showed you yesterday, when I called your attention to
the fact that he did not believe in the Holy Ghost, though
he believes that human spirits do these works.

Scott's handbook, page 121: "Spiritualistic literature
is full of the most insidious and seductive doctrines, cal-
culated to undermine the very foundations of morality
and virtue, and lead to the most unbridled licentiousness." *Facts, Fancies and Follies of Spiritualism Explained.* Again, on the same page: "For seven years
I held daily intercourse with what purported to be my
mother's spirit. I am now firmly persuaded that it was
nothing but an evil spirit and infernal demon, who in
that guise gained my soul's confidence, and lead me to
the very brink of ruin. * * * * Five of my friends
destroyed themselves, and I attempted it, by direct spiritual influences. Every crime in the calendar has been

committed by mortals moved by viewless beings! Adultery, fornication, suicides, etc." Again, on the same page: "I have a volume of sixty closely written pages, of names of those who have been drawn down from respectability, morality, wealth and intelligence, to the filth of free love, poverty, and to insanity itself. Spiritualism is a synonym of all falsities and lies; a cloak for all kinds of crimes, adultery, murder and lust; it weakens man's intellect and individuality; changes his worship of God to a worship of ghosts." Before I pass on to my fourth specification, I wish to give one more quotation on this point. It is from *"Evans-Fishback Debate—page* 51. I want to read this because it is from A. Jack Davis—*Andrew Jackson Davis.* "A. J. Davis, in answer to a question concerning the appearance of spirits, in the Herald of Progress, February 1, 1862, says: 'These appearances are intended merely as reminders and tests of identity. All intelligent spirits are great artists. They can psychologize a medium to see them and to describe them in the style that would produce the greatest impression on the receiver. * * * They can easily represent themselves as being old or young, as in the worldly dress or in flowing robes, as is best suited to accomplish the ends of the visitation. They substitute pantomime and appearance for oral explanation." Thus, you see, it is a confessed deception—they *confess* it themselves. Hence the third point, "giving heed to seducing spirits and doctrines of devils," is identified.

The fourth specification is *"Speaking lies in hypocrisy."* We have instanced a number of these in another speech. Here I will call your attention to only one. Scott's handbook, page 124: "After all our investigations for seven or eight years, we must say that we have as much evidence that they are lying spirits as we have that there are any spirits at all. * * * The doctrines they teach * * * are mostly contradictory and absurd." *Spiritualism Unveiled, page* 100. This was from Joel Tiffany, a well-known Spiritualist, who once debated with Eld. Isaac Errett. With this one quotation I shall leave this point. There are others I might read, but the time is short, so I leave them off.

My fifth specification is, *"Their conscience seared with a hot iron* (the Greek says "cauterized"). On this point I do not need to call your attention to that which is written in their books. I have the evidence in my opponent. A man that will stand before an intelligent people, debating for truth, and *misread a passage in God's word,* and when asked to correct it, *refuse to do so until* the moderators call on him, and then have to be *made* to read it right—that man, I maintain, is such a man as is here mentioned, his conscience seared and cauterized. Then again, reading from Isaiah 11:6, "A little child shall lead them," he said that this referred to the little Fox girls. But I read this passage, verse 6, "The wolf also shall dwell with the lamb, and the leopard shall lie down with the kid; and the calf and the young lion and the fatling together; and a little child shall lead THEM." (Pointing to his opponent) Here is the man that stood before you and quoted that passage as applying to the Fox girls, misleading the people. I need no further evidence to support this charge, though I have much more that shows that their conscience IS *seared with a hot iron."*

Fifth Specification: *"forbidding to marry."* I read, if you please, from Scott's handbook, page 135. "The

Spiritualists oppose marriage, and advocate *free love.* They feel the force of this passage, as is evinced by the fact that the word *"priest"* is added in a perverted New Testament, which they claim was revised by the spirits, making it read, *"forbidding the priest to marry."* Again, in the same book, page 138: "In a speech at the Spiritualist Convention at Ravenna, Ohio, July 4 and 5, 1857, Mrs. Lewis said that to confine her love to one man was an abridgment of her rights. * * * Although she had one husband in Cleveland, she considered herself married to the whole human race. All men were her husbands, and she had an undying love for them. What business is it of the world whether one man is the father of my children, or ten men are? I have a right to say who shall be the father of my offspring. Such comes from one of the great woman Spiritualists.

One more quotation, this time from the Evans-Fishback Debate, pages 143-4. I shall begin down in the middle of the quotation, as I have but a short time. "The spiritual world is the counterpart of the earth world, in this as in other matters; and as the generative organs are the proper vehicles for the impartation and propagation of natural life, so the same organs in the higher life, and, of course, in a higher plane, are vehicles through which spiritual life is often, though by no means always, caused to flow. They affirm that any positive spirit has access to any negative spirit where there is affinity; that though the male may have a female companion who is constitutionally adapted to be to him a better helpmate, on the whole, than any other, and so generally accompanies him, yet the latter has no jealousy and knows no exclusiveness; that she is glad to have the life of God increased in any way and anywhere; that the same liberty will ere long be given to men on earth, who are found worthy to obtain that world and the resurrection of the dead, which can be done without putting off the body." So the claim that "forbidding to marry" is applicable to Spiritualists is sustained.

Last Specification: *"Commanding to abstain from meats."* On this point I shall read but a single sentence, written concerning Andrew Jackson Davis: "Who opposed the killing of deer and all other animals." Of course, if they can not kill them they can not eat them. So we identify Spiritualism to be that which was prophesied by Paul.

TIME EXPIRED.

J. W. Ring makes his last speech in the affirmative:

No doubt you very readily understand that these lengthy references are given with the anticipation that it will divert your mind from the issue at point. These are the statements of men, so we can read the statements of men concerning their interpretation of the religion of Jesus. Infidels and Atheists, even those who are yet retained as ministers of respective churches differ in their interpretations and declare that this or that is not doctrinal, and vary in their conclusions. These statements read are not the fundamental principles of Spiritualism. I have held these clean, pure and lofty principles before this Jury, until I feel confident that every intelligent individual has become saturated with the cleanliness of Spiritualism, and the beauty of its purport. The Spiritualists, as a body of people, are ready to be called upon to stand in line and give answer as to their morality, as to the good which they are doing the world, in comparison with members of any denomination. If we can depend upon the records of our country, there are certainly no more individuals in the insane asylums who have been driven there from modern spiritualism than through revivals in churches. Whom do we find in the penitentiaries? Go and look! To what denominations do they belong? I am not here to bemean the character of any individual, nor am I here to attack the character of any religion. I come in the sweet spirit of Christ that lifted up the Magdalen, that sat down and ate with the publicans and sinners, and I proclaim to this Jury that I am a follower of that man in his purity and in his cleanliness, and insofar as I am capacitated, represent this declaration of principles which presents to the world these same ideas. That I might defame the character of individuals or attack the general methods of any religion would be a very easy matter, but I can not stoop to such attempts at argument, or reason; but I present in a concise manner those ideas which I believe will appeal to the thoughtful members of my jury. If it were not to digress from that which I know will weigh heavily upon the intelligence of those who are to determine this thought, I would like to refer to this matter of transmediumship. I hope that I shall have the time some evening to dwell extensively upon this—upon the matter of cabinets and conditions attendant upon the manifestations in those days and the manifestations to-day. The light surrounding the Holy of Holies is identical wth the cloud, with the presence of the spirit forces that surround our cabinets to-day. I leave it for you to determine this. You, not my opponent, are the Jury. Referring again to James, chapter one, 27th verse, we have his definition of religion—"Pure religion and undefiled before God and the Father is this, to visit the fatherless and widows in their affliction, and to keep himself unspotted from the world." It is for you to determine who possesses the pure religion. It is not for you to refer to the statement of some individual. We are not called here to pass judgment on the belief of any individual, and determine therefrom what his moral status may be; we are to look to the principles by which he lives. Because a minister is put in the penitentiary, am I to say ministers are frauds, and should be put out of the world? Just simply one that has fallen by the road-side, and alas, many of them have fallen thus. I believe that Paul was imbued with the same spirit that touches me this afternoon when he wrote the following, recorded in First Corinthians, chapter 13—"Though I speak with the tongues of men and of angels, and have not charity, I am become as sounding brass, or a tinkling cymbal. And though I have the gift of prophecy, and understand all mysteries, and all knowledge; and though I have *all faith,* so that I could remove mountains, and have not charity, I am nothing. And though I bestow all my goods to feed the poor, and though I give my body to be burned, and have not charity, it profiteth me nothing. Charity suffereth long, and is kind; charity envieth not; charity vaunteth not itself, is not puffed up, doth not behave itself unseemly, seeketh not her own, is not easily provoked, thinketh no evil; rejoiceth not in iniquity, but rejoiceth in the truth; beareth all things, believeth all things, hopeth all things, endureth all things. Charity never faileth: but whether there be prophecies, they shall fail; whether there be tongues, they shall cease; whether there be knowledge, it shall vanish away. For we know in part, and we prophesy in part. But when that which is perfect is come, then that which is in part shall be done away. When I was a child, I spake as a child, I understood as a child, I thought as a child; but when I became a man, I put away childish things. For now we see through a glass, darkly; but then face to face: now I know in part; but then I shall know even as also I am known. And now abideth faith, hope, charity, these three; but the greatest of these is charity."

Our fourth declaration—"We affirm that the existence and personal identity of the individual continue after the change called death." How beauteous to know that our personal identity continues, and as Paul says, "I shall know even as also I am known." We shall recognize ourselves, because we are the same individuals, moved by the same emotions as here, and we can progress and advance until we attain to that high degree of development that brings us to the fullness of spiritual development. Reverend Talmage said: "Men shall do in heaven what in their best moments they did on earth; the tombstone is not the terminus, but the starting point." To know that we are going higher and higher, and that all mankind, through love (the principle of their salvation) that manifests itself to every tribe and nation, to the children of men, shall all come to a realization of the truth.

Were it my purpose to lower your attention to ridicule—were it my intention to bring you to a lower concept of things (surely no individual would stand before an intelligent audience and presume to misquote from a book that each individual holds in his hand—surely none could be so foolish) I could invite your attention to some of the doctrines that have arisen from the creeds and the concepts of certain denominations, as my opponent has called your attention to the conclusions of certain individuals concerning our modern Spiritualism, and tell you of the time where we are declared to enter into hell or heaven to remain forever; that we shall so change in heaven, that we shall enjoy looking over into hell and seeing our loved ones in that condition.

We retain our personal identity. The mother loves her child, and if she sees her child is suffering she retains her mother-desire to save that child. If the hands of the Almighty have been shortened until he can not bring every one to himself, alas, alas, and alas again.

I have already referred you to the fact that Samuel retained his personal identity—that he came clothed in the mantle which he had worn that he might be recognized. Had my opponent any understanding of the principles of spiritual phenomena under its modern advent, he would know that these individuals make themselves known that they may be truly recognized, and that there may be no question that they are the individuals which they purport to be. We realize the existence of false prophets, even as in the days of old. I am trying to show you the comparison. Where false prophets existed in those days, they exist today; and we realize that we must have something to identify those with whom we are communicating, even as they did in the days gone by. The several appearances of Jesus after his transition and resurrection indicate that he retained his personal identity.

Our fifth declaration—"We affirm that communication with the so-called dead is a fact, scientifically proven by the phenomena of Spiritualism." This does not indicate the purity or the impurity of spirit communication; it simply proves that spirit communication is a fact, and to scientific people, it has come as evidence for the fact. The quality of the mediumship depends upon the conditions attendant. It depends upon the capacity of reception—the power of spiritual discernment. Demonstration does not satisfy the prejudiced. Overwhelming evidences of spirit communication would in no wise convince the prejudiced,—the bigoted, and the one who "already knows that it is the works of the devil" or that there is nothing in it. I realize that many of you have already settled in your mind concerning this issue —you are not honest in yours—you could not be placed in a jury to determine upon an issue of law, because you are prejudiced. You have conclusions already made. I am talking to the individual that wants to know the truth; I know that I am talking to his mind; I know I am touching his heart. I have seen evidences of it every hour I have been in your midst, and I rejoice in the power of the Spirit that I am more staid in the beauty of my philosophy than I have ever been before.

Scientific demonstration in no wise satisfies the prejudiced. There are many individuals in the world today who yet believe the world is not round. Do you suppose that the world were any less round when people thought it was flat? Do you suppose that the fact of spirit communication was any less true before it made its modern advent, and was declared to be of natural law? Recognized as a special dispensation, divine providence, by the people of old, was simply their concept, and I have endeavored to show you how this has led up to the present time. Our sixth and last Declaration which I present to you—"We believe that the highest morality is contained in the Golden Rule, 'Whatsoever ye would

that others should do unto you do ye also unto them.' "
As Jesus stated, his statement was an echo of Buddha,
and of Confucius. My honorable opponent called
your attention to the fact (I supposed, of course that
you already knew it) that these two gentlemen stated
it in the negative while Jesus stated it in the affirmative.
This simply denotes the advancement of the people. Our
concept of truth varies. Day unto day are we adding
unto ourselves evidences and facts concerning this
great Infinite, Supreme and Eternal Whole, and so our
concepts enlarge and our conclusions vary. That you
may be confident that we, as disputants, agree upon
one matter at least, you will notice this sixth declaration
and recall the fact on the first day of our explanation
of these things my worthy opponent said "the golden
rule is the foundation of Christian morality." If this
be the foundation, then, with Paul and Jesus, we stand,
for charity and love as the fulfillment of the law. Leaving this matter entirely in your hands, realizing that
you can decide it only yourselves, I simply ask you to
look into the beauteous light of truth as it appeals to
you to-day. Pray to the all-presiding Presence of Infinite Intelligence that to-morrow a broader concept of
truth may be yours; that your hearts may have the
greater charity. It is useless for individuals to attack
one another as to their concept of things; it brings the
principles they are endeavoring to elucidate down to
our personality. We can not demonstrate the principles;
we can only hope to attain thereto, and in our personali-
ties we are only climbing higher and higher that we
may attain to these heights, that we may conceive Infinite Intelligence in all things. Spirit communication has
brought to the children of men who sought for truth—

truth; it has elevated and exalted the mentality and the character of individuals. Look over the rank and file of Spiritualists and see the work they are doing as evidence. Use your individual reasoning powers, your capacity of thinking, of concluding, of discriminating— to know whether or not these fundamental principles of modern Spiritualism are identical with the spiritual base of the religion of Jesus Christ, as we are able to discern it from the brief accepted record which is made of his works, teachings, and ministrations to the children of men. Your intelligence must be the judge; yet it is only to judge for self. "No man liveth unto himself nor dieth unto himself; but whether we are living or dead we are the Lord's." We are parts of this supreme whole; we are children of that great Parent in whom, living and moving and having our beings, we evolve and progress; round by round, step by step draw nearer to that perfection of life made manifest through unfolding charity and bounteous love one for the other.

Completes his speech five minutes before his allowance ends.

J. W. CHISM—LAST SPEECH FOR NEGATIVE.

Gentlemen Moderators, Brethren and Friends:

I am before you for the closing speech of the afternoon and of the proposition, and I ask you to bear with me while I notice some of the things the gentleman has said.

I will begin with the beginning of his last speech. I submit that it is a very easy matter for a man to deliver good words and fair speeches, to deliver them in a soft flowing tongue and will almost make every one weep.

9 — 129 —

You remember the anecdote—the boy telling about the dog catching the rabbit and killing it, and how his mother wept because of the tone of voice in which he told it. Just strip the gentleman of his tone of voice and there is nothing left. His manner of address is all there is to his speech. I confess he is a pretty good orator. But oratory does not make truth. The Apostle Paul said that men would come with "good words and fair speeches" to deceive the hearts of the simple, and it would be, he said, those who had turned from the faith. And I have shown you conclusively, from God's word—the Bible, that these Spiritualists have "departed from the faith." But my opponent says these statements that I read—these long quotations—were for the purpose of diverting your attention from the issue. Beg pardon, sir. But I must deny the charge. I plead not guilty. They were read for the purpose of showing you people that, after you had been deceived by "good words and fair speeches," then it will be attempted to lead you onward and onward, until it will finally allow them to the privilege of gratifying the most unholy lusts. I have shown you from the writings of their men—he says they are from "men." True! But what kind of men? From Spiritualists, and leading men among them at that. If they have lied, it is spiritualists that have lied. I have read their statements—not mine. The gentleman tried to offset the force of it by saying, "Oh, I could read things against the Bible from the pens of infidels." Yes! Of course you can! Of course you can. But. Read statements that, Bible teaching leads men into such corruption as this from teachers who believe the Bible, can you? Can you do it? No! But I read from your own authors, sir. He says again, "Look in the penitentiaries and see what churches they are of," and after, while he sees what he is getting into, and, "Oh!" he says, "I don't accuse any one of these corruptions. I come in the sweet spirit of Christ; I am a follower of Christ." (Addressing his opponent) You are no such thing. Jesus Christ emphatically said "Go teach all nations, baptizing them," and you have not been baptized, and you know it. You are not a follower of Jesus Christ at all sir. Jesus Christ said to Peter "I give unto you the keys of the kingdom of heaven, and whatsoever thou shalt bind on earth shall be bound in heaven, and whatsoever thou shalt loose on earth shall be lost in heaven." (Matthew 16: 16-20.) You stood before this people, sir, and said 'Peter was trying to "force them to do what he said." As though the Apostle had no authority from Jesus, when he was doing the very thing that Jesus Christ told him to do. And yet you have the audacity to stand before this people and say "I am a follower of Jesus." Oh, shame! Where is thy blush?" "Conscience seared with a hot iron!" I have identified them.

But as the gentleman speaks of the "sweet spirit of Jesus" I want to show you that in denouncing false doctrine and false teachers Jesus Christ spoke as bitterly as ever did J. W. Chism. Listen—(Matthew 23: 23-28) "Woe unto you, scribes and Pharisees, hypocrites! for ye pay tithe of mint and anise and cummin and have omitted the weightier matters of the law, judgment, mercy and faith; these ought ye to have done, and not to leave the other undone." (27th verse) "Woe unto you, scribes and Pharisees, hypocrites! for ye are like unto whited sepulchres, which indeed appear beautiful outward, but are within full of dead men's bones, and of all uncleanness. Even so ye also outwardly appear righteous unto men, but within ye are full of hypocrisy and iniquity."

Doesn't that sound something like what Chism has been saying? Is not Chism following the Spirit of Christ when he tells you that men are whited sepulchres, when without they appear beautiful, but within they are full of iniquity? One of his own kind said, "I have the right to say who shall be the Father of my children." "What is it to the world whether one man or ten men be their father." There is the inside of the whited sepulchre. It came from a Spiritualist in good standing. You have seen in my opponent the outside.

But he tells us that the light around their cabinets is just the same as that light which was about the Holy of Holies. "Conscience seared with a hot iron identified." I can make all the light that he produces about his cabinet with a bit of phosphorus. Here is a light, dazzling into the skies above the Holy of Holies, the Shekinah of Glory, a cloud in the day time and fire at night time, a bright light that shone around, so the people could see to walk in the darkest night by its light. Have you anything like that? Where is that light you produce that is similar to that above the Temple, sir? Where is your Shekinah of Glory that gives light to the inhabitants of the city at night? Ah! Echo answers "where?"

But he says, "James speaks (James 1:26-27), of pure and undefiled religion." Sure, and James says it is this, "To visit the fatherless and the widows in their affliction and to keep yourself unspotted from the world." Do not walk in adultery, do not walk in lust, nor shall you nullify the marriage vow. But the husband shall depart from father and mother and cleave to his wife, for these two are one flesh. These are the things that are taught in the Bible; that spiritualism would erase, and give you the liberty of libertines and free love.

"I believe that Paul was imbued with the same spirit that toucheth me this evening." So says the gentleman, and he read from the 13th chapter of 1st Corinthians, "tho I speak with the tongues of men and of angels and have not charity I am nothing." Ah, I believe that. But, I would ask the gentleman, what is charity? As this very passage will be under discussion in my proposition when I am in the affirmative, I will give him the privilege, even in that proposition, to answer it. What is charity? You answer, "Love?" All right. John said, "This is the love of God, that you keep his commandments." Again John says that, "He that says he loves God and keepeth not his commandments is a liar." Then, a man to love God must keep his commandments. Christ says, "He that believeth and is baptized shall be saved." Do you love him? Do you keep his commandments? His *(my opponent's) commandments are all from the finite nature of man. As we showed you yesterday evening in his concept of it.

But he says, "Would any man stand before an intelligent people and presume to misquote from a book that every one had in their hand?" He seems to thing that they would not. Why did you do it? You did that very thing yesterday. Did you do it ignorantly? Do you plead ignorance on it? He must either plead ignorance or wilful perversion, because he left out a clause and I had to call him and press him hard to get him to put it in. That little clause "for the remission of sins," he wanted to leave out. The passage would not fit his theory with that in it.

Again he says, Had my opponent any knowledge of spiritual manifestations he would know that the spirits make themselves known. Well, I have called his attention to the fact, time and time again, that his own leading men say that you "cannot tell who they are." I read from his great men, his Apostle A. Jack Davis (Andrew Jackson Davis), who said that they could "impersonate" and represent themselves as "old" or "young," and were great "artists," and would appear in such manner as to make the best impression. If they can impersonate, then they can deceive, and if they can do that you cannot tell whether it is the spirit you want or some other. But again, in Evans-Fishback debate, pages 48-49, the Spiritual Telegraph, July 11, 1867, in the leading editorial on the Identification of Spirits, says, "The question is continually being asked, especially by novitiates in spiritual investigation, 'How shall we know that the spirits who communicate with us are really the ones they pretend to be?' And, for want of a satisfactory answer, many minds are thrown into perplexity, and even doubt, as to whether the so-called manifestations are really such. In giving the result of our own experience and observation upon this subject we would promise that spirits unquestionably can, and often do, personate other spirits, and that, too, often with such perfection as, for the time being, to defy every effort to detect the deception. Not only can they represent the leading personal characteristics of the spirits whom they purport to be, but they can relate such facts in the history of said spirits as may be known to the inquirer, or to some one else with whom the communicating spirit is, or has been, *en rapport;* and this, in our opinion, is done so often as to very materially diminish the value of any specific tests that may be designedly instituted by the inquirer for the purpose of proving identity; and if direct tests are demanded at all, we would recommend that they be asked for the purpose of proving that the manifesting influence is spirit rather than to prove what particular spirit is the agent of its production." So much for Spiritualists themselves. Some of them, their leading men, say they cannot identify them. My opponent says they can. It is just left with you, ladies and gentlemen, whether you believe a Spiritualist or, a Spiritualist, I am out of it.

I call your attention, now, to a brief review, and I will make it as brief as I can, and may close before the time is out, owing to the fact that it is looking like rain.

He refers to Genesis, "Six days." We called your attention to that in the first speech, and showed you the meaning of the word "day." Has the gentleman attempted to refute it? His silence gives consent that my argument is right. I thought I would have a fight on it, and I was prepared for the fight.

In second Timothy 4:3, I called your attention to the fact that Paul said, "The time will come when they will not endure sound doctrine; but after their own lusts shall they heap to themselves teachers, having itching ears; and they shall turn away their ears from the truth and shall be turned unto fables." I called your attention to the fact that this was done in turning after the fables, the Fox girls.

In 2d Thessalonians 2, verses 1 to 9, we called attention to the fact that miracles would be wrought in our age of the world; that God Almighty testified by his apostle that it would be done. But the Apostle says the miracles, so-called, are lying wonders. Again, there were to be three unclean spirits, like frogs, that would go forth working miracles to deceive the people by the miracles that they could work. Here comes a gentleman to tell you that he has miracles, and they prove he is right. Hence, to deceive the people with the miracles that he works. In Matthew 24-24, Jesus tells you that false prophets would come, and false christs, and would show great signs and wonders in so much that if it were possible they would deceive the very elect.

Just here let me call your attention to one "sweet" statement the gentleman made. He who comes "in the 'sweet' spirit of Christ," but says to the people assembled here, "You are not honest jurors." Such is the spirit, "the sweet spirit of Christ," in which he comes, with his sweet words, "You are not honest jurors; I am speaking to the few that want to believe; that want to know." He is speaking to the few that want to believe Spiritualism. If they want to believe Spiritualism, why then, he is speaking to them. That would be a fair interpretation of the gentleman's language. But, "you are not honest jurors." Men and women who realize that they are passing from time to eternity, and that their eternal welfare depends on their being right while in this world, and who say you cannot be saved unless you are right. He tells you that "You are not honest jurors."

But again, "Spiritualism is the soul of religion." I denied it, and the gentleman never came back to his statement again. But he comes with a different statement, now. He tells us that the religion of Jesus Christ is based on spiritual manifestations. Amen. Who denied it? The other day he said it was on a dream of Mary, on a clairvoyant vision. I showed him it was not. Then he said it was a dream of Joseph and I showed him it was not. Now he says "On spiritual manifestations." Sure! Manifestations of the spirit controlling Jesus Christ. Jesus walking on the water, sea obeying him, wind obeying him; such things as these show that he was a divine being.

Again he asserted that Jehovah was created by the Jews. I denied it. He never submitted one particle of evidence, but dropped it like it was hot.

He asserted again that, "No history was written of Jesus Christ until after Christ had passed away seventy years." I showed him, according to Luke, whom he had introduced as his own witness, that he had missed it something like thirty-nine years, and he has never denied it.

Again he says, "In this arena of spiritual conception we realize that all is divine." Again, that, "Live as education and environments say to you." I called your attention to the fact that that would justify life as corrupt as the black villain ravisher of the South lives. When I called his attention to this he said that it was "best" at any rate, showing you that he considers that these awful crimes are best. Such are the teachings of Spiritualism, that comes in such a "sweet spirit" before you to try to get you to believe that all is purity. He has confessed before you that the black villain who outrages a white woman has done the best.

But he tells us that Nicodemus went in the night, because he believed that he understood the law. Strange indeed! And now he is going to give things in the light, where they did work in Nicodemus' time.

We come next to Saul. The gentleman has brought this up, and we have had it up several times. I called your attention to the fact then, and do again, that Saul was not expecting Samuel in person, nor in spirit to come. He said to the woman, "Divine unto me by the familiar spirit." Then it was by the spirit, the familiar spirit of the woman. And "Saul perceived that it was Samuel." I called your attention to the fact that the word "perceived" in Hebrew was to perceive by sight, or, feeling. Hence, Saul "felt" like it was Samuel. This is evidenced again in Saul's language when he said to the woman "divine to me by the familiar spirit." Then Saul talked with Samuel. In first Samuel 28:15, he talked with Samuel, and in first Chronicles 13, he says it was the familiar spirit that he talked with. Hence, the spirit that Saul talked with was the familiar spirit of the woman. Hence, he says "bring up," or as we would use it to-day, "bring out," Samuel. Did she bring him in spirit? Oh, no. She just impersonated Samuel. That is all. The familiar spirit divined or impersonated Samuel. He could not "bring up" Samuel in the literal sense; that would make Samuel to be down in the earth. Spiritualists do not teach that the spirits are down in the earth, nor does the Bible so teach. Hence, they would have to say, according to Spiritualists, "Bring me down Samuel." He would have to use a different word entirely. Then Samuel was not "brought up" literally, either in spirit or person. But he was brought up in impersonation by the familiar spirit.

Again to the statement, "A little child shall lead them." Did he try to explain that? "A little child shall lead them." He was applying it to Spiritualism, to the Fox girls. But I called your attention to the fact that the Prophet applied it to some one else. He simply dropped it, never attempted to explain it.

Again he says, that, Jesus could do no mighty works because of the unbelief of the people. I illustrated that at the time that the doctor could not cure the sick child because of the unbelief of the father. The father's unbelief would prevent the doctor curing the child, because, the father would not give the medicine to the child, and thereby permit the doctor to cure him. So the unbelief of the people would not allow Jesus the privilege of working the miracles; they would not bring their people to him to be cured. Because they did not believe that he could cure them. Hence, because of their unbelief, he could do no mighty works there.

Then the spiritual photograph was in order. I challenged him to produce a spiritual photograph. He refused to even try. When he makes a spiritual photograph I am ready to make them right out there in the open sunlight, before this people, and you cannot tell how it is done either. I am ready to do it. Again, whenever he gets into his cabinet and sews himself up in a sack, and the spirit comes out and walks across the floor, I am ready to go in the cabinet and be sewed up in a sack and walk out in person, and yet you will find me still sewed up in the sack. I am ready to go to the test wher he is.

Again, he asserted that, Jesus firmly believed that he would be a temporal king on this earth. But when I called his attention to the fact that Jesus Christ himself said that he would go up to Jerusalem and be killed, and the third day rise again, he dropped the thing like it was hot.

Then he came to the Golden Rule, Confucius and Buddha gave it, and said that they spoke by the same spirit of inspiration that Christ spoke by. And that it was the same spirit in Christ. I denied it and challenged him to quote the Golden Rule as given by Buddha and Confucius. Though I quoted it yesterday, he made no attempt to quote it to-day. I have never yet heard a man who would stand on the rostrum and make the statement that he did—that the Golden Rule as given by Christ was the same as that given by Buddha and Confucius—I say, I have never heard one that could quote what Buddha and Confucius did say. I quoted it yesterday; I quote it again. "Whatsoever ye would that men should not do to you, do not you do to them." Jesus Christ put it otherwise. "All things whatsoever ye would that men should do to you, do ye even so to them." Hence, Buddha and Confucius only gave the half of what Jesus Christ did. Now, he tries to admit it, and avoid it's force by saying it is "development." Yes, I should say it was. But that does not indicate that the spirit was speaking through Buddha and Confucius, by a good deal.

But he says, "Paul saw Jesus Christ in a clairvoyant vision." I denied it and called your attention to the fact, that, the men with him heard a voice and saw the light. Has he ever even asserted that I was wrong. By his silence he has confessed again that his statement was wrong. You understand, in a debate, when a man comes with a proposition and the other man denies it, and the affirmant never touches it again, even after his attention has been called to it, he admits that he was wrong and the other man was right.

Again he called attention to socialism at Jerusalem, and spoke of the treasurer getting the money   And I showed him he was wrong, and he dropped that. When a man does not know any more about the Bible than that, when he does not know the teaching of the Bible on the subject, he does not know enough to teach the people.

Then he says that "Paul magnetized handkerchiefs." I denied that and he has never come back at it again. Hence, he admits that it was not true.

Now as to their wonderful cures and such like, that they claim. As I told you in the beginning, I am ready to undertake the job of healing five to his one, without medicine. I know the law of healing, and I know the law of suggestion. I understand the laws they work through, having studied it thoroughly. And I am ready to go to the test. But he is afraid of the issue.

In conclusion, I call your attention to what has been said on the proposition, pro and con. The proposition is before you. I read it again, and ask you to be the jurors, believing as I do, that you are honest jurors, that is, the majority of you at least, are honest jurors, I believe you to make the decision in your own minds. The proposition is "Resolved, that, the fundamental principles of modern spiritualism are identical with the spiritual basis of the religion of Jesus Christ." We have called your attention to the statements he has made, concerning this, and showed you, according to the teachings of God's word, that his proposition is untrue. We have called your attention to the fact that in order to make out his case he could not read the scriptures as they read. But he had to leave out a part, and make others apply to a different thing than that to which they referred.

Hence, in conclusion his proposition stands simply this,
Indicating hot air by his gestures.

TIME EXPIRED.

Thank you, ladies and gentlemen.

4:00 p. m., August 23d, 1907.
By Presiding Moderator T. W. Head:

Now the time is drawing close for the next proposition to be taken up, and I will read the proposition, so that you can all understand what it is.

"Resolved, That the Scriptures teach, that, with the

close of the apostolic age, spiritual gifts, such as are mentioned in the Bible, ceased."

J. W. Chism affirms—John W. Ring denies.

This is a new proposition, now, and Brother Chism will take the lead.

J. W. CHISM—FIRST AFFIRMATIVE.

Gentlemen Moderators, Brethren and Respected Friends:

I feel thankful, this afternoon, that I have the privilege of meeting with you once again, for the purpose, this time, of affirming the proposition which has been read It becomes my part, as an affirmant, to so define the terms used in the proposition, that there can be no misunderstanding with regard to them, so I invite your attention first, to a definition of the terms.

"The Scriptures teach." By this statement I simply mean, first, by the Scriptures, the writings of the Old and New Testament—the book that is commonly called the Bible. By the statement, "they teach," I mean to convey the idea that, they either say so in so many words, or, that, by a combination of passages relative to the proposition, the conclusion is inevitable. Note, I do not say that, the conclusion may follow, but I say that "it is inevitable"—must follow, "that, with the close of the apostolic age." What I mean by "the apostolic age" is, the life time of the Apostles. The time that they lived on this earth, before they died, and then such an age of the world following them as would bring us to the death of the last person upon whom these Apostles had bestowed spiritual gifts, through the imposition of their hands.

With the death of the last one of these, I would mark the close of the "apostolic age," and hence, that the Scriptures teach the spiritual gifts, such as are mentioned in the Bible, would cease at that time. By spiritual gifts that are mentioned in the Bible I mean such as we find recorded in the 12th chapter of first Corinthians. I read this passage in order that the people may have the understanding of what we mean. I read the first eleven verses.

"Now, concerning spiritual gifts, brethren, I would not have you ignorant. Ye know that ye were Gentiles, carried away unto these dumb idols, even as ye were led. Wherefore I give you to understand that no man speaking by the spirit of God calleth Jesus accursed, and that no man can say that Jesus is the Lord, but by the Holy Ghost. Now, there are diversities of gifts, but the same spirit. And there are differences of administrations, but the same Lord. And there were diversities of operations, but it is the same God which worketh all in all. But the manifestations of the spirit are given to every man to profit withal. For to one is given by the spirit the word of wisdom; to another the word of knowledge by the same spirit; to another faith by the same spirit; to another the gifts of healing by the same spirit; to another the working of miracles; to another prophecy; to another discerning of spirits; to another divers kinds of tongues; to another the interpretation of tongues. But all these worketh that one and the selfsame spirit, dividing to every man severally as he will." These are the things that we speak of. There are nine of them mentioned in this reading, and these are they to which we make reference, as spiritual gifts. The proposition, then, I affirm, says that these would cease at the close of the apostolic age. I mean by that word "cease" that the spirit would not give men these particular and peculiar powers any more after that time. That there would be no miracles, in reality, wrought in this world after that age. That when the last one, who had received these spiritual gifts through the imposition of apostolic hands, had passed from the stage of action, beneath the skies, that, then, there would be no more miracles of the nature that they wrought; that these manifestations of the spirit would all cease. This is the proposition that I am affirming in its definition. So I shall expect my opponent to meet me upon the ground of the proposition as defined. To this then I call your attention.

In order that we may understand the proposition I will begin with, first, the purpose of spiritual gifts and miracles, as wrought by the prophets of the Old Testament, as wrought by the men of God in olden times, and as wrought by Jesus Christ and by his Apostles. Not only shall we consider the purpose or object of these miracles and spiritual gifts, but we shall consider the nature and kind of miracles wrought, the place where and the circumstances surrounding, under which these manifestations of the spirit were brought to light. When we shall have found this, then we are prepared to examine the proposition as to when they ceased, if at all.

To get this understanding in your minds I call your attention to the times of the Old Testament writings, commonly called "patriarchal," beginning with righteous Abel. The Apostle Paul tells us that Abel offered a sacrifice by faith. Again the same Apostle tells us that "faith comes by hearing and hearing by the Word of God." This being true, we learn from the statement that he offered "by faith," that he had a commandment or entreaty in the word of God to do that thing which he did. Passing from Abel, when he offered a sacrifice by faith, we pass down to Noah and learn that, "Noah found favor with God;" that, Noah offered sacrifices; that God delivered him by the Ark through the flood. Passing on, to this side of the flood, we find Noah offering sacrifice again. These things were in the world until we come to Abraham. With Abraham we find still the same order of worship. It seems that it had obtained that the oldest man of the family was the high priest to offer the gifts and sacrifices for the family. This is that which is commonly called the Patriarchal age. We find this order of worship commonly known as the "family worship. But with Abraham we have the same worship. Turn to Genesis 22:7 to 14 and here we have a particular statement made concerning Abraham. I will read it, "And Isaac spake unto Abraham his father, and said, My father: and he said, Here am I, my son. And he said, Behold the fire and the wood; but where is the lamb for a burnt offering? And Abraham said, My son, God will provide himself a lamb for a burnt offering: So they went both of them together. And they came to the place which God had told him of; and Abraham built an altar there, and laid the wood in order, and bound Isaac his son, and laid him on the altar upon the wood. And Abraham stretched forth his hand, and took the knife to slay his son, And the anged of the Lord called upon him out of heaven, and said, Abraham, Abraham: And he said, Here am I. And he said, Lay not thine hand upon the lad, neither do thou any thing unto him: for now I know that thou fearest God, seeing thou hast not withheld thy son, thine only son from me. And Abraham lifted up his eyes, and looked, and behold behind him a ram caught in a thicket by his horns: and Abraham went and took the ram, and offered him up for a burnt offering, in the stead of his son. And Abraham called the name of that place Jehovah-jireh: as it is said to this day, In the mount of the Lord it shall be seen. And the angel of the Lord called unto Abraham out of heaven the second time, And said By myself have I sworn, saith the Lord, for because thou hast done this thing, and hast not withheld thy son, thine only son: That in blessing I will bless thee, and in multiplying I will multiply thy seed as the stars of the heaven, and as the sand which is upon the sea shore; and thy seed shall possess the gate of his enemies; And in thy seed shall all the nations of the earth be blessed; because thou hast obeyed my voice." I read to the 18th verse inclusive. Here God talked with Abraham and confirmed the promise which he had made unto Abraham, with an oath. This hope of this promise had obtained in Abraham's family. We find the same recorded in Genesis 26:1 to 5, to Isaac the same oath because that Abraham "had obeyed my voice." The Lord says again the same thing in Genesis 28:1 to 4, promised to Jacob by Isaac, as Jacob was going down to Padanaram. Again, in Genesis 28:10 to 15, where God appeared to him in a dream, and on this I would call your attention to the reading of the 14th verse carefully, beginning with the 13th verse we read, "And, behold, the Lord stood above it" (above the ladder), "and said, I am the Lord God of Abraham thy father, and the God of Isaac; the land whereon thou liest, to thee will I give it, and to thy seed; And thy seed shall be as the dust of the earth, and thou shalt spread abroad to the west, and to the east, and to the north, and to the south; and in thee and in thy seed shall all the families of the earth be blessed." Here we find a peculiar promise made to Jacob. A promise that he was to spread forth toward the west and the east, the north and the south, that his seed was to go forth, not only in the Land of Palestine, but the promise tells us it was to go into the regions beyond. This

promise has been verified. Israel's children to-day are
in every nation of earth; in every civilized nation of earth
we find the children of Israel a distinct and separate
people, yet. Hence, that word that God Almighty spoke
to Jacob there in dream is verified in the Jewish people
that multiplied and are in every nation of earth to-day.

But again, not only was this true, but in Genesis
25:9-15, as Jacob was coming back from his journey the
Lord appeared to him and repeated his promise again,
and changed his name from Jacob to Israel. This gives
us another thought, that these people had kept this hope.
This worship, that had been established, family worship,
was now confirmed over and over again, until Joseph,
down in Egypt, when he came to die (Genesis 50-25) told
the children of Israel that God would surely visit them
and deliver them, and made them take an oath that they
would carry his bonds up out of the land of Egypt. In
all this we learn that the religion, family worship, was
establish upon that people; fixed so firm in their minds,
by the fact that God Almighty had talked with these men,
face to face, and had delivered them this order. And the
miracles that had been wrought, and the dreams that had
been interpreted by Joseph. These things had been
shown them until it was fixed in the minds of the people
that it was right. To come to these people and tell them
that God is going to change the order from this family
worship to a national worship would be sacrilegious; the
very thought. Hence, when God determined to make a
change by Moses, to deliver them out of the land of
Egypt, and establish a different kind of a worship, Moses
said, when the Lord appeared to him in the burning bush,
"The people will not hear me." This you will find in
Ex. 3:1-6, and again in verses 20 to 22 is where Moses

said, "they will not hear me." I will read this passage because it is an important one. The Lord is speaking to Moses concerning this, says (beginning with the 19th verse) "And I am sure that the king of Egypt will not let you go, no, not by a mighty hand. And I will stretch out my hand, and smite Egypt with all my wonders which I will do in the midst thereof; and after that he will let you go. And I will give this people favor in the sight of the Egyptians; and it shall come to pass, that, when ye go, ye shall not go empty; But every woman shall borrow of her neighbor, and of her that sojourneth in her house, jewels of silver, and jewels of gold, and raiment; and ye shall put them upon your sons, and upon your daughters; and ye shall spoil the Egyptians."

Beginning with the 4th chapter, "And Moses answered and said, But, behold, they will not believe me, nor hearken unto my voice; for they will say, The Lord hath not appeared unto thee: And the Lord said until him, What is that in thine hand? And he said, A rod. And he said, Cast it on the ground. And he cast it on the ground, and it became a serpent; and Moses fled from before it. And the Lord said unto Moses, Put forth thine hand, and take it by the tail. And he put forth his hand, and caught it, and it became a rod in his hand: That they may believe that the Lord God of their fathers, the God of Abraham, the God of Isaac and the God of Jacob, hath appeared unto thee. And the Lord said furthermore unto him, Put now thine hand into thy bosom. And he put his hand into his bosom: and when he took it out, behold his hand was leprous as snow, And, he said, Put thine hand into thy bosom again. And he put his hand into his bosom again, and plucked it out of his bosom, and, behold, it was turned again as his other flesh. And it shall come to pass, if they will not believe thee, neither hearken to the voice of the first sign, that they will believe the voice of the latter sign. And it shall come to pass, if they will not believe also these two signs, neither harken unto thy voice, that thou shalt take of the water of the river, and pour it upon the dry land; and the water which thou takest out of the river shall become blood upon the dry land." Note, please, the Lord tells him that these things are given him for the purpose of proving to that people that the God of Abraham, the God of Isaac and the God of Jacob had sent him. So we see the purpose of miracles. They were given as credentials to prove to the people that the man doing them was prepared to deliver a message to them, from high heaven.

But again, Moses realized that something else was necessary. He had not only to deal with the people of Israel, but he had to deal also with Pharaoh. So the Lord gives him signs to Pharaoh. Pharaoh said, "Who is the Lord that I should obey his voice to let Israel go?" Here Pharaoh, if you please, was to be dealt with. And again, in Exodus 6:1-9 is recorded God's promise made to all Israel, and God's pledge and charge to Moses and Aaron. This is in the 26th and 27th verses of the same chapter. But the question comes up again. Exodus 7:8-9, "And the Lord spake unto Moses and unto Aaron, saying, When Pharaoh shall speak unto you, saying, Shew a miracle for you: then thou shalt say unto Aaron, Take thy rod, and cast it before Pharaoh, and it shall become a serpent." We give next the miracles that were to be wrought. I will name them in succession and give you the scriptural references to them, and especially call attention to the nature of these miracles, eleven in number. And later we will take them up, as time permits, and read and discuss each one, if the gentleman calls them in question.

First, the miracle of the rod. This we find the magicians did also, by their enchantments. Every one threw down his rod and they became serpents, but Aaron's rod swallowed them all up.

The next one was to "Smite the waters of the rivers, and the waters were to become blood." This was not in darkness, but in the day time. Exodus 7:20-22, "And smote the waters that were in the river, in the sight of Pharaoh, and in the sight of his servants; and all the waters that were in the river were turned to blood." But the magicians did the same, by their enchantments.

Third miracle was, that, they were to "call up frogs into the land among the people." In Exodus 8:1-4, is the charge. And in Exodus 8:5-7 we find the same fulfilled. Verse 6 "Aaron did what the Lord commanded. Verse 7 the magicians did the same thing. Not that here are three that the magicians did. But again, Pharaoh called Moses and said, "Entreat the Lord, that he may take away the frogs from me, and from my people; and I will let the people go, that they may do sacrifice unto the Lord." And Moses asked him when he should entreat for him, and Pharoah said, "To-morrow," and he said "Be it so." And it happened as Moses said.

Again, the 4th; which was, that they were to smite the dust and the dust was to become lice through all the land of Egypt. Exodus 8:8-16, They did so, and in Exodus 8:16-19 the magicians attempted to do so, but failed. And when they failed they said "This is the hand of God." They had gone as far as they could by magic, to even make an appearance of the same thing. They said, "This is the finger of God."

Fifth sign, Flies to be in all the land of Egypt, but not in Goshen among the children of Israel. The flies were to come up among the people of Egypt, but not to bother Israel. Exodus 8:23-24 was where they did so, and in Exodus 8:25-32 Moses entreated that the flies should be taken away.

The sixth miracle. Murrain in the cattle throughout the land of Egypt. Exodus 9:1-5, Though it was not to strike the children of Israel's cattle. This was fulfilled, the murrain came, and Exodus 9:6-7 we find them entreating that it be taken away, and it was taken away.

Again, the 7th, "Take to you handfuls of ashes of the furnace, and let Moses sprinkle it toward the heaven in the sight of Pharaoh. And it shall become small dust in all the land of Egypt, and it shall be a boil breaking forth with blains upon man, and upon beast, throughout all the land of Egypt." They did so and the people were sore with the boils.

The eighth miracle, "And Moses said about this time to-morrow the hail shall come." Did it? It did. Pharaoh asked him to stop it, and Moses gave him the sign that when he got out of the city it shall stop, and it stopped at the given sign.

Again, the 9th miracle, The locusts came and ate up everything. In Exodus 10:3-6 the charge was given. And in 16th to 20th verses, the locusts were taken away.

The 10th miracle was darkness. Three days darkness in all the land, the darkness that was so dark it could be felt, but in Israel they had light. Here again it was entreated to be taken away. And in Exodus 12-39th verses, at the conclsion of this, Pharaoh commanded Moses to show his face no more, under penalty of death. Moses goes out and now he gives the 11th miracle.

The Passover. At a given time they were to take a lamb without blemish, a male of the first year, keep it from the 10th to the 14th day of the month, and on the 14th day of the month, in the evening, they were to kill the lamb, and with a bunch of hyssop strike the blood of it on the lintel and on the side posts of the door. It was to be done in every house of Israel, and wherever that blood was sprinkled the Angel of Death passed over that house. But wherever that blood was not sprinkled, in every family of Egypt, at a given time, at a given hour, the first born of that died, according to the sign. Pharaoh let them go and they went by the way of the wilderness to the Red Sea. But Pharaoh followed them. They were being led by the fire in the night time, and the cloud in the day time. When they came to the Red Sea Moses stretched forth his hand and the waters parted for them, and they passed over dryshod. But when the Egyptians attempted to do the same thing Moses stretched forth his hand over the sea and the sea returned to his strength again, and they were all destroyed.

Again, on the top of Mount Sinai, the Lord Almighty, descending in clouds and darkness, thundered forth the law, the ten commandments in the ears of all the people. Here we find Him speaking it, so the whole people could hear it. We see wondrous miracles wrought up to and including Joshua leading them across the Jordan. The waters were up, overflowing all the banks. But when God's covenant ark was brought the waters stayed back, and the people passed over Jordan, after which the waters went on as before. Note, please, these miracles wrought, in establishing that order of worship, which Moses had come to establish. Changing from a family to a national worship. And this worship had remained for a period of nearly two thousand years, when Jesus Christ came into the world. But the question comes, "Why all this?" Exodus 10:1-2 says, "That ye may know how that I am the Lord," The God of Abraham, of Isaac and Jacob. Exodus 11:7, "That ye may know the Lord sent me."

But Exodus 12-21-24-27 special verses, The passover was to be kept, after they possessed the other land, as a memorial. In other words, as a monumental institution, that God Almighty had delivered his people. A monument coming down the line until Jesus Christ comes, keeping this ordinance of the passover, stands as a memorial of the miracles that had been wrought in ages past. But when God sees proper to change the worship, again, from a national worship, back to a patriarchal, instead of being just a family worship, it comes this time to an individual worship. When he determines to change this the man that comes to make the change must have credentials to show that he is of God. Hence, we see Jesus Christ and his Apostles coming with these credentials. Jesus Christ comes with various kinds of miracles, wrought in the presence of friend and foe, wrought in public places, that the people might all see and know. The nature of these miracles will be taken up at another time. I see my time is drawing to a close. (By Mr. Head—you have two minutes yet). Then, I call your attention to John the Baptist, as recorded in Luke 1:60 to 63. In this case we learn that John opened his mouth and praised God when he was but eight days old. Here is something of John the Baptist. I know you have been reading it, and thinking that it was Zacharias who was speaking, but the next verse, the 67th verse, tells you about Zacharias' mouth being opened. When the people heard it they kept the matter in their heart and wondered what kind of a child he would be. So John comes the forerunner of the Christ. John came baptizing to make manifest the Messiah. Turn to Matthew 3:17, where the voice says "This is my beloved son, in whom I am well pleased." This is a demonstration public, before the assembly. Again Matthew 4:23-24 we find the miracles that Christ wrought—healing of various kinds of diseases. They brought all that were sick and he healed them.

TIME.

J. W. RING—NEGATIVE.

Gentlemen Moderators, Ladies and Gentlemen:

If affords me unspeakable pleasure to be before you this afternoon denying the proposition which has been read to you, presuming that at any time God has withdrawn from the children of men the sweetness and power or fruits of inspiration. I hope to present such thought, reason and evidence as will enable you to look through clear sight and spiritual vision, and behold the Most High that changeth not, but is from beginning to beginning and forever the same. Giving the power of his spirit, the inspiration of truth and love and life, bearing light and joy and peace that "passeth understanding" to the children of men. If we are to look only to the Scriptures (Old and New Testament) we certainly have abundant ground to find the fruition of the spirit, the power of its inspiration and the sweetness of its voice. We cannot fail to comprehend that each and every one of these phenomena, as recorded, as read to you in the half hour just past, are evidences of the power of the

"word of God" (of inspiration said to be from the
Most High), coming through the spirit of Jehovah.
Surely you can but have heard the reading of these and
realize that they are evidence of a power that existed
in and under the jurisdiction of the spirit of God. If
you continue to read the history of these people you will
find that the selfsame things continued to occur, increasing
in power and magnitude. That these manifestations were
met by the magicians, necromancers, "mediums" of the
nations about, that the vied with each other as to who
might be the strongest, is self-evident by the passages read
in your hearing. That in some instances the prophets
of other nations succeeded, and in others they failed,
is evident to you. But we are speaking of the spiritual
gifts and truly the manifestations of these spiritual gifts
came not only to the prophets of Jehovah, but to the
prophets of other Gods, of other nations. If they were
only similar, it is evidence that they were results of the
same power. We certainly do not refute any of these
phenomena, aye, we would add unto them, that the self-
same phenomena occurs in our modern days. Referring
especially to the statement of our opponent of the infant
John the Baptist speaking, we gladly parallel this with
the case of the infant of Kate Fox, born in England,
that wrote a message that was recognized as coming from
an ex-carnate spirit. That this message, through the infant of Mrs. Jenkins, was any less a message or phenomenon than that received through the lips of John the
Baptist is for you to determine—not for any one individual to decide. ("Missing Link," by Leah Fox Underhill.) That the spirit who spoke through John the Baptist was Elias is a statement which I make to you upon
the authority of Jesus, for he said, "John comes in the

power and the spirit of Elias." I emphasize the statement that this was the spirit of John the Baptist speaking, upon the authority of the Angel Gabriel, for he had promised that John would come in the power and spirit of Elias.

Denying that spiritual gifts are no longer visited upon the children of men, I shall take up a series of thoughts which I believe, when presented to your intelligent consideration, you will see indicates that the word of God, the Christos of the Apostolic age, and the spiritual gifts demonstrated by modern spiritualism to-day are identical, affording conclusive evidence that spiritual gifts do not continue. In first Corinthians, chapter 10, Paul is recorded to have said "And were all baptized of Moses in the cloud and in the sea and did all eat of the spiritual meat and did all drink the same spiritual drink for they drank of that spiritual rock that followed them." "And that word was Christ." In other words, the "word of God" in the days of Moses was Christ. Surely it could not have been Christ, if Christ had come at a latter time as a sacrifice, for the sins of the people. Surely, my beloved friends, the "word of God" in the days of Moses that is declared by Paul to have been Christ must have been mediumship,, must have been the power of the spirit to speak, to manifest, to proclaim itself, even as has been read in your hearing this afternoon when the "word of God" was sounded to the people." I declared to you that the Holy of Holies in the temple was a cabinet for spirit manifestation. I present this again to your consideration for evidence, for you as a jury to decide; not for any individual to determine, whether or not these curtains in any way manifested the appearance of our cabinets of to-day. The manner in which the "word of

God" made its manifestation to the people in those days varied, even as it did in the apostolic days, even as it varies to-day; even as Paul said, a diversity of gifts yet by the same spirit. You cannot read a book of the Old Testament that you do not find divers ways in which the "word of God" manifested. What was the "word of God?" It was the voice of the spirit that came through the prophets, or as we would call them to-day, mediums; or a latter term, suggested as scientific by Professor Crookes of England, a "Psychic." The Scripture which has been read in your hearing indicates that at times the "word of God" manifested itself to the individual, to the individual prophet; at another time it became sufficiently intense in volume that it was heard by all. So in our spiritual seances of to-day sometimes the spirit comes and speaks only to the individual; at other times it is heard by all who are present. At times the manifestations that attended the "teacher of Galilee" were for his disciples only, as upon the Mount of Transfiguration. At other times it was for the multitude. When he returned to his disciples they not always recognized him, as he appeared in another form (Mark 16 c. 12 v., Luke 24 c. 13 to 31 v.), until he gave them some test, until he spoke some message by which they were able to recognize him. So to-day, our spirit friends make themselves known by some test. In the 9th chapter of Deut. we find that Jehovah, the "word of God," made itself known through writings upon tablets of stone and slate writing. The conditions attendant thereunto, it seems to me, I should not occupy your time to delineate. Surely, you have read and understand that Moses was forty days and forty nights upon the mountain in a thick cloud to receive these messages, and that all Israel waited at the foot of the

mountain that Moses might bring down the commandments, the message from their spirit guide, Jehovah.
Our seances to-day are conducted with order and precis-
ion, as Paul instructed his followers to conduct these
meetings with order. Oftentimes skeptical friends say
"how does it come that some one entering the room pre-
vents these phenomena or breaks the condition?" Because
you break the conditions that are formed. Why could
not the children of Israel go upon the mountain where
these phenomena were taking place? Because of the
presence of Jehovah; he was their spirit guide—God.
While Israel was deprived of the privilege of the mountain they were taking unto themselves other privileges;
if their God was going to conceal himself in a thick cloud
they chose to make for themselves another God, and so
they had made a molten calf. When Moses came down
from the mountain his spirit guide, Jehovah, was an-
gered. I cannot occupy your time in a relation of these
details. The Most High, the God of this universe, an-
gered because a little tribe of people had made a molten
calf. And if you read carefully this chapter (Exodus 32)
you will see how Moses appealed to Jehovah to appease
his wrath, and persuaded him to not destroy the children
of Israel. So the "word of God," at that time, came
through a prophet, but written upon tablets of stone. A
few evenings since I described to you the conditions attending the slate-written message which I received. The
same is placed upon exhibition in your town, and I leave
it to you, fellow jurors, which conditions appeal to you
as the most convincing of spirit power. The tablets of
stone upon which I received the message, never passed
from my hands; the words which I received were words
of joy and of comfort to my soul, for it assured me that

my "mother friend" retained her personal identity and proved to me conclusively the continuation of spiritual gifts, because she assured me of her continued love for the work which I was doing for the children of men. Under these conditions, that precluded any possible fraudulent practice or collusion, I received the little picture which is placed before you that proclaims the glad message that it is my delight to proclaim to you. "Spiritualism, the light across the waters of Death." You will probably hear much more of the phenomena recorded in the Old Testament; it is extensively recorded there. It was attended by no small degree of attempted duplication, by the necromancers, prophets, seers and mediums of other nations, even as it was in the apostolic age, even as it is at the present time, we have the true and the genuine. I believe I have emphasized this sufficiently for your intelligence, and you feel the dictation of Paul to try the spirits and to see if they are good or otherwise.

We have had our attention called to the enumeration of the spiritual gifts as Paul proclaimed them in his letter to the Corinthians and can say no more of these than "Amen, Amen.' We can parallel every one of them in our modern Spiritualism to-day. Continuing in the same 12th chapter, beginning with the 28th verse, "And God hath set some in the church as Apostles, secondly prophets, third, teachers, after that miracles, then gifts of healing, to others diversities of tongues." Here all are not teachers, all are not prophets, all are not workers of miracles. Have all the gifts of healing? Do all speak with tongues? "To covet honestly the best gifts, and yet show I unto you a most excellent way." (By Mr. Chism—You did not read it right—"More excellent.") He then continued with the 13th chapter, which I read you in full yesterday, emphasizing the beauty and power of charity, and assuring us that when we have laid off our physical garments we shall know even as we are known. Continuing 14th chapter with this good teacher Paul, "Follow after charity and desire spiritual gifts, but rather that ye prophesy. For he that speaketh in an unknown tongue speaketh not unto men, but to God, for no man understandeth him. Howbeit in the spirit he speaketh," so I invite your attention to the entire chapter. Again, in the 24th verse, "But if all prophesy and there come in one that believeth not, or one unlearned, he is convinced of all, he is judged of all: and thus are the secrets of his heart made manifest; and so falling down on his face he will worship God, and report that God is in you of a truth." Can there be any interpretation of this other than that with the power of prophesy we will be able to give to our seeking friends a test, a message even as Jesus gave a test to the woman at the well, even as he read the minds of those who came to him to know of his teachings; if you turn to the right or to the left to-day among the prophets of modern spiritualism, the seers, mediums, psychics, you will find those who by the power of prophecy can, in many instances, speak the name of the one who attends their seances, and many times describe the spirits that attend, thus in various manners proving the continuation of the same power by which Moses received the "word of God," that Jesus received "the word of God;" that Paul advised his followers they would receive the word of God. 39th and 40th verses, "Wherefore, brethren, covet to prophesy, and forbade not to speak with tongues. let all things be done decently and in order." Covet to prophesy that you may- be able to give the message; the test that will enable you to make the investigator to know that you are possessed of the "Word of God," of the power of the spirit, of the gift of mediumship. If you will take the time to read carefully the history of Jehovah you will find the various manners in which he manifested, even in the 32d chapter of Genesis, where he "wrestled with Jacob through the night," but when the morning came he begged to be released; he was in a hurry to go, when the light began to come.

I feel to refrain from calling your attention to the admonition which these people received to borrow from their Egyptian friends their belongings, and spoil Egypt. Advised to take that which did not belong to them, and make way with it. I regret to call your attention to this condition of affairs, but it seems necessary at this time, for, after all, in those olden times, even as when the Lord sent a lying spirit to deceive all the prophets of Israel, so were they advised to take that which did not belong to them, indicating the character of the "word of God," of the revelation of the spirit, of the message which they received at that time. My beloved friends, my thinking jurors, if these evidences which my honorable opponent has kindly assisted me in presenting to you do not indicate conclusively that the "word of God," which came to Moses, the power of the spirit which rested upon Jesus, the spiritual gifts which Paul promised to those that followed after his teachings, and the manifestations of the modern advent of spiritualism are identical, else you have not the power of spiritual discernment, of seeing the comparison of similar things. The "word of God" has revealed itself unto the children of men in every nation and tribe, according to the capacity of that respective nation to receive, and through chosen media, prophet, seer, Christ, psychics. The inspiration of spiritual gifts has blessed the children of men and increased as their intelligence permitted it to rest upon them until to-day the spirit world is drawn so near to the world in which we are living that the presence of our friends oftentimes fan our burning cheeks and brush away the scalding tears that doubt has brought into our eyes; until hope springs up in our hearts and illuminates our countenance with sweet smiles. Through our clouds of doubt we can look and behold the shining faces of those who have only passed a little higher and realize that they are our own friends, and that through the power of spiritual gifts do they make their presence known unto us, even as did the individuals make their presence known in the days of Moses, of Jacob, of Jesus and of Paul.

TIME.

J. W. CHISM—SECOND AFFIRMATIVE.

Gentlemen Moderators, Brethren and Friends:

Inasmuch as I am in the affirmative, and the work of my affirmation was not completed, before I shall examine anything, whatever, the gentleman has said in his last speech, I shall continue my affirmation to the conclusion of the argument. Having established the proposition, then I will turn back and examine everything he has said, that needs examination.

I was on the subject of the nature of miracles wrought by Jesus Christ and his Apostles. Just here I might introduce into this thought a statement that my opponent made, that they propose in this age to parallel every one of these spiritual gifts mentioned by Paul. Well! I would like to see you speak a little Hebrew. They spoke with

tongues, with "divers kinds of tongues." Will you give
us just a verse in Hebrew? Quote the first verse of
Genesis in Hebrew? Don't say you can't! You say
you can; for you say you can parallel every one of these
gifts—these miracles. What is the trouble? Can he do
it? No. He has not a man in his crew that can do it.
Have I not challenged them from the beginning, if they
could not tell what the Hebrew words were, to get
Samuel's spirit. "Call up Samuel" and let him tell them?
Have they done it? Have they accepted the challenge?
No. Why? Because they know they can not; that is
why. "Beraashith bara Elohim eth hashamayim weeth
haarets." Will you tell us what that means in English?
Paul says they could interpret tongues. Tell us what it
means. Can you tell us? "Call up Samuel" and let him
tell. Can you do it? No. But so much for paralleling
these spiritual gifts. He knows he can not do it.

I was on the subject of Jesus Christ and the miracles
that he wrought. I desire now to show you the nature
of these miracles. Matthew 4:23-24, I had called your
attention to these. But now I shall turn and read them.
"And Jesus went about all Galilee, teaching in their
synagogues, and preaching the gospel of the kingdom,
and healing all manner of sickness and all manner of
disease among the people. And his fame went throughout all Syria; and they brought unto him all sick people
that were taken with divers diseases and torments and
those which were possessed with devils, and those which
were lunatick, and those that had the palsy; and he
healed them." Do you see Spiritualists doing such work
as this? Do any of them claim that everybody that is
sick, of every disease, is healed by them, or do they find
a person once in a while that they can heal without medi-

cine, and hail it as a miracle? I have challenged him to undertake the job of healing one to my five without medicine, because I know how it is done and the law that it is done by. Has he accepted the challenge? No. I dare make the assertion that he will not; neither will his whole combined force. But again, Matthew 8:5-13, We have here the case of the servant that was sick. In verse 8 the centurion said, "Speak the word only and my servant shall be healed." Get the thought. "Speak the word only and my servant shall be healed." As Luke records it, "I also am a man under authority, having under me soldiers, and I say to this man go, and he goeth, and to that man come, and he comes, and to my servant do this, and he does it." This man recognized that Jesus was under the authority of God Jehovah, and that he had back of him creative power, and it was necessary only for him to speak the word, to put it in operation. He did not need to go in person; he did not have to go into the cabinet; he did not have to get his colleagues around him. But, "Speak the word only and my servant shall be healed." This man was under authority and when he said to his soldier, Go; there was the authority of the Government of Rome back of that commandment to enforce it. When Jesus said, "Be healed," there was the authority of heaven back of that command to enforce it. Will he parallel that? No. He cannot.

Matthew 8:14-15, Peter's wife's mother lay sick of a fever. Jesus entered in and touched her. The fever was cured, and immediately she rose and ministered unto them. Will he parallel that? No.

Again, Matthew 8:23-27, I want to read this one, "And when he was entered into the ship his disciples followed him. And, behold, there arose a great tempest in the sea, insomuch that the ship was covered with the waves; but he was asleep. And his disciples came to him, and awoke him, saying, Lord, save us; we perish. And he saith unto them, Why are ye fearful, O ye of little faith? Then he arose and rebuked the winds and the sea; and there was a great calm. But the men marvelled, saying, What manner of man is this, that even the winds and the sea obey him!" Again, Matthew 9:1-8 we find a man sick of the palsy healed. When Jesus saw their faith he healed the man that was sick of the palsy. Again, Matthew 9:18-23-26 we find in the 18th verse, "While he spake these things unto them, behold, there came a certain ruler, and worshipped him, saying, My daughter is even now dead; but come and lay thy hand upon her, and she shall live." 20th verse, "And, behold, a woman, which was diseased with an issue of blood twelve years, came behind him and touched the hem of his garment; For she said within herself, If I may but touch his garment, I shall be whole. But Jesus turned him about, and when he saw her, he said, Daughter, be of good comfort; thy faith hath made thee whole. And the woman was made whole from that hour." Again 23d to 25th we read, "And when Jesus came into the ruler's house, and saw the minstrels and the people making a noise, He said unto them, Give place; for the maid is not dead, but sleepeth, And they laughed him to scorn. But when the people were put forth, he went in, and took her by the hand, and the maid arose. And the fame hereof went abroad into all that land." Do you see Spiritualists paralleling that? I remember one time of hearing of a man that claimed he had the power to work these miracles. A man came in the community and stopped to stay all night, and suddenly, about midnight, or a little after, he took sick, violently sick, and before they could get a physician he was dead. The next morning, as they could not find out who he was, the people were preparing to bury him. So about 9 o'clock in the morning, this man that claimed he could work miracles, came as though passing by, but stopped and asked what was the matter, and when they told him he said, "I can raise him from the dead. He died just to show the power of the Lord. I can heal the man. The Lord has sent me to raise him up." And when he came in by the bedside the man of the house asked, "Hold on, are you sure you can raise him up?" He replied "Yes." So the man of the house ran out of doors and got a broad-ax and said, "If he is dead and you can raise him up you can do it just as well with his head chopped off," and just as he raised the ax the dead man jumped up. Your miracles are like that. Only pretense. But you do as Jesus was done, thrust a spear right into his heart and see what will be done. Can you raise him up? No!

In Matthew 9:27-31 we find two blind men healed. In Matthew 9:32-35 a dumb man healed. Thus we find in the miracles of Jesus every kind of work, and in public.

Again, he gives the twelve Apostles power. Matthew, 10 and 1, commanding them to go and preach and heal the sick, giving them power over unclean spirits. But we pass on from the power of the Apostles in their first commission to Matthew 12:13, where a withered hand was restored, by Jesus. Again, Matthew 12:22-23 we find a blind and dumb man healed. Next in Matthew 14:15-21 we find five thousand people fed by Jesus of a few loaves and fishes, and much more food gathered up after they had eaten that there was to begin with. Do Spiritualists parallel that?

Again, following this; Jesus walks on the sea, in the midst of the sea, the record tells us. Matthew 14:22-23. John 6:18-21 recording the same. I want to read John's statement, and whenever Spiritualists parallel this I am ready to go into the secret chamber to investigate with them. Otherwise I believe what my Saviour said, "If they shall say unto you . . . behold he is in the secret chambers; believe it not." (Matthew 24:26). John 6:18-21, "And the sea arose by reason of the great wind that blew. So when they had rowed about five and twenty or thirty furlongs, they saw Jesus walking on the sea, and drawing nigh unto the ship, and they were afraid; but he said unto them 'It is I, be not afraid.' Then they willingly received him into the ship, and immediately the ship was at the land whither they went." Matthew tells us that it was in the midst of the sea when Jesus entered it. It was the sea of Galilee. John says about five and twenty furlongs. About three or four miles from shore, putting them right in the midst of the sea, three and a half or four miles from land. Jesus entered the ship "and immediately the ship was at the land, whither they went." Do Spiritualists parallel this? See them carry the ship three and a half miles immediately, by stepping into it. Can they do it? No, and he knows they can't.

Again, in Matthew 14:34-36, "All that came to Jesus were made perfectly whole," whatever their diseases might be. Matthew 15:32-39, we find the miracle of the four thousand fed. Matthew 17:1-13 the transfiguration of Jesus before the three Apostles. Then, when he came down, Matthew 1:4-8, the epileptic healed, amid friend and foe, at the foot of the mountain. Again, John 11:1-46, especially verses 41 to 45, is the case of Lazarus being raised from the dead, after he had been dead four days. Here, then, we find such miracles as were wrought by Jesus Christ. But, finally, after all these, comes the resurrection of himself. He says: "My father has given me power to lay down my life; he has given me power to take it again." So he laid down his life, being crucified. And to show he was dead, the spear was thrust right into his heart, and there came forth blood and water. Death must have ensued, scientists tell us, when blood separates into blood and water. It was not what could be called a case of "suspended animation," for in that condition the blood remains pure. But in Jesus' case the blood and water had separated. And Jesus Christ on the appointed day, the third day, came forth triumphant, bringing his body with the wounds in it, and showing himself to his disciples. But when Thomas doubted, he said, "Put your finger in the print of the nails and thrust your hand into my side, and doubt no more." Here we see the final miracle, the triumphant one, of Jesus Christ, showing that he was of God. Now, he commissions his disciples and tells them to "Go into all the world and preach the gospel to every creature, he that believeth and is baptized shall be saved, but he that believeth not shall be damned." Mark 16: 15-16. But I read right on, verse 17, "And these signs shall follow them that believe. In my name shall they cast out devils; they shall speak with new tongues; They shall take up serpents; and if they drink any deadly thing, it shall not hurt them; they shall lay hands on the sick, and they shall recover. So then, after the Lord had spoken unto them, he was received up into heaven, and sat on the right hand of God. And they went forth and preached every where, the Lord working with them, and

confirming the word with signs following. Amen." I
read to the 20th verse, inclusive, the end of the chapter.
Here is the commission given by Jesus Christ. Here are
the miracles which he says, "shall follow" the believer.
I turn to Acts of the Apostles, the 2d chapter, there I
find the Holy Spirit given, and demonstration of cloven
tongues, as of fire, sitting upon each of them. And there
were dwelling at Jerusalem, "Parthians, and Medes, and
Elamites, and the dwellers in Mesopotamia, and in
Judea, and Cappadocia, in Pontus, and Asia, Phrygia, and
Pamphylia, in Egypt, and in the parts of Libya about
Cyrene, and strangers of Rome, Jews and proselytes,
Cretes and Arabians," and they said, "we do hear them
speak in our tongues the wonderful works of God."
Here then the spirit so gave speech to the Apostles that
they could speak in the seventeen dialects. Do Spiritualists parallel that? Let him try it. Has any German in
this audience heard him yet, in the German tongue? He
claimed the other night that he was speaking by the spirit
of inspiration. Did you hear him in the German tongue,
you who are Germans? But in these tongues is the
great demonstration of the spirit. Peter used it to show
that his message was of God.

But again, in the 3d chapter of Acts, we find the record
of Peter healing the impotent man, who was lame from
his birth. Peter said to him, "In the name of Jesus Christ
of Nazareth rise up," and he arose immediately and
walked. But the Apostle 'Peter said it was through faith,
in the name of Jesus, whom ye crucified, that this man is
made whole in the midst of you all.

On another occasion I see the Apostle Paul gathering
an armful of sticks. When putting it on the fire a viper
clings to his hand and he shakes it into the fire and

receives no harm. Again, I see the Apostle Paul preaching to a deputy, and a sorcerer was trying to turn the deputy from the faith. That sorcerer stood to him as I stand to this man (pointing to his opponent). Paul says to him, "thou shalt be blind and not see the sun for a season," and immediately he was blind, and sought for some one to lead him. I challenge him (turning to his opponent), yea I dare you, with all your gods, to even act like you want, to try to speak me blind. Go at it. There sits the man who is self-condemned, who realizes that he cannot do it. I am not meeting this doctrine for the first time. I have met other men who claimed to possess these powers. That challenge has gone forth every time, and I see yet without the use of spectacles and am forty-two years old past. Besides, I have used my eyes a great deal, too, reading. Why don't they strike me blind? Just because they can't, and they know it.

pose of them. Paul says that God bore them witness with signs and wonders and divers miracles and gifts of the Holy Ghost, according to His own will. Then, of

Having shown these miracles I now take up the purthe ones that were making the revelation to us, who heard Jesus Christ, and who were to confirm that word to us, Paul says, "God bore them witness" with these signs. And Mark says that, "The Lord worked with them, confirming the word" with these signs following those who believed. Hence, the purpose of these things was to confirm the revelation. To show that the revelation given was of God. Having found this to be true, the next question comes, "Were these things to cease?" My proposition says, "the Scriptures teach that they ceased" at a certain time—that the Scriptures teach it. To this I invite your attention.

Jesus Christ says, "these signs shall follow." The language does not say how long. If they followed but one week after the commission was given the language is fulfilled, and no more than fulfilled. If they did not follow but one day the language is fulfilled. Even if they follow to the present day the language is fulfilled and no more than fulfilled. The language has no limit to it; but Jesus Christ told the Apostles, "Whatsoever you shall bind on earth shall be bound in heaven, and whatsoever you loose on earth shall be loosed in heaven." Matthew 16:16-19. Again, in Matthew 18:18 he uses the same language. Then it was left with the Apostles to bind or to loose. If the Apostles tell us that these things were to continue to the present time they would continue to now. Let us see what we can find. First Corinthians, the gifts as recorded in the 12th chapter, 11th verse, "Dividing to every man severally as he will." Note, if you please, that he says the spirit "divides" these gifts unto every man. Hence, one man received one part and another man another part. He was dividing to every man "severally as he will." Continuing in that chapter to the 31st verse, Paul says, to "covet earnestly the best gifts, and yet shew I unto you a more excellent way," "and yet shew I unto you a more excellent way." (Not a most excellent way, as the gentleman cited it.) A more excellent way? More excellent than what? More excellent than having these diversities of gifts of the spirit. I will show you a more excellent way. "Though I speak with the tongues of men and of angels, and have not charity, I am become as sounding brass or tinkling cymbal." "And though I have all faith, so that I could remove mountains and have not charity I am nothing." Note, please, the Apostle is teaching us that these spiritual gifts were not equal to charity. Here is something that is a more excellent way than having spiritual gifts. "Charity vaunteth not itself; is not puffed up," and after giving the characteristics of charity, he says, in the 8th verse, "Charity never faileth, but whether there be prophecies, they shall fail." This was one of the diversities of gifts, "whether there be tongues, they shall cease." That was another of the diversities of gifts. "Whether there be knowledge, it shall vanish away." Here was another of the diversities of gifts. Question, will the gentleman tell us that when a man passes into the great beyond that knowledge ceases? Most assuredly he will not. He has told us many times that they carry their personal characteristics with them. What knowledge was Paul talking about? Most assuredly it was that knowledge that came through God Almighty, through the Spirit. Listen, "For we know in part and we prophesy in part." Verse 9, "But when that which is perfect is come, then that which is in part shall be done away." But what is that which is in part, Paul? "The spirit divides to every man severally as he will." (1 Cor. 12:11.) These diversities of gifts of the spirit are the things which Paul calls the parts. But he says, "when the perfect is come then that which is in part shall be done away." When? "At the time when the perfect is come." Listen, Paul says, verse 11, "When I was a child I spake as a child, I understood as a child, I thought as a child, but when I became a man I put away childish things. For now we see through a glass, darkly; but then face to face; now I know in part; but then I shall know even as also I am known. And now abideth faith, hope and charity, these three; but the greatest of these is charity." Then at a given time the miracles were to cease. At what time? When the perfect is come. Has the perfect come yet? That is the next question to engage your attention. Paul says that God "gave some Apostles, and some prophets, and some pastors and teachers, for the perfecting of the saints, * * * * till we all come in the unity of the faith, and of the knowledge of the Son of God, unto a perfect man, unto the measure of the stature of the fullness of Christ." Ephesians the 4th, chapter 8-14, I will quote the whole passage at another time. Time is short now. Here he tells us that certain things were given to do a certain thing, and that this thing was to perfect the saints. Well, Paul, what did you do with it? Timothy, second letter, 4th chapter, 7th verse. "I have finished my course." What was your course, Paul? To perfect the saints. What was to happen then, Paul? "Then that which is in part shall be done away." What was that which was in part, Paul? Dividing to every man severally as he will. But what was divided? The spiritual gifts. Hence, when Paul said "when that which is perfect is come, then that which is in part shall be done away." He simply said these spiritual gifts would be done away. Then, with the death of the Apostles, the church having been perfected, with its officers and everything in it, with a "perfect law of liberty" to guide it into the perfect truth. There was no further need for the miracles, because they were the credentials of the ambassadors who were giving or establishing the law. Hence, The Lord's Supper, given in this law, stands as a monument from the days of the Apostles to the present time, showing us conclusively that these things come from the Apostles, and at the very time and place which they claim. So we find the Scriptures teach that the gifts would cease with the close of apostolic age.

This thought, which I now introduce, has been before you, but it will complete this argument. After the time, when the last one possessing these gifts had passed away, there is no power that is recorded in the Bible, as one that would ever work miracles save the spirit of the devil. Revelation 16:13-14, "And I saw three unclean spirits like frogs come out of the mouth of the dragon, and out of the mouth of the beast, and out of the mouth of the false prophet. For they are the spirits of devils, working miracles, which go forth unto the kings of the earth and of the whole world, to gather them to the battle of that great day of God Almighty." Again, Revelation 13:13-14, This little beast had power to do great signs and wonders, "And he doeth great wonders, so that he maketh fire come down from heaven on the earth in the sight of men. And deceiveth them that dwell on the earth by the means of those miracles which he had power to do in the sight of the beast; saying to them that dwell on the earth, that they should make an image to the beast, which had the wound by a sword, and did live." Now second Thess. 2:9-13, Paul says, they would come with lying wonders, shewing miracles. But they were not true miracles. Jesus says, Matthew 24:24, that, False prophets would come and would show great signs and wonders, and that they would deceive the very elect, if it were possible. "If they say He is in the secret chamber, do not believe it;" if they say He is in the cabinet, do not believe it. Jesus said it, not I.

TIME.

J. W. RING—NEGATIVE.

Gentlemen Moderators and Friends:

I rejoice that each individual is permitted in this glorious land of liberty to believe as he pleases. It matter not what doctrines or creeds may fling at me, it matters not what throttles may be attempted to be placed upon our reason, we are still permitted in this glorious land, in which we live, to reason, to think, to believe and to act as we will, so long as we do not infringe upon the equal privilege of others. Have I at any time attempted to insinuate that my opponent was teaching that which is false? I believe you will bear with me in my declaration, lady and gentlemen jurors, that I have declared that every individual teaches the truth as he sees it; however high or low his concept may be, he proclaims it. I am glad that I live in a land, and am present in a community where I can meet ladies and gentlemen who do not conceive truth as I conceive it, yet will come in the kindly spirit of the Most High and of the Christ—that has made its presence felt in all ages, and greet me as brother. The end of an age, the passing of a dispensation, the entrance into another epoch, has been the point of argument with every religion that has attempted cemented organization, from the foundation of the world. Jehovah constantly proclaimed to his followers, "I am the Lord thy God; thou shalt have no other Gods before me." In like imperative intonations has the presiding spirit of their cult attempted to hold in restraint his followers lest they might investigate and find something concerning another creed, religion or doctrine. We have received in the last half hour a wonderful account of spiritual gifts. My spirit swells within me when I hear all of these, and to know that they are evidences of the presence of the "word of God;" I rejoice that my spiritual perception permits me to look out through the extended horizon down to that time, and enables me to behold the unfolding of the same tide of spiritual power and gift that bears to this age, to-day, the like power and phenomena.

We do not stand before you posing as capable of demonstrating all of this diversity of gifts, nor even of imitating it, as our honorable opponent has promised us to imitate some of these phenomena. Spiritualism has not come into the world to convert any one to any belief, for you already have your beliefs, but since spiritual gifts have come along down through the past, recognized only as spiritual revelations or divine providences, it is the mission of the modern advent of spiritualism to bring to us a comprehension of the naturalness of these phenomena, that we may know they are the result of natural law. I invited your attention on the first day of our thought along these lines to the fact—if there be a difference between ancient and modern spiritualism it is not in these phenomena, but in the acceptance of the same; under the modern advent they are recognized as the natural result of an equally natural law, because the children of men have grown to a point of development where they can appreciate the naturalness of things, rather than that which is a miracle. That spiritual gifts have been cut off or withdrawn I openly deny, and repeatedly declare is in no way true. We have constantly had placed before us as a fact the statement that in the last days there would come these wondrous and terrible things. "Now the spirit speaketh expressly that in the latter times some shall depart from the faith, giving heed to seducing spirits and doctrines of devils (Timothy, chap 4.) Haven't you memorized that? It has been repeated so frequently. I wish to invite your attention to the fact that when Paul wrote this he and his associates fully realized that they are living in the last days. "This text has been used whenever there has been a departure from the mother church—poor Martin Luther suffered under this text when he renounced Catholicism. It was hurled at him with all its force. Wesley when he departed from the Church of England, found it could be and was used against him. It was again weiled into requisition when the Adventists started out. But the Adventists have had their revenge by beating Spiritualists over the head with it," and then, just lately, have had another knock of it in another hand. Why do I say they knew these were the last days in which they were living? Because on the day of Pentecost, as recorded in Acts, chapter 2, when all of these phenomena which have been read to you were occuring, then the Holy Ghost was upon the Apostles, and these phenomena were taking place and the people marveling, "Peter, standing up with the eleven, lifted up his voice and said unto them, Ye men of Judea, and all ye that dwell at Jerusalem, be this known unto you and hearken to my words, for these are not drunken as ye supposed, seeing it is but the third hour of the day, and this is that which was spoken by the Prophet Joel, and it shall come to pass in the last days, saith God, I will pour out my spirit upon all flesh, and your sons and daughters shall prophesy, and your young men shall see visions, and your old men shall dream dreams," etc., referring to the prophesy of Joel, declaring that when these took place it would be the last days. Did these things occur? They were occuring there upon the day of Pentecost. These Apostles were endeavoring to present their concept of religion. They had many obstacles in their way—the unbelief of the people who were satisfied with the religions they had, the materialism of the age, that had come to exist because of the doctrines that had been taught, but could not be accepted. Even as to-day Spiritualists find as an organization that there is a great spread of materialism in the world because men and women have turned away from their former concepts of religion, because they find themselves unable to conform with the laws prescribed by these respective doctrines. I invite your attention, respected jurors, to a consideration of the materialists, agnostics and people among your acquaintance, either by personal contact or reputation, who have turned away from their previous religious precepts, and appeal to you to decide if they have not turned away because the doctrines of those religions were beyond their power of acceptance? Are not the men and women that stand in the world and say "I don't know" the legitimate children of churchanity? I want to parenthetically call your attention here to another consideration of these individuals and ask you if you do not find them to be intelligent, thoughtful, kindly people? They say, "I don't know of but one world, and I am going to make it just as happy as I can for myself and others," and it seems to me that in the quiver of their voice of failure to know I detect the spirit of the Christ that said "love is the fulfillment of the law." In other words, would you and I not give more for the man that loves his fellowman and serves him as best he can than we would for the individual that believes in a God that has the reputation of sending a small majority of the human race to a place where they will so change their natures that they will delight in the torture and torment of the overwhelming majority of the human race that have been sent by this self-same God to Hell? Oh, for the man that, after all, is a man, that feels the pains of mankind and strives to appease sorrows, dry tears and soothe bleeding hearts. It is the grandest faith, it is the broadest concept of life after all, and it must be the embodiment of the Most High in the children of men. These Apostles were working under adverse circumstances to present their religion and to gain for it a hold. They were teaching, and, as has been stated to you this afternoon, their teachings were substantiated by these signs and these miracles, and Peter declares that these phenomena, which substantiates their teachings and were the prophesy of Joel that would come in the last days. It is recorded in first Peter, chapter 1, verse 20, "who verily was for-ordained before the foundation of the world, but was manifested in these last times for you." These last times. These Apostles were having trials to establish their belief, even contentions among themselves, as described in Acts, chapter 15, where Paul and Barnabas disagreed concerning the commission and other doctrinal points and as to the places about the country where they should go. That there were many who had departed from the faith, that there were many who still clung to their old ideas of mediumship of "the word of God" is found in many instances, as recorded by these Apostles and teachers. In the 15th chapter of Acts is the story of the damsel possessed of a spirit of divination. Paul commanded the spirit to come out and it came out, showing the superiority of Paul as a medium over this young girl medium. Read the story. When Paul and Silas were thrown into prison, as recorded in this self-same chapter, for teaching customs not lawful, comes the phenomena of the prison opening. Paralleling that by Dr. Luke and Rand in Oswego, N. Y., jail, in 1855, and if my word amounts to anything as an individual, I have seen prison doors fly open in broad daylight by the simple touch of a physical medium's hand. In these days—it was not more than thirty years ago, for I will be thirty-one next month (Sept. 7.)—it seems to be popular to tell your ages. I ask you to accept this, respected jurors, as my statement upon the honor of whatever you consider me to be. That the days of the Apostles were the last days it seems to me you cannot fail to see. That these spiritual gifts were abundant, not only among the Apostles, but those individuals who were associated with their religious movement as well, and that they were declared by Paul and 'Peter to be what spiritualism is to-day. Would I attempt by proclamation of good words, or even by the presentation of convincing phenomena, to convert you to a belief? No, the world is too full of beliefs already. But I would beg of you, my beloved brethren, in the spirit of the Most High, to try the spirits to see if they are of God, and to use your own reason and judgment that you may be convinced of the truth. When a man is once convinced he will not depart from the things that have convinced him, but though he may be converted over and over again he may backslide. Once convince a man by reason and common sense and he will cling to it as tenaciously as possible; so I only beg of you, as respected jurors, to search for the truth. The truth will appeal to you according to your development; and your concept thereof will be as your spiritual discernment may impart. The matter of interpretation seems to be rather a serious one sometimes. You heard stated this afternoon that since there was no time specifically indicated, that the Scripture would be fulfilled if these signs followed one day, or even if they followed to this day. I beg to impart to you the honest statement of an individual that according to my interpretation they continue to the present day, and they will so continue until every child of the Most High shall have developed that spirituality of his nature that will bring him into a perfect at-one-ment with all of the spiritual powers of the universe and all failures will be swallowed up in victory, and all sins will be wiped away by the fullness of grace. Praise to the philosophy of light that cannot be put under a bushel. We anticipate the time when all the children of men shall know the truth and the truth shall make them free. Why do we anticipate this? The "Teacher of Galilee" said "These signs shall follow them that believe." The world is filled with a few millions of believers to-day, and the signs are following them even until to-day; the signs are following the members of the Modern Spiritualist's Organization because they are believers. You must decide from the evidence which has been given you this afternoon. This is left optional with you to interpret and I beg of you to be unbiased and interpret it after your own reason. Brethren, in the spirit of the Most High can I give to you a broader spirit of charity? Can I give to you a fuller spirit of Christ than to present to you my conception of these things and say, "believe it if it appeals to your concept of truth?" I do not come to you with doctrine, nor with faith, nor with any seducing sign, but simply to reason with you that as children of the Most High you will use the powers with which you are possessed and investigate the surrounding powers of the universe and see in what manner they appeal to your spiritual power of perception; that you live after the manner of the highest truth and light within you, giving unto every other individual the same privilege. If you can attain to that lofty point where you, with me, can believe that the Most High is able to draw unto himself all men, then let us draw near to each other in that spirit of Christ, and anticipate the time in the vast eons of the unfoldment that lies before us, when we shall all have come to know the truth, thus made free, clean and holy, to sit down at the bridegroom's feast with not a place vacant. You are to judge of these statements made upon this declaration that is before you for consideration, and if the broad plain of thought and reason which I have given to you, invites you to walk in this broad plain, where the light of truth shines upon the just and the unjust, to teach the spirit that is within, until it shall leap into expression and receive this light, come and walk and let us live as brethren in the fullness of the power of the spirit of truth, of light and of wisdom.

TIME.

(4:00 p. m., August 24th, 1907.)

J. W. CHISM'S THIRD AFFIRMATIVE.

Gentlemen Moderators, Brethren and Friends:

Glad am I, indeed, that I have the privilege again of standing in your presence, to further continue the investigation of the proposition, that "The Scriptures teach, that with the close of the apostolic age spiritual gifts, such as are mentioned in the Bible, ceased."

I must confess that I am somewhat amused. I have had a few debates in my life, and it has, generally, been my privilege, when I was in the affirmative, to see the negative at least attempt a refutation of the arguments that I made. But if there has been an attempt yet, in this debate, I do not remember it. While I was occupied in the whole of my two speeches yesterday in the affirmation I passed by what my opponent said. But I come this afternoon to a review of everything that was said by the negative.

There was one thought submitted by the negative that impressed me very much. He put it in the form of a question. "Have I at any time insinuated that his teaching was false?" I would like to know why he signed the proposition in the negative if he has not come on this rostrum to prove that what I said was false? What did he come here for? In the name of common sense! He has signed his name J. W. Ring, negative to the proposition. It seems to me that that would be more than an insinuation that the proposition was false. When I signed my name to the negative of his proposition I meant that I was at least attempting to show the people that everything he said, that was peculiar to the Spiritualists, was false. You understand, I do not call a man a liar, because I say his teaching is false. But do you suppose that I am to stand before the people and say "your teaching is true," when I stand just exactly cross to what you teach? I would ask the gentleman this afternoon, if he can, will he at least attempt to review the arguments that I made upon the proposition, on the cessation of miracles? He told us in one place that miracles continued to the present time, according to his interpretation. You understand, my dear sir, my proposition does not say "your interpretation." It says "the Scriptures teach." Will you please turn to the chapter and verse in either the Old or the New Testament that

— 183 —

says that miracles would continue to the present time? I have shown you conclusively that the Apostle says that they "will cease" when the perfect is come; and I showed you that the perfect was to come at that time when the church was perfected, had reached manhood; and that Paul said, "I have finished my course," and that he said the course of the Apostles was "to perfect the saints." And that Paul says, "then that which is in part shall be done away." I showed you that these spiritual gifts were the identical things mentioned as "part." Why does not the gentleman take them up, and try, at least, to show that the arguments are inconclusive? But I will review him.

Beginning with the first of his speech he says, "I deny that God has withdrawn the spirit of inspiration." I know you deny it, but who are you? Where is the evidence to sustain your denial? I have submitted from God's word the evidence that Christ and the Apostles came from God Jehovah. I gave it in those signs that I cited, which the gentleman acknowledges to be true, and said he would not even try to refute them. Then, if that word came from God under these signs, wonders and miracles, and God Almighty in that word says that these signs would cease at such a time. Will he dare stand in the face of this people and say that God Almighty lied about it? That it is untrue? He says, "If we are to look only into the Scriptures." My dear sir, my proposition says, "The Scriptures teach." If you are convinced that the Scriptures do teach that these things would cease, and you now desire to turn this debate into a scientific investigation, I am ready for it.

Again, he says, "After having heard these phenomena you can but believe in the mighty power of the God that gave them." This being true, I ask him why he does not accept it and follow it? Why does he deny it, since he acknowledges that the mighty power was evidence that the Lord Almighty gave it.

But he tells us that Jehovah, the presiding spirit of the Jewish God, was striving to fasten his teachings on these people, and again he says, the presiding spirits of the other nations have done the same thing. We would like to have a little evidence, please. Assertions are cheap articles, any man may deal in them. But he says "the self-same thing is continued with his people and comes on down to us." Now I would like to see some of the phenomena, or, even have mention of some of it. He told us he was going to parallel these things. Where is the parallel of any of those things I mentioned yesterday?

Then I called attention to John the Baptist speaking when he was but eight days old, and he said he would parallel that by one of the Fox girls' infant baby writing a message with her hand. I submit, ladies and gentlemen, that he has never as yet submitted any evidence that the child did it. Those things I have stated to you I have turned to authority—in the Bible—and read it. Where is the authority that he has produced? I deny the statement and challenge for authority. You understand, I am not prepared to receive his ipsi dixit and his assertions. But, granting that it was done—that the message was written in the child's hand, it is nothing more than magic can do. Why do they do only such as magic can do? Why do they not present phenomena that magic—slight of hand performances—cannot do. Nor need he claim the things done by the known laws of psychic phenomena, which are known to thousands and thousands of people, who know that it is not spirits of dead men doing this work? Why do they not present the phenomena that cannot be done by these things? Because they can't.

Then I note him referring to the people as "most worthy jurors." It seems the gentleman has changed his mind a little since he told you yesterday, or the day before, that you were a "dishonest jury." For now he says "most worthy jurors." It seems he is changing his mind some!

But he tells us that Modern Spiritualism has the same gifts to-day as mentioned by the Apostle Paul, and he cites first Cor. 10:1-7. Paul says, "Moreover, brethren, I would not that ye should be ignorant, how that all our fathers were under the cloud, and all passed through the sea; And were all baptized unto Moses in the cloud and in the sea; And did eat the same spiritual meat; and did all drink the same spiritual drink; for they drank of that spiritual Rock that followed them; and that Rock was Christ. But with many of them God was not well pleased; for they were overthrown in the wilderness. Now these things were our examples, to the intent we should not lust after evil things, as they also lusted." He cites us this and says that the word that was with them in the wilderness was Christ. I deny it. Is it possible that with the Bible open in his hand he makes such a statement as this. Open at the very chapter where the Apostle says "and that rock was Christ," and presume to tell the people that the "word was Christ." My dear sir, do you not know the difference between "rock" and "word." Paul says "and that rock was Christ." Go back to the wilderness, if you please, and see Moses, as he stands by the great rock, Horeb, and smites it with his staff, and out gushes the water, to water all that great congregation of people. This is that rock, i. e., the literal one, and that spiritual rock was Christ. Not the word was Christ. But he says again, "surely it could not be Christ if he was to come afterwards as a sacrifice, but it was a medium, or mediumship." I did not exactly get his word there, mediumship though, I think. That is, it was mediumship that was to come. Spiritualists can see mediumship in everything under the sun. Just here I want to submit some questions. I submit them in writing and demand an answer. I have eleven of them. The gentleman has been telling you of his confidence in Christ, and of the "sweet spirit of Christ, and sometimes he talks so sweet that he would hardly melt sugar in his mouth. So I desire to ask him some questions. I want to show you people that he does not believe in Jesus Christ.

First—Do you believe that Jesus is the Christ, the Son of the living God?

Second—If yes, do you believe that Jesus of Nazareth is any more the son of God than you yourself are?

Third—Do you believe that Jesus is the Christ, the Son of God as taught in the New Testament?

Fourth—Do you believe all that Jesus of Nazareth taught?

Fifth—Do you believe that Jesus of Nazareth was, and is, what he claimed to be?

Sixth—Do you believe that Jesus of Nazareth made the sacrifice for the sins of the whole world, as taught in the New Testament?

Seventh—Do you believe that his blood was shed for the remission of sins?

Eighth—Do you believe that Jesus of Nazareth rose from the dead as taught in the New Testament?

Ninth—Do you believe that all power in heaven and

in earth was given to Jesus of Nazareth as claimed by him
in Matthew 28:18?

Tenth—Do you believe that Jesus of Nazareth told the
truth in the statement to the Apostles recorded in Matthew 16:16-19, where he says, "Upon this rock I will
build my church, and the gates of death shall not prevail
against it, and I will give unto thee the keys of the kingdom of heaven; and whatsoever thou shalt bind on earth
shall be bound in heaven; and whatsoever thou shalt loose
on earth shall be loosed in heaven?" And in John 20:21-
23, where he said, "Whose soever sins ye remit, they are
remitted unto them; and whose soever sins ye retain,
they are retained?"

Eleventh—Do you believe what Jesus Christ said when
he said (John 10:7-10), "All that came before me are
thieves and robbers?"

I would like for the gentleman to answer these questions. He has been telling us of Confucius and Buddha
as great prophets before. Now Jesus Christ said that,
"all that came before me are thieves and robbers," and
he has told you that he believed what Jesus Christ said.
Now, does he believe what he said? Will he answer the
questions? Then he comes to the prophets, seers, mediums, or he says, scientifically called psychics." I have
been a bit amused ever since this debate began by the
gentleman attempting all the while to twist in the common law of hypnotism as spiritualism. Right here I desire to make a little bit of explanation. You saw the
gentleman the other evening, as he stood by this table
with his fingers placed upon it—you saw him standing
silently for a few moments of time, following which he
proposed to give you a demonstration in poetry, of the
"spirit's inspiration." The gentleman stood for a while

— 188 —

and then began reciting what most people would call "doggerel poetry," scarcely good enough to make good doggerel, but anyway he recited it. I called attention of some friends on the street—I told them that, as the gentleman was standing there he suggested to himself that the spirit of some poet would possess him, that he went into a condition that hypnotists called hypnotic, or a subjective condition. Just as soon as he went into that condition he became en rapport with the thought that he had suggested to himself. As soon as he became en rapport with that thought he began to do just what he thought that spirit would do. I take a man and put him in the same condition, hypnotize him, and I tell him he is a horse, "there is some good hay, and you are hungry," and he will walk right out on his feet and hands, go through the motion of eating hay, where there is none before him. The congregation may roar and laugh, but he never moves a muscle of his face; he is as sober as a judge; the same as a horse eating the grass. That man sees himself "as a horse." Why? Spirit got hold of him? No. My suggestions got hold of him. But the gentleman though he was possessed of a spirit. Why? He had his own suggestion hold of him; and that is all. I might take the boy, again, from the place he is eating straw, with a snap of the fingers, "follow me. You are now a doctor, a dentist," and tell him that here is a patient that wants a tooth pulled, pointing to a chair, and he will look in the mouth of it, of the imaginary man, and get his imaginary forceps and immediately begin to pull the tooth. He thinks he is a dentist. Is he a dentist? No. In that condition his reasoning faculty is laid aside and whatever is suggested to him by one who is en rapport with him puts him en rapport with that

— 189 —

thought; and takes that suggestion for reason, and there is no doubt about it at the time. If a man suggests to himself that the spirit of Samuel will come on him when he gets en rapport with that thought the thought in his suggestion, he will begin to act just like he thinks Samuel would act. These things have been demonstrated time and time again, in the psychic world, and prove that it is true and that it is not spiritualism, nor within a thousand miles of it; yet the gentleman has been trying to twist it in all the time as spiritualism.

But he tells us the disciples did not always recognize Christ until he gave them the test. Well, sir, do your spirits give you that kind of a test? Do they eat a piece of bread and fish before you? Do they say, "thrust your hand into my side, and be no more doubting, but believing?"

But he tells us when Moses brought messages to the people that he set a boundary lest the people in going up to the mountain should break the psychic condition. The Bible says no such thing. The Bible says the people should not go up to the mountain lest they die. But he says "Jehovah was not aware of what was being done in the camp while they were in the mountain, and when Moses came down off of the mount, with Jehovah attending him, that Jehovah got mad when he saw they had gone into idolatry." Turn to Exodus 24:18. You find Moses commanded to go up into the mountain and he went up. Turn now to Exodus 32, and I will begin with the 5th verse and read you this record to show you that the gentleman has twisted it again, "And when Aaron saw it, he built an altar before it; and Aaron made a proclamation, and said, To-morrow is a feast to the Lord. And they rose up early on the morrow, and offered burnt offerings, and brought peace offerings; and the people sat down to eat and to drink, and rose up to play. And the Lord said unto Moses, Go, get thee down; for thy people, which thou broughtest out of the land of Egypt, have corrupted themselves; They have turned aside quickly out of the way which I commanded them; they have made them a molten calf, and have worshipped it, and have sacrificed thereunto, and said, These be thy Gods, O Israel, which have brought thee up out of the land of Egypt." Israel, to the 8th verse inclusive. Here, then, we find, when they did the thing, the Lord knew it, and told Moses at once about it, while in the mountain. He asserted that the Lord did not know it until he came down. Then he asserted that Jehovah came down off the mountain with Moses. Say, can't you read? Don't you know the difference between "Joshua" and "Jehovah?" Say, it was Joshua that came down off the mountain with Moses, and not Jehovah. Exodus 32:17, "And when Joshua heard the noise of the people, as they shouted, he said unto Moses, there is a noise of war in the camp." It was Joshua and not Jehovah that came down off of the mountain. Is it possible that he looked at the word "Joshua" and thought it was "Jehovah," or, does he stand before the people handling the word of God deceitfully, thinking that J. W. Chism does not know what is in that book? Does he think that I have been debating for the number of years that I have, and preaching it for a number of years, and yet not know what is in it? Sir, when you come to reading that word know you are in the right. I do not have to turn to the chapter to see when you are reading it right. A man with another man after him, to take charge of him for misreading, that would pervert God's truth like that, to make out his case; in the name of common sense, what would he do if there was nobody to follow him?

Now I come to the slate messages. Why, anybody could write some messages on a slate and put them down in the town, and tell you that they were written by spirits. But, where is the evidence that they were written by spirits. But he says, "I give you my word on my honor, of whatever you think me to be." I must confess, my dear sir, that a man that would handle the word of God as deceitfully as you have before this people I am not prepared to accept your statement on such an important proposition as this. But, while we are talking about the spirit's writing, I know one time of spirit writing. There came forth the fingers of a man's hand and wrote on the plaster of the wall, in the presence of the King, in the presence of his Lords and his Concubines, and the King saw the part of the hand that did the writing, and it was right against the candlestick, right in the lightest part of the house.

But he says, "we can parallel the spiritual gifts" as Paul gave them, "every one of them." Speak some Hebrew, please.

Again, he tells us, that, "Jehovah came to Jacob, and was talking to Jacob, that it was at night, and he was wrestling with him, and when the morning came he wanted to get away." If he will turn to Genesis 22:24 the record says it was a man—"m-a-n"—that does not spell Jehovah. This is another case of his handling the word of God deceitfully. In the 29th verse he says, "Why asketh thou after my name." In the 30th verse Jacob says, "I have seen God face to face," called the name Peniel, that is, the face of God. In Genesis 23:10, when Jacob met Esau, he said, "I saw thy face, as it were the face of God." Esau had come to his brother by night, and Esau was evidently the man who wrestled with Jacob. But when the daylight began to come he said, "Let me go." And Jacob said "I will not let you go until you bless me." He said "What is your name?" And he answered "it is Jacob; what is your name?" He said, why asketh thou after my name? But when Jacob met him in open daylight he knew him—knew it was the face he had seen at night, as it was the face of God.

Next we come to the spoiling of Egypt, and he talks—Oh, about spoiling Egypt, that was awful. After the Egyptians had robbed them for four hundred years, the idea of their going out with substance—enough to live on, being "robbing the Egyptians."

I have another thought to which I call your attention. The gentleman seems not to be satisfied with the proposition gone before, and is now trying to patch up by going over it again. He calls your attention to first Timothy 4:1-3 and tells us that, Paul "lived in the latter times." My dear sir, you should look into your Bible! He then cited us Acts 2:16-17, where Peter speaks of the prophesy of Joel, and says it is fulfilled, making that the last days. The phrases are not the same either in English or Greek. The Greek for "last days" is "eschatais hemerais," acts 2:17, last days. But in the other place, in 1 Tim. 4:1-3, it is "husterois kairois," which does not mean "last days," but latter times." Now I will turn to the lexicon and read you the meaning of both these words. I read from Dr. George Ricker Berry, Ph. D., Kairos, ou, ho—"a fixed time, season, opportunity. Kronos is time in general, viewed simply as such. Kairos, definite, suitable time, the time of some decisive event, crises, opportunity. Such is the word that Paul used in the letter to Timothy.

But Hemera, as, he, "a day, *i. e.,* from sunrise to sunset, a day of twenty-four hours. Figuratively, in various senses." In Acts 2 Peter uses the word "Hemera," "day." In 1 Tim 4 Paul uses the word "Kairos," which is not "day," but "times." Paul then says, "In the latter times;" using a phrase that distinguishes it from the last days. "In the latter appointed time." A specific time to come hereafter. Latter times. Not "In the last days," which began on the Pentecost. But the latter tmies, * a specific time to come, an opportune time. Such is the time Paul speaks of, and we have identified it with the time that Modern Spiritualism came up. And I promise you every time the gentleman attempts to make an argument to get out of it, his head is turned downward and I will sink him deeper.

Oh, he says, "Send them to hell," and he almost cries about it. The God of the Bible never made hell for man. He made it for that deceptive being that deceives men; but if men prefer to take that, instead of God, all right; he gives man his privilege and his choice.

But he has been telling you how he believes in Christ. Jesus Christ says in Matthew 45:46, "These shall go away in everlasting punishment." In John 5:29 he says, "And shall come forth; they that have done good, unto the resurrection of life; and they that have done evil, unto the resurrection of damnation." He does not believe these statements. Does he believe in Jesus Christ or not?

TIME.

J. W. RING—NEGATIVE.

Gentlemen Moderators and Friends:

Any reason, evidence, argument or question which may be presented by the opposition bearing upon the point at issue we believe we have from time to time brought intelligently before your consideration. The question which we are discussing is not to determine whether I, as an individual, believe in Jesus as a man, saviour, son of God or in any way whatsoever. We are endeavoring to talk about spiritual gifts, not the belief of an individual. I most assuredly would not occupy one moment of your valuable time to invite your attention to my belief, nor to any man's belief. The world is too full of beliefs already. We have our concepts of truth, and these concepts of truth have been labeled our beliefs, our doctrines, our creeds, and as indicated to you on yesterday afternoon, it has been the attempt of organized churchanity at all times to force their belief upon other individuals. It is my hope that, because of this series of thought exchange, a few individuals will become so interested (not in my belief, nor my opponent's belief, nor any other belief than your own) that they will endeavor to follow the reasoning of personal belief into such investigation as will enable them to gain a few facts, a little demonstration of knowledge. Thus closer to a conclusion of truth, may you be broader and more charitable, until you will be moved to say, with a mighty host of individuals in the world everywhere, "we anticipate the time when all of the children of men will be drawn into a 'unity of spirit,' where they will permit each individual to believe as his education and environment compels, and not have this constant spirit of enmity to compel individuals to believe this or that doctrine, nor present such doctrines as will intimidate the people to believe lest they be damned." To-day we have perhaps five or six hundreds of denominations in the world, each of which proclaim "Unless you believe these doctrines you shall be damned." (Mr. Chism—Gentlemen moderators, I raise a point of order. The gentleman is entirely off of the proposition. The proposition is that the Scriptures teach that the spiritual gifts, such as are mentioned in the Bible, ceased with the close of the apostolic age. I demand that he make an attempt to refer to what I have said. Debating is debating; lecturing is lecturing, and he should at least make an attempt to reply). I believe I am speaking to the jury, not to an individual. Some questions have been placed here for me to answer. I say that I am not here to answer questions to prove whether I am a believer of Jesus in one sense of the word or another, and as a preface to what I am to say upon the point which I have stated I claim the privilege of explaining why I am not immediately referring to these questions. They are irrelevant, they are not to the question. Because of personal attack I claim the privilege to further state I did not say this was a jury irresponsible nor unworthy. I said if any individual juror had come prejudiced that he could not sit honestly upon a jury in any point of law; when I address my respected jurors I am speaking to those who are not prejudiced, but who come to listen to the reason, logic and evidence that may be presented by either side, and then decide. He sneers at the connected evidence which we placed before you yesterday, as to the rock to which Peter referred being the gift of mediumship, and says that way back in Israel we see the rock, and see issuing therefrom the water to water the children of

Israel. Was the rock the gift, or was the power by which the water was brought the gift? Was Jesus as a Christ the rock or was he the one endowed with the self-same spiritual gifts as moved the prophet of old to produce this phenomena? I leave the matter to your consideration.

He again attacks the personal actions of his opponent in referring to an incident that took place the other evening in your presence. (Improvised rhyme.) I would like to see the gentleman, and I believe you would as well, hypnotize some subject and produce a few verses of "doggerel." There is an opportunity perhaps for evidence along the line.

Lest we lose sight of the thought of spiritual gifts, may we refer you to the fact that on yesterday afternoon we invited your attention to the consideration of the prophesy of the prophets of old (which are claimed by the followers of Jesus in the church to indicate the prophesy of the advent of Jesus) in connection with the statement of our opponent when he said, the language, in Mark, chap. 16, does not indicate the duration of the spiritual gifts. We further led you into a consideration of evidence as presented by us that they did continue, and "surely these signs shall follow them that believe," indicates conclusively as to who they shall follow; and intimates at least concerning the time of its continuation. Since in my denial of this proposition, under consideration, I affirm that spiritual gifts, such as are recorded in the Old and New Testament, continue to-day, we will consider the purport or object of these spiritual gifts. Our worthy opponent tells us that Paul has emphatically stated that they came for the perfecting of faith for the perfecting of the saints, and we are in search of these things made perfect; of evidence, if you please, that there is a perfect church, that there is a perfected denomination or following of this belief or of this religion established. We must remember that these books or epistles from which we are reading are translations from letters written by Paul to various people. They were speaking concerning the efforts of the Apostles to establish their concept of this religion, where it was at that time unpopular. These translations have later been canonized and declared to be the inspired Scripture, and are so accepted by us. In this 4th chapter of Ephesians Paul says, I therefore, the prisoner of the Lord, beseech you that ye walk worthy of the vocation wherewith ye are called, With all lowliness and meekness, with long suffering, forbearing one another in love; Endeavoring to keep the unity of the Spirit in the bond of peace." Remembering the differences that had arisen between the Apostles themselves and endeavoring to keep the "unity of the Spirit" in the bond of peace. "There is one body, and one Spirit, even as ye are called in one hope of your calling; One Lord, one faith, one baptism. One God and Father of all who is above all, and through all, and in you all. But unto every one of us is given grace according to the measure of the gift of Christ. Wherefore he saith, When he ascended up on high, he led captivity captive, and gave gifts unto men." "And he gave some, Apostles; and some, prophets; and some evangelists; and some, pastors and teachers. For the perfecting of the saints, for the work of the ministry, for the edifying of the body of Christ; Till we all come in the unity of the faith, and of the knowledge of the Son of God, unto a perfect man, unto the measure of the stature of the fulness of Christ;" Did they? And have we come to the fulness of the stature of Christ? Have we become perfect even as Christ was perfect? Are there any evidences of any of these perfect people? Does the Scriptures give us any record of them? Have we ever heard or seen them? Are we to understand that the "Son of God" indicate the personality of the individual, or that it indicate the power of the spirit, the spiritual gift, that rested upon the prophets of old, that manifested itself through Jesus and the Apostles and continues to manifest itself through the children of men to-day? It was Paul's intention to convey to these individuals the necessity of perfecting the gifts of mediumship, of perfecting spiritual gifts that they might be able to produce such phenomena as would be superior to that which had already been produced by other media, and by the prophets that stood in other denominations. There were other sects, creeds, doctrines, and they had their prophets and their mediums. They were giving their manifestations, and Paul was admonishing his disciples to perfect themselves in spiritual gifts until they would be able to produce greater phenomena than their adversaries. Was there or is there any intimation in this that the spiritual gifts were to be withdrawn? I beg of you, respected jurors; it was an admonition that they perfect themselves in spiritual gfts, as he said in first Cor. in the 13th chapter, "for we know in part and we prophesy in part, but when that which is perfect is come." When we have perfected our powers, when we have perfected the development of our spiritual gifts then "that which is in part shall be done away." The development which takes place in the early enfoldment of an individual for his mediumship is passed by, and we then enter into the higher phases of the special gift. "When I was a child I spoke as a child, I understood as a child, I thought as a child, but when I became a man I put away childish things," using the illustration, that even as a child puts away childish things, so we may be able to perfect ourselves to become Christs. Well, then, we will certainly have the fulness of the spiritual gifts. Continuing in the 14th verse of the 4th chapter of Ephesians, "That we henceforth be no more children, tossed to and fro, and carried about with every wind of doctrne, by the sleight of men, and cunning craftiness, whereby they lie in wait to deceive ;" Was he referring to something to take place in 1848, or was he referring to the things which were then occurring? They were upon every side hedged about by the necromancers and by the prophets and mediums of other denominations that were moving their believers to desert their ranks and go into the other denominations and he wanted them to perfect themselves that they might be able to give greater demonstrations and greater phenomena. Continuing, as we were asked to, in second Timothy, chapter 4, we have another letter from Paul to one of his younger teachers. Paul was getting along in years. He felt the weight of the experiences through which he had passed. He felt that it was nearing the time when he would go from this world, and he said, "for the time will come when they will not endure sound doctrine," speaking to his disciples, realizing that there would be many of them that would go back into their former beliefs, "but after their own lusts shall they heap to themselves teachers having itching ears— and shall be turned unto fables—" "Make full proof of thy ministry for I am now ready to be offered, and the time of my departure is at hand." Is there anything to indicate here that there is going to be an end of these spiritual gifts? Since he has just admonished them to per-

fect themselves in spiritual gifts? "I have fought a good
fight." Would not any of us say as much if we had
fought by the faith we believed? "I have finished my
course." The course of finishing the perfect church?
Where is the perfect church? Where is the unit of a
congregation, that there is not a difference of opinion
among the individuals? Do you not, my beloved jurors,
disagree among yourselves in the matter of religion or
doctrinal points as to baptism, as to the condition of the
individual after the change called death, as to how many
shall be in heaven? Where is the perfect church?
"Henceforth, there is laid up for me a crown of righteousness, which the Lord, the righteous Judge, shall give
to me that day——" "Do thou, by thy diligence, come
shortly unto me." This is a letter to those that are following along with him, admonishing them to remain true
and sincere to the faith by which they have lived, and to
above all things perfect themselves in those spiritual
gifts that will enable them to demonstrate their religion,
and lead others into an understanding of the power and
worth of that respective religion. That I further impress you with the fact that these spiritual gifts continue
it is my privilege, in denying this proposition, to present
you all possible evidence. I want to thoroughly establish before your consideration the fact that they were
sought for in those days, and I want to inform you that
in those days individuals sought to receive these spiritual
gifts through baptism. They realized that baptism in the
Bible was primarily for spiritual gifts. When Jesus was
baptized by John, as recorded in Matthew 3, verse 16,
"And Jesus, when he was baptized, went up straightway
out of the water, and lo, the heavens were opened unto
him, and he saw the Spirit of God descending like a dove,

and lighting upon him, and lo, the voice from heaven saying 'This is my beloved Son, in whom I am well pleased.' " It does not say the multitude saw it, but he saw it; he was baptized and received the gift, the spiritual gift, the power of the Spirit of God, mediumship, even as the apostles of old had received it, and had sought to receive it through the laying on of hands and in various manners. Peter, in explaining how this Spirit of God, Holy Ghost, or spiritual gift might be received reason in Acts, chapter 2—"Therefore being by the right hand of God exalted, and having received of the Father the promise of the Holy Ghost, he hath shed forth this which ye now see and hear." What was the Holy Ghost? These manifestations, these things which we now see and hear. "For David is not ascended into the heavens; but he saith himself, The Lord said unto my Lord, Sit thou on my right hand, until I make thy foes thy footstool. Therefore let all the house of Israel know assuredly, that God hath made that same Jesus, whom ye have crucified, both Lord and Christ. (Made him a medium.) Now when they heard this, they were pricked in their heart, and said unto Peter and to the rest of the apostles, Men and brethren, what shall we do? Then Peter said unto them, Repent, and be baptized every one of you in the name of Jesus Christ for the remission of sins, and ye shall receive the gift of the Holy Ghost." What was the Holy Ghost? The gift, the spiritual gift, the power of mediumship that these men had received, that the men and women of earth were enjoying, that the prophets had enjoyed, that the men and women of earth are enjoying today. "For the promise is unto you, and to your children, and to all that are afar off, even as many as the Lord our God

shall call." Thus, afar off in some other country, afar
off in some other age. "Now as many as God may call."
Has God called a cessation of these spiritual gifts? Have
we any evidence in the Scripture that there has been a
cessation of these spirtual gifts? If there can be proven
authentically, a single phenomenon, it is sufficient to
show that these spiritual gifts have continued. Paul
was admonishing his followers to perfect themselves
in spiritual gifts, to grow into the "unity of spirit," that
they might so develop these spiritual gifts that they would
be one united body. Evidently, the attempt is going on
yet. We have never seen the church that existed in
unity yet. The horrors of the history of the world, the
crimes that have been committed, and in the name of
religion, to compel to believe this or that doctrine, to believe that spiritual gifts have been discontinued, or that
they have not been discontinued, are sore spots upon
the history of humanity who claim to believe in the for-
giving Christ. I beg of you to consider that all of the
history of the world, religiously considered, is a history
of warfare to attempt to make people believe a certain
doctrine. There has not been a unity of spirit among
the churches, not among the church members (among
the self-declared churches of Christ), nor is there a unity
among them today. You know, as well as I, that one
denomination says "Our membership will be found in
heaven." Another church says, "Our membership will
be found in heaven." Another will say emphatically,
"that church membership will not be found in heaven."
I do not want to bring these matters before your consideration in order to refute such flimsy ideas as trying
to determine my personal belief in Jesus. I accept these
books as the Scripture, else I would not have signed my

name to this proposition. I want that broad spirit of liberality that says to each individual: See the light that shines in glory from the heavens above, live by this light and perfect yourself until you can live in unity with yourself and then at unity with each other, for "he that overcometh himself is greater than he that taketh a city." I beg for personal development, for personal unfoldment and for the accomplishment of those things that will enable us to live together in the unity that we have never seen yet manifested by the followers of this great "Teacher or Prophet of Galilee."

TIME.

J. W. CHISM'S FOURTH AFFIRMATIVE.

Gentlemen Moderators, Brethren, Friends:

I must confess that I am still a bit amused. I have asked the gentleman eleven questions. He stubbornly refuses to answer. Do you know why I asked them? I maintain that no man has a right to stand before the people, and tell them that he believes a doctrine that is taught by Christ, and believes Christ, until he tells the people whether he believes in him. But he refuses to answer. He continuously makes his appeal to the teachings of Christ, or says he believes what Christ said here and yonder and tries to leave the impression that he accepts Christ, and I have asked him some questions to prove to you that he does not believe in Jesus Christ. His refusal to answer the questions shows this intelligent people that he does not accept Christ. Had he believed in Christ he would have answered every question, "Yes, sir;" but knowing that he does not believe in him, he realizes if he answers "No," that his little cob-house,

— 204 —

that he has builded on those smooth, oily tongued statements, will come to the ground. You see why he does
not answer. Ah! I did not expect him to answer. I
asked those questions to show this people that he
could not answer them and hold his job, to show you
that he is an infidel to the Christ. There were one or
two things that I had not examined in the other speech,
to which I wish to call your attention, because I want to
review everything that he said.

He called your attention yesterday afternoon to Paul,
and Barnabas, and said, they quarreled, in a difference
about these "spiritual gifts," and about where they should
go. I submit that if the gentleman thought he was telling the facts, he is too ignorant to stand before the people to teach them. But if he knew he was telling the
facts, then he is too dishonest to teach. But then you
may be the judges in the case as to his sincerity in
what he was teaching. I simply call your attention to
Acts 15:36-40, where the writer, Luke, gives the record
of this case; beginning with the 36th verse, I read:
"And some days after, Paul said unto Barnabas, Let us
go again and visit our brethren in every city where
we have preached the word of the Lord and see how
they do, and Barnabas determined to take with them
John, whose surname was Mark. But Paul thought not
good to take him with them, who departed from them
at Pamphylia and went not with them to the work. And
the contention was so sharp between them, that they
departed asunder one from the other: and so Barnabas
took Mark and sailed into Cypress, and Paul departed,
being recommended by the brethren unto the grace of
God, and he went through Syria and Cilicia, confirming
the churches." (I read to the conclusion of the chap-

ter.) This is the record of the case. Why did he stand before you and tell you it was a contention about spiritual gifts, and about where they should go? You judge.

But he told us he had seen prison doors opened by the touch of a physical medium. I must confess, ladies and gentlemen, without evidence I am unable to believe. And I am unprepared to accept the simple statements of a man who handles the word of God so deceitfully as does this man.

Again, he says, "I do not come to you with doctrines and faith." Well, I have told you, all the time, that Paul said, "In the latter times some would depart from the faith."

Then he says, "If you can attain to the lofty point with me," Umph! Me! I!—I am the what I am, for if I am not, what am I? I am the "it." If you can just get up by the side of Me, up my Me—this lofty point. Oh, shame! where is thy blush?

I submit one more thought in connection with these signs, these spiritual gifts. I read from I Cor. 14:22, which the gentleman said, in his last speech, were letters from the apostles, "claimed to be inspired revelations, and they accepted them as such, as well as we." Well, if he accepts them as such, I will try him as one, by Paul's writing. "Wherefore tongues are for a sign, not to them that believe, but to them that believe not: but prophesying serveth not for them that believeth not, but for them which believe." He and his people, relative to Spiritualism, are the believers. Me and my brethren are the unbelievers, relative to Spiritualism. Tongues are for a sign to the unbelievers. Speak a few words in Hebrew, please, or, interpret that Hebrew I gave you the other day. Can you speak it? Let us hear a word of that tongue.

But he says, It is not a question of whether I believe in Jesus as a person, and so on. My dear sir, you have been begging sympathy on that one point ever since this debate began; you have been talking about your belief in Jesus, and that you wanted them to follow the spirit of Christ, when you don't want any such thing. You want them to follow the Spirit of YOU KNOW NOT WHAT. But he said right after that, "There were too many beliefs;" and he wanted you to be at liberty so you could reach out on broader grounds. I confess there are too many beliefs. The apostle Paul says, "There is one faith, and one spirit." How many do you people teach? Many? Remember you said, in your last speech, that these writings of Paul were inspired revelations; and Paul says, "There is one body and one spirit." How many do you people teach?

Then he speaks about a "personal attack." Humph! He was the man who said before these people, "You are not honest jurors." I did not say it. I just called the people's attention to the fact that he had said it, and that today he was calling you by a different name, "most worthy jurors."

Again he said, that rock was the "gift of mediumship," if I understood him rightly. Paul said, "they drank of that spiritual rock that followed them, and that rock was Christ." Where did you learn that it was the spirit of mediumship? But he says he would like to see my hypnotism. I have been ready ever since this debate commenced, when they begin to show their spirit demonstrations, to parallel them. I challenged him to allow me in the room where the medium was at work, with my hands loose, and at liberty to strike a match when I please. Would he grant it? He has not yet. But he says, we come to the purpose of spiritual gifts, and that I said, the gifts were to perfect the saints. Beg pardon, sir. I quoted the apostle Paul, and Paul said, speaking of the apostles and prophets, evangelists, pastors and teachers that they were given to perfect the saints. Who were the apostles and prophets? These were the men who possessed these spiritual gifts. Then when the saints were perfected, the apostles and prophets who had these gifts would pass away, and the gifts that came to others through the imposition of apostolic hands would pass away when these who possessed them died.

In reading the Ephesian letter, he read it, "till we all come in the knowledge of the son of man;" but it reads, the "knowledge of the Son of God to a perfect man."

In commenting on this he tries his hand once, on a reply to an argument. I am glad he did so. I shall now take up his attempted reply and examine it. He says, "Have we come to the perfect man?" I will let Paul answer that question. Paul, what do you mean by "the perfect man?" In the same Ephesian letter, in the second chapter, beginning with the 15th verse, Paul says, "Having abolished in his flesh the enmity, even the law of commandments contained in ordinances; for to make in himself of twain one new man, so making peace; and that he might reconcile both unto God in one body by the cross, having slain the enmity thereby." Then, they are both to be found the "one new man"—the "one body." What is that one body, Paul? Colossians the first chapter and 18th verse: "And he is the head of the body, the church: who is the beginning, the first born from the dead; that in all things he might have the pre-eminence." Then the church is the body to be made one, one new man—one church. So making peace. This, then, is conclusive as to the thing that was to be perfected, the new man. When the wall of partition was broken down by the death of Jesus Christ; and the covenant of Christ was erected, and Jew and Gentile had both entered into that covenant with Christ, thus, the two making one body, one church; when that body had been completed, with its officers to take the oversight thereof; with its evangelists for the work of the ministry; with its pastors and teachers for the edifying of the body of Christ; when this had been perfected; and, then, the "perfect law of liberty"—the law of the spirit of life—the New Testament had been completed; the perfect came. "Then," says Paul, "That which is in part shall be done away." But what was it in part, Paul? First Corinthians 12:11, "the spirit dividing unto every man severally as he will." Then the nine diversities of gifts, tongues, healings, miracles and such like. These nine diversities were the parts that Paul spoke of, for he said himself they were the divisions; and the thing that is divided, is in parts. Paul specifies three of these parts in I Cor. 13th chapter, to tell you what he is talking about. In the 8th to the 11th verses, he tells us that these parts were to cease when the perfect came. But is that come yet? I will read once again from Paul in his writings, II Timothy, 4th chapter, beginning with the 6th verse, "I am now ready to be offered, and the time of my departure is at hand; I have fought a good fight; I have finished my course; I have kept the faith." Paul says, "I have finished my course." What were you, Paul? Gal. 1: "An apostle of Jesus Christ." Then since Paul was an apostle of Jesus

Christ, and says, "'I have finished my course." What was the course of the apostle Paul? Listen—"He gave some apostles and some prophets and some evangelists and some pastors and teachers for the perfecting of the saints for the work of the ministry, for the edifying of the body of Christ." Here are three classes of individuals, or teachers, given. 1st, "apostles and prophets," men possessed of spiritual gifts; 2nd, evangelists; 3rd, pastors and teachers. Again, three classes of work to be done—1st, perfecting of the saints; 2nd, work of the ministry; 2rd, edifying the body of Christ. Hence, the conclusion is inevitable, that the apostles and prophets were given for the perfecting of the saints. These were the ones possessed of spiritual gifts. When Paul said, "I have finished my course," he but said he had finished the work of the apostles, hence the saints perfected, and the last one of these apostles to finish his course so far as we have any record, was the apostle John. But, I call your attention to his final statement. Revelation 22:18-21, "For I testify unto every man that heareth the words of the prophecy of this book, If any man shall add unto these things, God shall add unto him the plagues that are written in this book; And if any man shall take away from the words of the book of the prophecy, God shall take away his part out of the book of life, and out of the holy city, and from the things which are written in this book. He which testifieth these things, saith, Surely I come quickly. Amen. Even so, come Lord Jesus. The grace of our Lord Jesus Christ be with you all Amen." There is the last message given from the last apostle of Jesus Christ, who lived on this earth, and when he completed his work, he said no man should dare add to it under the penalty of the plagues of that book being added unto him. One of those plagues was he should be cast alive into the lake of fire, that burns with fire and brim-stone. If a man takes from these things, his part shall be taken out of the book of life. Hence, lost on either score. We conclude from this, that the revelation of God is completed; the perfect law of liberty is completed with this writing, and under the penalty of eternal death, no man dare add to, or take from that law. What happened then, Paul? "Then that which is in part shall be done away." What is the part, Paul? First Cor. 12th chapter, 1st to 11th verses, he gives us nine diversities of gifts. I will read them once again for the benefit of the hearer. Beginning with the 4th verse, "Now there are diversities of gifts, but the same spirit. And there are differences of administrations, but the same Lord. And there are diversities of operations, but it is the same God which worketh in all. But the manifestation of the Spirit is given to every man to profit withal. For to one is given by the Spirit the word of wisdom; to another the word of knowledge by the same Spirit; To another faith by the same Spirit; to another the gifts of healing by the same Spirit; To another the working of miracles; to another prophecy; to another discerning of spirits; to another divers kinds of tongues; to another the interpretation of tongues; But all these worketh that one and the selfsame Spirit, dividing to every man severally as he will." Here are the parts. Paul says, "Yet shew I unto you a more excellent way." He is to show us a more excellent way than to have these spiritual gifts. I have showed you that the perfect had come, and Paul says when the perfect is come, that which is in part shall be done away. But my opponent has gone to record, telling us that these were accepted by him as letters of inspiration. Being such, Paul says it is one spirit that worketh all these. You (addressing his opponent) teach that there are many spirits and that they come in diverse ways, to teach you. Paul says there is one spirit that taught them, and operated in the different ways. See the difference, ladies and gentlemen, You now see why I asked him if he believed in Jesus Christ, and what Jesus Christ said. But this is not all yet. He says Paul's idea was to perfect the mediumship. Then he tells us that that which is in part should be done away when the mediumship was perfected. I thought you said that when mediumship was perfected, that was the time the spiritual gifts would come. Spiritual gifts were the parts. When mediumship is perfected, spiritual gifts cease. You cross yourself. Paul does not leave us to guess what the parts are. But he mentions three of them by name in I. Cor., 13th chapter. Then if my opponent was right, when his mediumship is perfected, they lose these spiritual powers.

But he wants to know in Ephesians 4:12 if Paul was referring to this age of the world. No, he was referring to the time that the perfect should come, thence onward to our time, and on to the end of the world. Again he says, that "from henceforth," that is, after we come into the "unity of faith." Not "unity of faith," as he quoted it. But the "unity of the faith," and the knowledge of the Son of God. There (holding the Bible up and pointing to it) we have the unity of "the faith" and the knowledge of the Son of God revealed. When we come to that, we have the revelation completed. (Of course, that little shake of the head over there don't amount to anything. I know it hurts but the directions say take it. (By Mr. Lee, a moderator, to whom the speaker referred—Why don't you take it, then?) I do take mine. But this is your medicine and I may have to hold your nose before you get through with it. II Timothy, 4th chapter, 1 to 8, "for the time will come when they will not endure sound doctrine, but after their own lusts shall they heap to themselves teachers having itching ears; And they shall turn away their ears from the truth, and shall be turned unto fables."

But again he says of Paul, "Did he say anything about spiritual gifts ceasing?" Let him take it in connection with the argument that I give him, and let him show that the argument is not conclusive. Will he try it? But again, Paul tells us "when that which is perfect is come, knowledge shall vanish away." Will he tell us that when the mediumship is completed the man's knowledge vanishes? Why, he said they were perfecting mediumship. Does that make the man cease to know anything? Some of them, I confess, do go to the asylum.

Next, he says, the "perfecting of spiritual gifts by baptism." Chapter and verse, please? He says, "baptism primarily was for spiritual gifts." I deny it emphatically and challenge for proof. There is not a statement in the Bible, from the first word in Genesis, which says "in," to the close of Revelation and the last word that says "all." Then, "in all" that Bible there is not a word that says a man must be baptized "for spiritual gifts." The record says John came baptizing "for the remission of sins" and preaching the baptism of repentance "for the remission of sins," and the record says that Peter said, "repent, and be baptized, every one of you, in the name of Jesus Christ, for the remission of sins." That is what the record says, when it is talking about the word baptism with the word for.

But he told us that "Christ was baptized, and when he was baptized the Holy Ghost came upon him." Jesus Christ was baptized and when he was baptized the Holy Ghost did come upon him. And the Father said, "Hear him," but you people will not do it. Then he reads Acts 2:32-36 and says that God has made him "medium." But the Bible says "Made him Lord." That means ruler. Made him Christ—that means "anointed." Anointed him the ruler of the universe, giving him all power in heaven and in earth. But in verse 37 "what shall we do?" My opponent says that means, "what shall we do to receive the gift of the Holy Ghost?" Where did you learn that? The import of a question, when not placed in the question itself, may be learned in the answer of the question. The import of this question is not given in the question. It says, "Men and brethren, what shall we do?" Then we must look to the answer for the import. Answer, "Repent and be baptized, every one of you, in the name of Jesus Christ, for the remission of sins, and you shall receive the gift of the Holy Ghost, for the promises unto you, and to your children, and to all that are afar off, even as many as the Lord our God shall call." Here the remission of sins is expressed connectedly with the commandment, showing it to be the import of the question. "And" comes in, showing us another clause added. Then, the promise to them and their children does not refer to the promise of the "gift of the Holy Ghost," but the promise of "the remission of sins." The thing that God had promised Abraham, back yonder. We drop the parenthetical clause and read it without the parenthesis, as we have both been reading Ephesians before. "Repent and be baptized, every one of you in the name of Jesus Christ, for the remission of sins (* * *), for the promise is unto you and to your children." Parenthesis thrown in, though it is not marked in parenthesis, set off, if you please, as parenthetic clauses are, and thrown in to explain a side thought to the subject at issue. Then the import of the question in the answer is, "for the remission of sins." This shows that the gentleman has missed his mark again.

But he keeps on talking about men "perfecting mediumship." I confess that I see one in the New Testament that did want to perfect his mediumship. He said to Peter, "give me this power," and offered him money. That was Simon, who had been a magician before, and he now wanted these great gifts. But Peter said, "You have neither part nor lot in this matter."

But he says, "Has God caused a cessation of these spiritual gifts—that it was not for me to assert that he had, but to prove it." Sir, I have just given you the argument that proves it conclusively. God's word says it, and places the penalty of death on any man that would subvert it.

But he says, he never saw the "churches united." Paul did not say we would. He said we would all come in unity of "The Faith," to the knowledge of the Son of God. Solomon says, "Out of his mouth comes knowledge and understanding."—Prov. 2:6. Then we were to come into the unity of "The Faith," the System of Faith. The knowledge of the Son of God, i. e., come to the unity of that which comes out of the mouth of the Son of God, "The Faith." Not into unity of believing. Not that everybody would believe the same thing. But unity of "The Faith."

TIME.

J. W. RING—NEGATIVE.

Gentlemen Moderators, Ladies and Gentlemen:

I am pleased to again deny that the Old and New Testament teach that spiritual gifts have ceased, or in any manner of the world been withdrawn. My worthiness as a witness, my testimony has been contested, but not by the jury. It seems to me that to this jury I have certainly made my position clear and distinct concerning the teachings of Jesus, the Christ. I continue to appeal for evidence that there has been or is a unity of faith concerning the teachings of Jesus, the Christ, as recorded in the books which we have before us for consideration. I yet contend for evidence that there has been or now exists any unity of faith in the acceptation of or interpretation of the teachings of the faith of the spiritual gifts, as recorded of Jesus.

Lest I might possibly be misunderstood in my position as to the acceptation of this great teacher, permit me to again recite to you in brief my position in this matter. In the history of the human race there has been one desire, above all others, manifest in the desire of his heart to know of the purpose of his being, to know whith-er he is tending, and the best mode of conducting himself while he associates with his fellow man here. The various faiths and doctrines that have arisen in connection with this desire of the human heart has been declared to be religion. These various denominations have contended for dominance, each claiming superiority; and endeavored to substantiate their claims with the production of such phenomena as their spiritual gifts would admit. Thus, we find that the human race has been divided and sub-divided in its "unity of faith," concerning religion in all ages of the world. Today we find that a very small percentage of the members of the human family look upon Jesus of Nazareth as their Saviour. We look into the vast hosts who do accept Jesus as a Christ, and behold them at variance in their conception, in their interpretation, in their unity of faith, if you please; many of these denominations declaring (as does my opponent in your presence) that spiritual gifts have been entirely withdrawn, other denominations declaring that these spiritual gifts are a part of the faith and the religion of the man Jesus. These conflicting acceptations of this man's teachings have caused the hosts of individuals who know concerning this religion (for but a small percentage of the human race knows anything about it) to depart from the membership with any of these organizations, because, pendulum like, they have swung to the other extreme, and said, "I don't know." The man and the woman standing in the world today declaring that they do not know of immortality, and that they do not accept the faith of Jesus Christ, have been driven to this position by the lack of the "unity of faith." Hence, when I come representing a vast denomination of people, thoroughly organized, respected and respectable, whose influence has been felt in every civilized nation of the earth, and say, "I accept this man as a great teacher. I accept this history which we have of him as beautiful," am in any way profaning the faith of this man? When I find similar spiritual gifts existing among people who have had equal faith in their respective Christs, Messiahs, Saviours and have demonstrated their belief by equally wonderful spiritual gifts, I, too, accept them as great spiritual teachers. I cannot see that this individuality of Jesus is the fullness of the spirit of Christ. I can but declare to you my honest belief. I leave it for you, in your mind, to censure, as you may, and I ask neither you nor any other individual to dictate to me what God has in store for me. I am a child of the "Most High," and I believe in the absolute justice of this same Most High. I firmly believe that through *Christos* (the Spirit of love) the fullness of God's spirit made manifest to me through a multiplicity of messiahs and saviours, that all men shall be brought into an understanding of the truth when the Spirit of God will quicken their hearts and they will enter into the possession of the fullness of life. If the charity of my platform and my position is too much for the narrowness of any individual's respected creed or doctrine or interpretation, I cannot help it. I am honest. The strength of my heart and my spirit leaps into my expressions, and the love that I have in my breast for each and every one of my fellow-men, irrespective of their belief, indicates the love that I have for the most high God. I cannot anticipate the time when we, living in our present condition of religions and of governmental affairs, can all agree upon the details of existence, but I do anticipate that we can come in the spirit of tolerance, and exchange thoughts and develop our intellectualities and unfold our spiritual gifts until our concepts will broaden and we will draw nearer to the great spirit of truth. I anticipate that the mantle of spiritual power may be dropped upon the children of men, from time to time, even as it has been placed upon them at other times. I rejoice to know that these spiritual gifts are constantly demonstrating to me a most substantial concept of the presence of the "Most High."

Permit me to call to your attention, you will kindly

read the connecting verses in this, II Kings, chapter 2, beginning with the 9th verse, "And it came to pass when they were gone over that Elijah said unto Elisha, Ask what I shall do for thee, before I be taken away from thee. And Elisha said, I pray thee, let a double portion of thy spirit be upon me." Was it this individual spirit of Elijah? Was it the spirit of inspiration? Paul said there is but one spirit, but a diversity of spirits or gifts. The one spirit of truth that is or has spoken through all the Messiahs of the world. They did not speak alone through Jesus, to the little people to whom that message has come, but spoke through Buddha and the people that have received that message; that spoke through Zoroaster and to those that received that; that spoke to those through Christ, the self-same spirit. Then he says, "Thou hast asked a hard thing; nevertheless, if thou see me when I am taken from thee, it shall be so unto thee; but if not, it shall not be so. And it came to pass, as they still went on, and talked, that, behold, there appeared a chariot of fire, and horses of fire, and parted them both asunder; and Elijah went up by a whirlwind into heaven. And Elisha saw it, and he cried, My Father, my father, the chariot of Israel, and the horsemen thereof. And he saw him no more: and he took hold of his own clothes, and rent them in two pieces. He took up also the mantle of Elijah that fell from him, and went back, and stood by the bank of Jordan; And he took the mantle of Elijah that fell from him, and smote the waters, and said, Where is the Lord God of Elijah? and when he also had smitten the waters, they parted hither and thither: and Elisha went over. And when the sons of the prophets which were to view at Jericho saw him, they said, The Spirit of Elijah doth rest on Elisha. And they came to meet him, and bowed themselves to the ground before him." Why? Because they found that the spiritual gift rested upon him. This is but the passing of the mediumship of one individual to that of another; the spiritual intelligences that surround one individual passed on to another. It seems to me that I have presented by reasonable logical thought, and thoroughly substantiated it with passages from the book that we have accepted as evidence, that Paul in no wise indicates the passing of these spiritual gifts, but the perfecting of them, until all men shall come to an understanding, the "unity of faith." I do not see it. I do not see that it existed then. I do not see that it exists now. We find that among our mediums there is a diversity of gifts, and that these work severally, according to the development of the same. Our mediums of today are able oftentimes to lay their hands upon those in whom this power of mediumship has not been developed until they become prophets, until they receive the gift of mediumship, as Moses did in laying his hands upon Joshua that he might become a prophet, being possessed of the spirit of the Lord. These are called developing mediums, and they continue, this self-same demonstration, in the midst of the children of earth today, and so we could occupy your time in naming the various phases of mediumship that apply to the spiritual gifts of today. But you, if you desire to inform yourselves, if you have not done so, can read extensively of books written along this line, and learn concerning these. We are not here to inform you particularly concerning these specifically, but to admonish you as did Paul that these spiritual gifts exist, and that you should cultivate them, and that in the cultivation thereof you will receive these manifestations. I wish to here say that we are still waiting for the presentation of evidence in the way of—well, either inspirational or hypnotized doggerel, either species would be acceptable.

I wish to place as evidence before this jury a spiritual experience that is recorded having taken place under the observation of Judge Edmonds, a noted Judge, who has now ascended, and also of Dr. J. M. Peebels, who still remains eighty-six years young in the physical, and if members of my jury wish to communicate with this gentleman relative to the authenticity of this phenomena, you will find his address "Battle Creek, Michigan." He writes to me under date of August 13th, 1907, "I am just home from my fifth journey around the world in the interests of Spiritualism—rational, religious Spiritualism, and it was the most successful trip that I have made. I spent much of my time in India and was the guest for awhile of His Highness the Maharajah, the King of Tagore, and I had fine opportunities of seeing the Yogis, Gosains, Adepts and wonder-workers." This pilgrim seer did not go abroad to teach people alone, but to be taught as well, recognizing the reciprocity of the east and the west, the universal spirit of searching for truth, which I proclaim to you. Read of this man, and hear his words as he relates the spiritual occurrence. Page 318, "Our Bible," by Hull. "It is related of Isaac T. Hopper, the well-known Philadelphia Quaker abolitionist, that at 4 o'clock Judge Edmonds bade him farewell, and at 7 o'clock the same evening, three hours after, Hopper came and controlled the Judge's daughter and said: 'Now I know what Paul meant when he said we shall not all sleep but shall be changed. I did not sleep; I never lost consciousness for a moment.'" The occurence transpired in one of Judge Edmonds' Thursday evening seances. His daughter Laura was the writing medium in this seance. Hopper, only a few hours in spirit life, wrote: "I am in the spirit world," signing it I. T. H. Who is that for? was the inquiry. All present were puzzled. The Judge, looking at the communication the second time, remarked: "Why, those are the initials of Isaac T. Hopper, but that cannot be, as I was there this afternoon, finding him feeble, but as comfortable as I expected. I will test the matter.' The Judge, throwing on his cloak, was soon at the Hopper residence, where he found his friend's body slumbering in death. The Judge, returning to his residence, and the seance reopened by a short prayer. Hopper again wrote: 'I am in the spirit world and I now understand what the apostle meant when he said, we shall not all sleep, but we shall all be changed. I have not slept; I was not unconscious for a moment, only a little dazed by the event called death; but I've been changed, or have changed worlds. I have met my companions and friends, many of whom I knew. Oh, it is blessed.' This fact establishes Hopper's continuity of consciousness, identity and memory." Would you anticipate that to substantiate the fact of the continuation of spiritual gifts, we are to appeal to other than your interpretation of and understanding of the unity of faith as set down in this book which has been accepted as the basis of our evidence? Would you anticipate that I am going to occupy your time in reading the multiplicity of evidence which we have, in the world today, of the actual presence of these spiritual gifts, and elaborate upon them extensively to you? Volumes have been written, volumes could be read, substantiating the communication between these two worlds, which would thoroughly establish the continuation of these spiritual gifts.

I would like to ask, where has been the "unity of faith" from the time we are told it was established, up to the time of the organization of the denomination that now proclaims this especial doctrine? What are you to understand, as jurors, in connections with all of the contentions among those who have lived in this "unity of faith" during all of these hundreds of years? To further demonstrate the broadness of my position, the extent of the plane of spiritual truth upon which I stand, I do not censure the claims of the Christian Scientists, nor of the Adventists, nor any of the several denominations whose names I might call in the gift of healing, nor any of their diversity of gifts; but in this broad spirit of Modern Spiritualism, I ask this jury to understand, all of these things are accepted. We have been informed that we cannot accept the testimony of an individual in part. We must believe it in its entirety. And yet we find so small a majority of the individuals of the world accepting any especial belief or doctrine or faith. Can we not then look for the time when we will agree to disagree, and when each sect and creed and doctrine will be permitted to use its interpretation of the religion for the betterment of its associates and the world at large. If some of these denominations can see that the spiritual gifts continue to the present time and belong only to them, and that any one else that uses them are workers under the influences of Beelzebub, it is not for you or for me to judge them and to say they are narrow. Judge them only by their works. If they are healing the sick, if they are soothing the bruised heart, if they are comforting the children of men, let us rejoice with them in their good work, feeling that they, in their own ways and after their own fashion, are administering unto the children of the "Most High."

I do not anticipate that "sweet speech, nor oily words" (or any other kind of words) will move my jury; but I do anticipate that the truths uttered will arouse the conception of truth which is in the mind of each individual, and he will begin to look about (not necessarily believe me or my belief, nor accept my ideas, nor bow down to my interpretation), seek for a broader concept of truth and live with a more extended horizon of righteousness, receiving such gifts of the spirit as will enable him to minister abundantly to the needs of humanity. The existence of these spiritual gifts at the present time, if substantiated, will lead you to conclude that I am right in my denial of this proposition. If you will investigate this personally, my respected jurors (you can find opportunity at almost any turn of the road), you can satisfy yourself as to the continuation of these spiritual gifts. I do not come before you claiming to be possessed of the power to demonstrate. I have come before you to claim the fact that these spiritual gifts have not ceased, that they do continue to exist, that they are in our midst today, and after my own fashion, I have referred you to instances, as recorded in the book upon which we agreed as evidence, I have invited your attention to an interpretation of such passages as have been declared evidence that they did cease, and declared unto you that according to my understanding, they had not ceased. I simply leave that matter with you.

I thank you.

TIME.

(4:00 p. m. August 25th, 1907—Sunday.)

J. W. CHISM—FIFTH AFFIRMATIVE.

Gentlemen Moderators, Brethren and Friends:

Once again do I feel thankful that I have the privilege of coming before you with the right use and exercise of my mind for the purpose of resuming the discussion of the proposition that, "The Scriptures teach that, with the close of the Apostolic age, spiritual gifts, such as are mentioned in the Bible, ceased." We have examined this proposition from the viewpoint of Scriptures, and have shown you conclusively from the language of the Apostle Paul as to when and where spiritual gifts ceased. My opponent has seen proper to say but very little about the proposition, as such, and the arguments that I introduce upon it. He has touched upon these a few times, especially in his next to last speech, his first speech yesterday. He said more about what I had said and the arguments that I had made, than at any other time.

You understand the proposition is not, that my friend thinks that they continue, nor that any one else thinks it; but "do the Scriptures teach it?" I defined the proposition, "Scriptures teach"—that they either said so in so many words, or by a combination of passages relative thereto, the conclusion is inevitable, I have shown you from the writings of the apostle Paul, that these spiritual gifts were given to last until a certain time. This was called in question, in the last speech that the gentleman made, as to whether that time had come. Paul says that these apostles and prophets were to continue "till we all come in the unity of the faith." My friend seems to have a little peculiar idea about it. He seems to think that Paul said that the apostles and prophets, and such things as he mentioned, would continue until we all come to "believe the same thing." Why, it doesn't say that. It says "till we all come in the unity of the faith" or "till we come to the unity of the faith." Reading it word for word from Greek text, "Till we all arrive at the unity of the faith." Question: What is meant by "the faith?" If we may learn the meaning of this statement, we may learn what the apostle Paul means by "unity of the faith." In the Roman letter the apostle speaks of "the faith" and "the law." "The faith," in his Roman writings, having reference to the New Testament teachings, "the law" having reference to the Old Testament. Paul uses the phrase continuously in the Roman letter, "faith," "law," "the faith," "the law," contrasting "the faith" with "the law." Hence, "The faith" has reference, not to man's believing, but to the system of faith. Again, in the Galatian letter, Paul speaks of "the faith of the Jesus Christ," using this phrase interchangeable with "the gospel of Jesus Christ." Hence, "the faith"—"the gospel," "the system of faith," all meaning the same thing. So when Paul says, "till we all arrive at the unity of the faith," he simply says, "till we all arrive at the time when that revelation shall have been completed." "The faith," unified, so that we might see it face to face. For, Paul says in the Corinthian letter, 13th chapter, "Now we see through a glass darkly, but then" (when that which is perfect is come, we shall see), "face to face." "Now we know in part, but then," he says, "we shall know even as also we are known." "Now we see in part

— 226 —

and prophecy in part." Here then, Paul contrasted the now—the time in which he lived, with the time when the unity in "The Faith," or, the perfect should come. What is meant by "seeing in part?" To illustrate this and get it before your minds perfectly, I would call your attention to the language of the apostle Peter on the day of Pentecost. Where he said, "The promise is unto you and to your children, and to all that are afar off, even as many as the Lord our God shall call." Notwithstanding Peter used that language (beginning with the 39th verse of the second chapter of Acts), yet, it seems that he himself did not understand it, for a few years after that it took a miracle to convince Peter than the Gentiles, the people of "afar off," should have the privileges or benefits of this gospel; hence, Peter "saw through a glass darlkly." He saw it, but he did not see it plain until afterward.

"See in part." What is meant by this? Turn again to the apostle Paul, as we find him (I believe it was at Antioch), when there came a disputation as to whether circumcision should be bound unto the Gentiles, when certain of the Jews which believed rose up and said "the Gentiles must be circumcised," and Paul and Barnabas had had a disputation with them, they sent men to Jerusalem, to the apostles, and in that assembly it was revealed to them by the Holy Spirit that circumcision should not be bound unto the Gentiles. Hence, "See in part, prophecy in part." As each part was necessary in the development of the church, the new man, to his full grown manhood, before it came to the measure of the stature of the fulness of Christ; and while it was in development, that part was given, as each part was needed to develop the church, that part was given and recorded by the pen of the apostle, the inspired penman, and when this was completed; when everything and every phase of trouble that might arise in the church had a part of "the faith" revealed covering that particular phase and circumstance; when this was all completed; with the Jew and Gentile builded into one family—one new man, one church, one body, as Paul calls it; "With the perfect law of liberty;" as James calls it; this constituted "the unity of the faith." "The law of liberty," the New Testament Scriptures being "the faith" that was spoken of. The system of faith, if you will have it. Then Paul did not say "till we all shall come to believe the same thing. But, "till we all arrive at the unity of the faith"—the unity of the gospel of Christ—the unity of the system. Until the system is completed, making it a complete system of teaching. "Then," says Paul, the apostles and prophets who possess "the parts shall be done away." The parts, i. e., Scriptural gifts, these, divided unto every man severally as he will, was to be done away, but we showed you that, the apostles had accomplished this work before they died.

But again, beginning with the first of the gentleman's speech, yesterday afternoon, he said, "I recite my position concerning Jesus of Nazareth." It seems that the gentleman is terribly hurt because I asked him eleven questions. I submit that the questions are pertinent, because of the fact that he had been trying to make this people believe, all the time, that he accepted Jesus, as the Christ. So I have asked him eleven question right on this point, and I am going to ask him, giving him the privilege of answering in his first speech. Remember, he will not have the privilege of answering in his second speech, but in his first.

First—Do you believe that Jesus is the Christ, the son of the living God?

Mr. Lee—"I raise a point of order."

Mr. Chism—"Will he tell the people whether he believes that Jesus is the Son of God?"

Mr. Lee—"We are not asserting that. The question is not what you believe or what you are trying to prove."

Mr. Chism—"The question, sir, is, 'Does he believe the proposition that he has been insinuating to this people that he does believe?'" (To the audience): "I told you people that he was an infidel."

Mr. Lee—"I ask that that be kept out, because it is not a point in order. I want some way to appeal to the people, because you are not the whole thing. These questions are irrelevant."

Mr. Chism—"They are not irrelevant, because you injected the questions into the proposition yourselves. You say these questions are irrelevant. Are you going to introduce a man's testimony whom you say is a liar, that his testimony is not true? I maintain, sir, that if you do not believe Christ you have no right to use him as a witness."

Mr. Lee—"I want to make an argument showing the point of order that we raised."

Mr. Head—"Just state the point of order."

Mr. Lee—"The point of order, ladies and gentlemen, is this: The gentleman speaking is in the affirmative; he is affirming that the spiritual gifts have ceased, according to the Scriptures. Now, understand, that is the proposition. He has stated it many times. He is affirming that, Mr. Moderator. Ladies and gentlemen, he is not here to pluck from his opponent by his cross-questioning his faith. His opponent, when he says J. W. Ring denies, gives you his faith as regards the proposition. Now in order to satisfy a private opinion, which the gentleman holds as regards the faith of his opponent, he should not be allowed to ask these questions; they are evidently irrelevant."

Mr. Chism—"Why did he injcet his faith into the proposition?"

Mr. Lee—"I ask the ruling of your moderator on this point. The question is, he is affirming it is not a question of what his opponent believes as to this proposition of spiritual gifts. He contends or believes that the spiritual gifts continue, and his definition in regard to what Jesus Christ is, is not the question. It is only a private matter of yours, concerning what that is, and your interpretation is, and I ask the ruling of your moderator, whom I believe is an honest and fair man."

Mr. Chism—"I would like to speak a word first. I did not introduce these into the proposition. I had affirmed two speeches without making reference to anything of the kind. The gentleman himself injected the question of Jesus Christ, and his belief in Jesus Christ, into this debate; he did it in his speech; and I have a right to review him. I find it in his last speech. Is he going to make a speech and give me no right to review it? He injected it himself; here is his speech, right here, which I started to review. Have I the right to review what he said, or shall you cut me off from what he said?"

Mr. Head—"It seems to me that owing to the fact that those things have come into the argument pro and con as to Jesus Christ, and Mr. Ring has appealed to Jesus Christ repeatedly, and all that; it seems to me that the point is relevant as to that."

Mr. Lee—"The principles of Jesus Christ have been debated and passed up to the jury for decision. Now, then, we are not, according to the rules of debate, permitted to return to them. The gentleman let his opportune time pass by. There was a time when he might have introduced those questions, as relevant, but this is not concerning Jesus Christ; this is, or, has nothing to do with Jesus Christ. That is the point—spiritual gifts and what the Scriptures teach in regard to spir-'tual gifts, not Jesus Christ."

Mr. Chism—"Well, you make your man stick to the proposition in his following two speeches. If you will make him stand to my proposition, and make a negative reply to what I say, I will drop these questions. But I am going to speak of what he said, relevant or irrelevant, and there is nothing beneath the high canopy of heaven that can keep me from it, unless you kill me. Do you understand it? He has asserted that he believes thus and so. Am I going to be cut off, and not be allowed to review him? Why, he did not follow my first two speeches; absolutely made no reference to them. The gentleman himself introduced the subject of Jesus Christ and insinuated his faith, and his regards for him, and I decided I would show the people that he did not believe in him. And I have done it."

In the beginning of his speech he says, "I recite my position of Jesus." He says again, " a very small percentage of the human family look on Jesus as a saviour."

I want you to get these statements. They are his. Again, he says, "I accept Jesus as a great teacher." I have asked him of his faith in Jesus Christ, and he refuses to answer the questions. If he answers in his last speech, he shows that he was afraid for me to get hold of his answer. I submit in review of this that if Jesus is not what he professed to be, he was the greatest imposter the world have ever seen, for he professed to be the Son of the Living God. He claimed that all power is given unto him, in heaven and in earth, and he says the man that comes to me and does my sayings, shall have life eternal, and he says the man that does it not shall be damned. You can see the predicament it would place my opponent in. If the questions had been answered "Yes," that he believed that Jesus was what he professed to be," then here comes the teaching of Jesus Christ to cut him off. If he says he does not believe it, if he says it right out in so many words, then the people see his insinuations of his faith in the Christ, what they are. If Jesus was nothing but a man, he was not a good man; he was as evil as his Satanic Majesty was ever represented in divine truth as being, since he claimed that he was the Son of God, that everything was given into his hands. If they were not, then he was an imposter and not a good man.

But he says, "When I find people believing in a similar Christ." Who injected that into the proposition? Had the proposition anything under the sun, anything, to do with that? He was the man that introduced, and asserted, that there were other Christs. I have denied it, but where is the authority that he has brought outside of his own "ipsi dixit?" I believe that through the Christus, that is, through a multiplicity of saviours."

What does Christus mean? It means Christ; it is a Greek word that simply means "Christ," or "the annointed." But here was this Christ that he was trying to insinuate on the people, when I asked those questions. I submit that if the gentleman's position is true, that me and my brethren and the balance of those people who believe in Jesus of Nazareth as the Son of God, are infalliby safe. But if our teaching be true, he is not safe.

But he says, "The love I have in my heart for my fellowman, indicates my love for God." You understand, ladies and gentlemen, that the man who speaks soft things is not every time the man that loves his fellowman. The man who has the courage to face a frowning world and speak truth, though unpopular, and speak it in plain terse language, that man can understand, that man shows himself a friend to humanity. When he realizes that their eternal welfare is hinged on right life; and he speaks to them right principles fearlessly, though it may not be pleasant things that he is saying, he shows himself their friend. While the other man comes with "fair speeches," as Paul says, "and deceives the heart of the simple."

Then he says again, "I come in the spirit of tolerance; we should come in the spirit of tolerance and develop ourselves into unity until we draw nearer the perfect truth." "In the spirit of tolerance." What is meant by that? That we shall tolerate everything, true or false; or, in his creed, is there anything false? What is meant by the language? That we shall let him go his way, and me go my way regardless of truth. I am willing to allow the gentleman the privilege of choosing for himself; but among my neighbors and my friends, citizens of my government; when I am present, I am not willing to let teaching go undisputed, that I realize is leading men in the downward course, to eternal ruin.

Then he cites II Kings, 2:9—speaks of Elijah and his mantle being left with Elisha, and his spirit being left upon Elisha. And asserts that it was the "passing of mediumship." My dear sir, why do you not prove that such things were mediumship? He has never attempted reasoning nor otherwise, to prove that it was mediumship, simply gets up and makes an assertion.

But I want to know, again, what right has mediumship in the discussion of this proposition? I did not bring it in. I am not the man that injected it. I gave you two speeches without reviewing a word that he said, save one, where he said he would parallel the Bible, and when I come to review his speeches I find it full of such things as these. Now shall I be cut off and not review him, because it is not rightly in my proposition, seeing he has interjected such things in this debate? Excuse me, ladies and gentlemen, I am here for that business. It is a part of my work to review him. Of course, if I should allow him to dictate as to what evidence I should introduce, what I shall say, they could very easily review it and set it aside.

But he says, "Among our mediums there are diversities of gifts." Therefore the Scriptures teach that the gifts would be continued? Ah! Is that his conclusion? The proposition says, "The Scriptures teach." Why does he not turn to their teaching and try to show that they declare that spiritual gifts would be continued?

He says he would like to see a hypnotic demonstration. I have gone to record before with a challenge, that, when they get their cabinet, and their man that will undertake to do these wonders you have heard him talk about, to allow me in the circle, that I have two colleagues with me, loose hands, free to do as I please, to strike a light in the midst of the darkness, when I get ready, that I will show you the trickery and the fakery of the thing they call spiritual mediumship. Has he said he will admit me? No. I have challenged again, that when they get ready to put their man on the stand and make the spirit of a man walk out of a closed cabinet, when the man is sewed up in a sack, as they profess sometimes to do, that I will come out of the sack, walk across the stage in person before you, and go back, and at the given signal and you will find me sewed up in the sack like you left me. I proposed the spiritual photograph with them. Have they accepted it? No. The challenge is still out and will stand to the judgment.

He recites a wonder which he says was under observation of Judge Edmonds, I believe. He cited a case from a book which is left out of court today.

Mr. Ring—"It is in the hands of the stenographer, sir."

Mr. Chism—"But it is left out of court today; it isn't here. When I use books for evidence I keep them in court."

He cited from page 318 and read to the 319th page. On page 318, in giving the statement of that thing he recited, it says, "It is related that" so and so took place. The writer did not even assert that it was true. He simply said "it is related" that so and so took place. I am not denying that it is related; I saw it in the print, but where is the evidence that it was true? Where is the evidence that it was true? This compliments all that the gentleman said in his last speech. I shall now begin a recapitulation of the proposition, and shall continue it until I shall have completed the entire work.

When I began the proposition on the purpose of miracles, I showed you that the dispensation commonly called patriarchal; that from Abel on down the line, sacrifices and offerings had been made; that these sacrifices were made by the father of the family. That this age was commonly known as the patriarchal dispensation; that Abraham, Isaac and Jacob lived in this age. I cited you to Genesis 22:22-24, where Abraham offered Isaac upon the altar, and the promise was made to him upon the oath of God.

Again, I cited you Genesis 26:1-5, the oath of God to Isaac. Genesis 28:14, the promise made by Isaac to Jacob, and again, Genesis 28-10-15, Jacob's dream, that wonderful dream that has been fulfilled by the Jews being scattered through all nations. Genesis 38:9-15, where God himself confirmed this language. I gave you then Joseph—how he had been down in Egypt, and the things that befell him there; and the people of Israel, at Joseph's death, were enjoined to carry his bones out of that land, for he had said, that God would surely visit and take them out of this land.

I showed you that this religion had obtained, possibly, for two thousand years, upon the Jews; that to attempt a change of this order of religious worship would require the man who brought the change to bring credentials to show that he had authority from the God of Abraham, Isaac and Jacob, to make this change in their religion. For it had been entailed upon the people until they were established in it, and would cling to that religion tenaciously. When Moses is called we find him saying, "If I go, the people will not believe." The Lord gave him three miracles, and told him that when he would

show these miracles, they would believe what he said—
the Lord giving Moses miracles as credentials, or evidence, that what he taught was of God. I then carried
you down into Egypt where Moses came to Pharaoh and
God told Moses he must have miracles before Pharaoh,
giving them as credentials again. I took up these miracles; the waters of the country turned to blood; the rods
turned to serpents, and the frogs that were called up into
the country, where the magicians said that this is the
finger of God, that the flies came over Egypt, murrain
in horses and cattle, ashes spread over the earth and became boils, hail destroying the crops, and again, the
locusts came, eating up the remaining portion of the
wheat, the darkness that covered the land for three days
and three nights, and lastly the miracle of the passover,
and then I carried you to the Red Sea over which the
Israelites crossed in safety, but the Egyptians were destroyed; on Sinai's smoking mount, where Jehovah spoke
in language that the people could hear, the ten commandments; the earth cleaving asunder at the time that
Moses said it would do so, swallowing up Karah Dathan
and Abiram alive. Then I carried you to the Jordan,
when it was overflowing, the waters congealing, standing
up on a heap above; and the walls of Jericho falling, having seen these miracles wrought by the hand of Moses
and Joshua. The water in the sea, the rushing water of
the mighty old Jordan as she was overflowing, that
rushing swift stream; here Moses controlled those;
Joshua this. But the gentleman told us he would parallel
these things. Where has his parallel come as yet? Have
you seen them controlling the elements of nature? No.
Here Moses says (coming with these things as credentials) that "God Almighty, the God of Abraham and of

Isaac and of Jacob, had sent him to deliver that people." Then comes the law, established under these mighty demonstrations, and when this law had been established, and the people had kept up the same, upwards of fifteen hundred years, right at two thousand years of the world's history again having passed away; Jesus Christ, the Son of the living God, came into this world to change now the national worship, that had been established by Moses to an individual worship; came to change the entire order of things; take away the law under which they had been living, and places men under faith instead of under law; places men where they could have the privilege of turning away from sin and being forgiven of these sins.

When Jesus Christ came to do this thing, it was necessary that he have credentials to prove that he was what he claimed to be. Hence, we see Jesus Christ coming with credentials as evidence, to prove that he was the Messiah, the Son of the living God.

Turning to these credentials, I find various kinds of miracles wrought by Jesus Christ. I find him healing the sick, casting out evil spirits, stilling the tempest in the midst of the sea when the winds were boisterous, at a word they ceased, and the sea became calm. I see him standing at the grave of Lazarus, who had been dead four days, and by his command, calling him forth. I see a blind man healed, and the dumb man made to speak. I see him giving the apostles power, and sending them out to perform the same wondrous signs and miracles. I see him again, the withered and restored. Again a blind man healed; again, five thousand people fed of just a few loaves and fishes; had plenty. Again, I see him walking in the midst of the sea, Matthew

14:22-23, walking on the waves, and came into the ship; and again in John 6:18-21, where the record tells us that the ship, when he entered, was in the middle of that sea, being then about 25 or 35 furlongs from land, but while it was thus, from 3½ to 4½ miles from land, when Jesus entered the ship, John says "immediately they were at the shore." Note, that that ponderous vessel passed immediately from the midst of the sea to the shore, three and a half miles distant. Here we find these miracles. Again, I pass on to where they that touch him were made perfectly whole. Again, four thousand fed on a few loaves and fishes. Again, the transfiguration of Jesus on the Mount. Again, we find, if you please, his own resurrection, the one that spoke mightier than all the rest. Here comes these miracles from Jesus Christ, if you please, establishing his mighty power, showing that he had the right to change this order of worship, and make it as God Almighty saw fit to make him. We see then, that every time a change is necessary, miracles are given as credentials; and I reason, then, that when the work was accomplished, that he was to do with the miracles, the miracles being needed no farther, ceased.

A QUESTION OF PRIVILEGE.

(By Robert G. Lee, Presiding Moderator.)

Ladies and Gentlemen:

Inasmuch as I had more to do with the arranging of this question than any other man here except Mr. Chism, I wish to make a statement in regard to it—I wish to be absolutely fair in this statement, although I am not a minister of the gospel. This gentleman wrote me, and

I have his letter present, that he would affirm that the Bible is the inspired Word of God. He wrote me that the Bible was the inspired Word of God and that he would affirm it. I want that made plain to your minds. I know there are many people that believe the Bible is the inspired Word of God in its entirety. I know that some eminent divines believed that—and Mr. Talmage was one of them (I didn't know for sure whether this gentleman believed that the Bible was the entire Word of God or not). I suggested to find out whether he did or not, that we put the word "entirety" in. I asked him if he would affirm that the Bible in its entirety is inspired, and he says "No," and I will meet any man in the world on that proposition. He told you yesterday and he told you today, and repeated it, that he had offered to affirm that the Bible was the Word of God and we could not deny it, and why did he do it? He wanted to leave the impression on your mind, that he believed the whole thing and we did not. Am I not fair in that statement? I have his letters to show to you if he disputes any word that I say—any statement that I make here in this matter. Now, then, inasmuch as he said that he would affirm that the Bible was the inspired Word of God, and when I have his statement in writing that he would affirm that it was the inspired Word of God in its entirety, and he acknowledged to you here in your presence that it contained an inspired record. I just want to explain to you or make plain to your minds that he occupies exactly the same position that we do. He wants the privilege of saying what part is inspired, and what is not. He wouldn't say every word is inspired, and he has acknowledged he wouldn't say it, and I want you to know that this is his position, and I am frank and free to acknowledge to you that this is our position, and that it is our representative's position. We do not deny that there is not inspired portions in that Bible—that is as much as he will acknowledge. He may swallow a little more than we do, but it is only a matter of degree.

J. W. CHISM'S REPLY TO MR. LEE.

Ladies and Gentlemen:

Just a word about it, while this thing is before us. I knew it would hurt; I proposed to affirm that "The Bible is the inspired Word of God." They refused to deny it. He wanted me to affirm that "it is inspired in every word." There are some words in it that were uttered by the Devil, and I did not care to take that proposition, because some of it was the language of the Devil, and I did not believe that such was the Word of God. That is what I said. He would say in the debate that I claimed this word of the Devil was the Word of God. I saw his trick. I proposed to affirm that "The Bible in ·its entirety is an inspired record." Will you deny it? Will you deny it? (By Mr. Lee—"Certainly, certainly.") Why did you not take it up before? I agreed in my letter to affirm that, and you refused it. I proposed to affirm that the Bible was the complete and whole inspired record and that even the record of the words of the Devil was an inspired record—recorded by inspiration. But I do not believe you can produce a man under the sun that would make every word of it come from God. There is no man under the sun whom I have ever seen that believed any such stuff as that. But we believe the Bible is the complete inspired record—that everything in it is a record by the pen of inspiration.

When I speak of the Bible, I do not mean the King James Version. This is the old book I am talking about (holding a Hebrew Bible) that is given in the Hebrew tongue, the tongue in which God Almighty gave it to the Hebrews. So if they will accept that proposition, I am ready to "hitch up" with them. I will have to send home and get some books. They will have to wait until I can send home and get them.

MEETING FOR THE DAY CLOSES.
J. W. RING—NEGATIVE.

Gentlemen Moderators, Ladies and Gentlemen:

You are called upon at all times to determine whether or not the evidence presented is relative to the proposition under consideration or no. It is furthermore left in your hands to determine whether or not the evidence presented by either side affirms or denies successfully the proposition which we have before us for consideration. I speak with all confidence to those members of my jury who have qualified themselves by removing all prejudice from their minds, to receive these evidences and determine therefrom, without personal prejudice, concerning the evidence which may be given; with perfect confidence that you know the difference between ideas, tersely presented, and doctrinal harangue. I have from time to time carefully reread the passages of Scripture quoted as having fallen from the lips of Jesus and of his apostles. There have not been very many of them relative to the attempt of my opponent to convince you that spiritual gifts have ceased with the passing of the apostolic age. After my own fashion (as is my privilege as a free citizen of a free land that recognizes no God,

— 242 —

but the will of the people) I asked you to reread these and see if in any way you can anticipate the possibility of the ascribed authors to convey the idea that spiritual gifts have been withdrawn. After having completed a reconsideration of all these citations I have called your attention repeatedly to a natural reasoning that spiritual gifts have not ceased, it is my purpose, it is my work, to present to you some tangible evidence of the continuation of these spiritual gifts. I have furthermore attempted to convey to your intelligent consideration the fact that the term "spiritual gift" in that day, and the fruits thereof, was identical with the term mediumship, and these phenomena of the present day. I feel assured that your intelligence is sufficient to comprehend. In order to present my position in the positive and determined denial of the proposition under consideration, I have endeavored to present to you repeatedly the fact that spiritual gifts have been the evidence of the followers of the "Most High" in all ages of the world, have emphasized my concept as a reasonably sane individual of the language of the Master Teacher, Jesus. When he declared that these signs would follow as many as believed, and my interpretation led me to believe (since my opponent said it did not convey the matter of time) that it was surely a continuation through the present day, and continuing on, he brought before our consideration a statement that it indicated the perfecting of the faith, I again read those passages and asked you if you could in any way discover an intimation that the author intended to convey the cessation of spiritual gifts. I do not presume to stand before you and tell you what shall be your verdict in this case. I depend upon your intelligence. It is not my place to act as a judge and tell you what verdict you shall return; it is my place. to present such evidence to your reason and common sense as will lead you to a careful investigation the subject which we are considering, that you will return an impartial verdict. If faiths must fall, and creeds must crumble to you as individuals, because of your verdict, let them pass. I firmly believe because of the words which I have read in our book of reference that all men are tending to the perfect unfoldment of an individual.

Evidently the reason for emphatic repetition of evidence would insinuate to you, as to me, that there is no more. If these passages that have been quoted, taken collectively, are the fullness of evidence that these spiritual gifts, as mentioned in the Scriptures, have ceased, it is well to repeat them. They must of necessity be repeated a great number of times yet to bring the world into "unity of faith," for as yet there is no semblance of such, even among the few who accept Jesus as Christ. If other men have declared themselves to be Christs, and to substantiate their declaration, have offered to the world miracles, signs and wonders, as the history of the sixteen crucified saviours tells us, they are at least worthy of your consideration, as intelligent people, and I commend them to your thought.

Since it has seemed wise to my opponent to take the inspiration, which was presented to you on an evening independent of this debate, and "drag it" as evidence into this debate, denominating it doggerel, and declare himself in readiness to parallel it, I will now place it in its entirety before you as a jury, and in the confines of this court, respectfully ask that you, as a jury, demand from this opponent a parallel of this "doggerel." Since this evidence has been received from the outside, would suggest that his presentation of the parallel be give immediately following the time of the debate this afternoon, tonight, or at any convenient time.

That I may make myself fully understood as to my position in the denial of this proposition, may I repeat the fact, as I have said before, that the belief in spirits has been and is universal among all the nations of the earth, from the lowest to the highest. I do not presume to bring to you an entire library and quote to you the things which you should read, if you are interested in the determination of the subject. (As to the evidence which was presented on a previous occasion concerning the written message by the child of Kate Fox, you will refer to the volume written by her sister, Leah Fox Underhill, "The Missing Link," which shows the affidavits of intelligent and respected citizens of England to the phenomena which occurred.) Your attention is called to the histories of the world, both sacred and profane. Not confined to the single Scripture of one God, but to the history of the gods of the world, indicating that they have all universally believed in spirits. It has been the foundation of their religions. Spirits, angels, ghosts, the visitants from the unseen world, have been revealed unto the children of men the advent of religions even as did they reveal the advent of John the Baptist as the forerunner of the great "Teacher of Galilee," and as they did of Jesus. It is recorded in the Old Testament that Jehovah employed the fruits of spiritual gifts as evidence, or "credentials," if you prefer the word, to convince his followers that he was God; to gain the confidence of his followers, he presented them these phenomena. My opponent has kindly read extensively of these phenomena, and has even called your attention to the fact that these prophets, or as we would call them today, seers or mediums, contested with the prophets or seers or mediums of other nations, religions and Gods to show by their phenomena, by their signs, by the fruits of their spiritual gifts that they were greater than the others. (The spirit of contention has always existed, it has been universal as the acceptation of the belief in spirits.) Jesus recognized the same necessity and substantiated his teachings with similar signs, then called miracles, endeavoring, however, to convey to the understanding of his followers the fact that they were the result of compliance with the will of the Father, and that they should follow, as signs, as many as believed upon the will of the Father. His reason for presenting these, as the opponent has stated, was to convince people. Of what? Simply that he was Christ? That he was endowed with this power to get them to follow after him, as well. To convince them he recognized the necessity of the continuation of these spiritual gifts by empowering his disciples and apostles to continue the use of them. You were just cited to the fact that at one time Peter was compelled to behold a miracle to remain steadfast in the faith. What is necessary for this materialistic age? If all spiritual gifts have been withdrawn, what is for us? The "unity of faith" that we have never seen? Surely it is made clear to you that Jesus was baptized in compliance with his request to John the Baptist. I hardly believe that any of you believe that he was baptized for the remission of sins, but we are told the result of the purpose of his baptism, was the reception of the Holy Ghost. (By Mr. Chism—Chapter and verse.) It is there recorded that the heavens were opened and the spirit descending upon him, and the signs and wonders that followed him indicates the possession of spiritual gifts, and certainly indicates to any rational man that he as a man became a Christ, one annointed, or a medium. The attempt to convince you that the Holy Ghost was a secondary matter, when it came to baptism for the remission of sins, by manipulating the reading of the verses which have been quoted repeatedly in your presence, I believe, respected jurors, has not impressed you. Those who received baptism from the hands of the apostles, received the gift of the Holy Ghost, and I have expended a sufficient amount of time, I believe, to convince you that if baptism was for the remission of sins, it was for the reception of the Holy Ghost, for the Scriptures said that these signs shall follow as many as believe, and I am showing with all possible evidence that he referred not only to an apostolic age, but he referred to the time when all men should receive the truth because they were endowed with these "credentials" that have been known from the beginning of the history of time; and these credentials have been spiritual gifts—the power to determine these phenomena. I have reread each passage as carefully as possible in your presence and called your attention to its consideration to see if it conveyed to you any semblance of the withdrawal of these spiritual gifts, and I believe that you who have come here unprejudiced and qualified yourselves as jurors, will not only consider the evidence that I have presented to you, but it will appeal to your reason, and that you will determine that there are a multiplicity of evidences, by the Scriptures, that these spiritual gifts have not ceased. I declare unto you that these spiritual gifts have not ceased, then it is a part of my work to present to you some evidence of their continuation. We have called your attention to a few specific evidences—it would appear very childish upon my part to insult your intelligence by occupying your entire time by reading of these phenomena since they are in the history of the world, both sacred and secular. I refer you to the history of the formation, organization and continuation of the church and its fathers, at any time, at all times, and you will find not only the belief that they continued but a history of these phenomena as they were presented. Lest you might conclude, lest you might fail to look into all of these evidences, lest you might think that these phenomena dropped out of existence and did not appear until the modern advent of Spiritualism (even as the interpretation of these Scriptures, which have been presented to you by my opponent, dropped out of existence and through all of these years, until this especial denomination came into existence) I want to call your attention to a phenomenon that occurred in 1772. I want to especially impress you again with the fact that if there be a distinction (not a difference) between the fruits of the spiritual gifts, or phenomena, of ancient days, and that of the present time, it was in the belief that it was a divine providence or a special revelation, while today it is accepted as natural law; it indicates the progress, the unfoldment of the concept of the people concerning these things; even as has been presented to your consideration by a comparison of the acceptance of these spiritual gifts, in the days of Moses and the prophets, of Jesus and his apostles, of the days following these, as recorded in the history of the world, leading up to the modern advent of Spiritualism.

Howett's History of the Supernatural, Volume 2, page 133: "Boswell, in his life of Johnson, also introduces the subject of apparitions on the occasion of a dinner at

General Oglethrop's, April 10, 1772, in which Johnson said that Mr. Cave, the publisher of the Gentleman's Magazine, assured him that he had seen a ghost. Goldsmith, who was present, stated that his brother, the Rev. Oliver Goldsmith, had seen one, and Gen. Oglethorp, that Pendergast, an officer in the Duke of Marlborough's army, told his brother officers that Sir John Friend, who was executed·for high treason, had appeared to him, and told him that he would die on a certain day. On that day a battle took place, but when it was over and Pendergast was alive, his brother officers railed him and asked him where was his prophecy now? Pendergast replied gravely, 'I shall die notwithstanding.' And soon after there came a shot from a French battery to which the order for the cessation of firing had not reached, and killed him on the spot. Oglethorp added that Col. Cecil, who took possession of Pendergast's effects, found in his pocket-book a memorandum containing the particulars of the intimation of his death on the day specified, and that he was with Cecil when Pope came to inquire into the facts of the case, which has made a great noise, and that they were confirmed by the colonel." (The use of the word ghost, spirit, spook or apparition indicates only the concept of the people who used those terms. I remember when as a boy I first attended spiritualistic meetings it was considered respectable to call them spook meetings; in other localities it was considered ridicule.) Here we have unspeakable evidence of the return of an individual spirit, and proves one possessed of the power of discerning spirits. Paul, although he believed in one spirit, believed that that one spirit of the Most High, the infinite intelligence, gave unto men the spiritual gift of discerning spirits. The spirit told the truth, its prophecy was fulfilled, even as was the prophecy of Samuel when he spoke through the medium of the woman of Endor; she declared that he would be killed and he was killed. It is useless to elaborate upon such statements as this because it is not the purpose of Spiritualism as an organization to prove phenomena, but to teach the people of its possible reception that they may abound in the fruits of the spirit. We know that these spiritual gifts continue, else I would not presume to stand before you and attempt to convince you that they do continue. I not only refer to this accepted book (Old and New Testament), but I refer you to the history of the world before and after, and the evidence of men possessed of the power of God, for the power of God possesseth every man that cometh into the world. We are all children of the "Most High." To further state my position I quote you from Professor Alfred Russell Willace, whose name is a synonym for integrity and character. "My position, therefore, is that the phenomena of Spiritualism in their entirety do not require further confirmation. They are proved quite as well as any facts are proved in other sciences and it is not quibbling or denial that can disprove any of them, but only fresh facts, and accurate deductions from facts. When the opponents of Spiritualism can give a record of their researches approaching in duration and completeness to those of its advocates, and when they can discover and show in detail either how the phenomena are produced, or how many sane and able men here referred to have been deluded into coincident belief that they have witnessed them; and when they can prove the correctness of their theory by producing a like belief in a body of equally sane and able unbelievers— then, and not till then, will it be necessary for Spiritualists to product fresh confirmation of facts which are, and always have been, sufficiently real aьd indisputable to satisfy any honest and persevering inquirer."—Miracles and Modern Spiritualism.

Have I no privilege to present to you the statements of men who live today concerning the standard of modern Spiritualism as a movement based upon the declaration of principles which I have presented to you? I most assurely have because the modern advent of Spiritualism is the continuation of these spiritual gifts which I declare unto you have never ceased but have always been poured out upon the children of men.

TIME.

J. W. CHISM—SIXTH AFFIRMATIVE.

Gentlemen Moderators, Brethren, Friends:

I am before you for the last speech on my proposition. You imagine my surprise, after the play that was made to keep me from introducing certain things, to find the gentleman turning off the proposition himself and scarcely touching it hair, head, top or bottom, and still he asserts that "I ought to debate it." Well, my dear sir, you are in the negative of that proposition and it becomes your duty to follow and examine the arguments that I make. Has he introduced to you evidence from the scriptures, the Old and New Testament, the Holy Bible? That was the way the proposition was defined. Has he introduced evidence therefrom, to show you that spiritual gifts were to be continued? Do you remember the chapter and verse which he read, that said they would be continued? Do you remember the passage in the Bible? O! he says, "Modern Spiritualism" does wonders today. What has that to do with what the Bible teaches? Suppose I grant, for the sake of argument, that they do all the wonders that they claim to do? Does that prove that "the Scriptures teach that they would continue?" Does it prove it? Would the admission disprove my proposition? Not a bit of it. My proposition says "the Scriptures teach." Why does he not turn to the Scriptures? For after that he had rambled like that; and I started to follow him in his rambles, they got very sore over it; did not want me to review him in his rambles. Gentlemen, may I have the privilege of reviewing that last speech? I shall take it anyway.

He makes one reference to the proposition, and I want to examine it fully, because, it is on the point I had reached when my time was called. I had just called your attention to the purpose of miracles; that they were given to the persons making the revelation as credentials, in evidence of the divine authority of the persons revealing the faith; and when the faith was unified—perfected, if you please; then, these gifts which were given as credentials for the purpose of unifying "the faith," would cease. Has the gentleman paid any attention to the argument I made on the "unity of the faith?" No, verily. He only comes back with the simple statement that we have not all come in the "unity of faith." Who said they would? Paul did not. Paul said, "in the unity of the faith." I showed you in my last speech what "the faith" meant. Has he denied it? No. If he denies it in his last speech; he admits that he was afraid for me to get hold of it. The unity of "the faith" is the unity of the "system," as I showed you conclusively. Until the system was completed. Miracles, then, were given as credentials to the men delivering this faith.

Now, I will show you the authority on which they rested and on which they ceased. Turn with me to Mark 16, beginning with the 17th verse. This is the passage to which the gentleman made reference. "And these signs shall follow them that believe; in my name shall they cast out devils; they shall speak with new tongues; they shall take up serpents, and if they drink any deadly thing it shall not hurt them; they shall lay hands on the sick and they shall recover. So, then, after the Lord had spoken unto them, he was received up into heaven, and sat on the right hand of God; and they went forth and preached everywhere; the Lord working with them and confirming the word with signs following. Amen." Here we find the miracles given. Jesus Christ said, "they should follow the believer." Luke said they did follow the believer. Hence the language of Christ is fulfilled. The question to be settled now is, How long should they follow the believer? Should they follow them to the present time, or, was there a limit set for it? We have learned, hitherto, that from the language of Jesus Christ there is an indefinite period. It does not say how long. The language is fulfilled if they followed but one week; if they follow up to the present time, the language is no more than fulfilled. The language is completely fulfilled in either instance; but how long were they to follow? We must look into some other passage for this. Turn with me, then, to Matthew 16-19, where I hear Jesus Christ saying to the apostle Peter, "And I will give unto thee the keys of the kingdom of heaven, and whatsoever thou shalt bind on earth shall be bound in heaven, and whatsoever thou shalt loose on earth, shall be loosed in heaven." Here Jesus told this apostle, that what he bound on earth should be bound in heaven and what he loosed on earth should be loosed in heaven. Did he mean what he said? Listen, again, Matthew 18:18, speaking to the twelve, he said, "Verily, I say unto you, Whatsoever ye shall bind on earth shall be bound in heaven: and whatsoever ye shall loose on earth shall be loosed in heaven." Then, Jesus certainly gave unto them the power to loose these gifts. If they say they are to be loosed at a certain time; if any one of the apostles said so, then they would be loosed at that time. But if they did not, then the common understanding would be that they would continue up to the present time. Look once again, Matthew 10:40. Here we find Jesus once more giving the apostles authority. "He that receiveth you receiveth me, and he that receiveth me receiveth him that sent me." Hence, we will be required to receive them. Again in I John 4, where John says, "try the spirits;" in the 6th verse he says, "the spirit that hears not us, is not of God." Then, the apostles teach that we must hear the apostles of Christ or we are not of God. Turn, once again, to John the 16th chapter and 13th verse. "Howbeit when he, the Spirit of truth, is come, he will guide you into all truth: for he shall not speak of himself; but whatsoever he shall hear, that shall he speak: and he will shew you things to come." Hence, the spirit was to come and guide these apostles. Turn now to John 20:22,23, "And when he had said this, he breathed on them, and said unto them, Receive ye the Holy Ghost; whose soever sins ye remit, they are remitted unto them; and whose soever sins ye retain, they are retained." Showing us that when this spirit came it would be the time when these apostles would have this great power committed unto them. Shall we find when this came? Turn to Acts 2:1-4. There you find the

Spirit did come. Hence, since the Spirit did come to them on that occasion, it shows us conclusively that they now onward have the power to "bind on earth and it shall be bound in heaven; to loose on earth and it shall be loosed in heaven." But another question arises. Was Paul speaking by inspiration? Hear him in Gal. 1:8-12: "But though we, or an angel from heaven, preach any other gospel unto you than that which we have preached unto you, let him be accursed. As we said before, so say I now again, If any man preach any other gospel unto you than that ye have received, let him be accursed. For do I now persuade men, or God? or do I seek to please men? for if I yet pleased men, I should not be the servant of Christ. But I certify you, brethren, that the Gospel which was preached of me is not of man. For I neither received it of man, neither was I taught it, but by the revelation of Jesus Christ." Again Paul tells us in the same chapter—I read connectedly—"For ye have heard of my conversation in time past in the Jews' religion, how that beyond measure I persecuted the church of God, and wasted it: And profited in the Jews' religion above many my equals in mine own nation, being more exceedingly zealous of the traditions of my fathers. But when it pleased God, who separated me from my mother's womb, and called my by his grade, to reveal his son in me, that I might preach him among the heathen; immediately I conferred not with flesh and blood: Neither went I up to Jerusalem to them which were apostles before me, but I went into Arabia, and returned again unto Damascus. Then after three years I went up to Jerusalem to see Peter, and abode with him fifteen days. But other of the apostles saw I none save James the Lord's brother. Now the things which I write unto you, behold, before God, I lie not. Afterwards I came into the regions of Syria and Cilicia; And was unknown by face unto the churches of Judea which were in Christ; But they had heard only That he which persecuted us in times past now preacheth the faith which once he destroyed. And they glorified God in me." (Chapter 2): "Then fourteen years after I went up again to Jerusalem with Barnabas, and took Titus with me also. And I went up by revelation, and communicated unto them that gospel which I preach among the Gentiles, but privately to them which were of reputation lest by any means I should run, or had run, in vain. But neither Titus, who was with me, being a Greek, was compelled to be circumcised; And that because of false brethren unawares brought in, who came in privily to spy out our liberty which we have in Christ Jesus, that they might bring us into bondage: To whom we gave place by subjection, no, not for an hour; that the truth of the gospel might continue with you. But of these who seemed to be somewhat, (whatsoever they were, it maketh no matter to me: God accepteth no man's person;) for they who seemed to be somewhat in conference added nothing to me; But contrariwise, when they saw that the gospel of the uncircumcision was committed unto me, as the gospel of the circumcision was unto Peter; (For he that wrought effectually in Peter to the apostleship of the circumcision, the same was mighty in me toward the Gentiles:) And when James, Cephas, and John, who seemed to be pillars, perceived the grace that was given unto me, they gave to me and Barnabas the right hands of fellowship; that we should go unto the heathen, and they unto the circumcision." I have read to the 9th verse of the second chapter, inclusive. This shows us that the authority of the apostle Paul was ac-

But he says, "All these teachers back here believed in spirits." Why, of course they did. God is a spirit. Who has ever denied that man believed in spirits? To believe in spirits is one thing, and to believe that human spirits come back and communicate with men by the knocking of a table, is quite a different thing.

But he tells you when I was in the affirmative I ought to take up the Scriptures on the proposition. I have done this, time and time again, but it seems that he thinks he does not need to stick to the proposition. It becomes your duty, my dear sir, as a negative, to review me first, in every argument that I make, then, you can introduce new matter. But he said we had record that Peter was compelled to behold. No, no, it was to convince him that the Gentiles were to come in. Why didn't he take up the language and try to show you that that was not what it meant? But he said, "nobody evidently would say that Jesus Christ was baptized for the remission of sins." My dear sir, had not Jesus Christ been baptized, the remission of sins for the world would have been lost. He was not baptized for the remission of his personal sins, he had none. But it became necessary for him to be baptized to obey God; for God had commanded it. Then he was baptized that he might be the mediator between God and man, to make reconciliation for the sins of the people. Hence for the remission of sins; other men's sins. But he says, "He (Christ) was baptized for the Holy Ghost, or that he might obtain this." I submit, there is not a statement in God's word, that records any such statement, nor anything that sounds like it. When Jesus came to John to be baptized, John said, "I have need to be baptized of thee, and comest thou to me?" Jesus said, "Suffer it to be now, for thus it becomes us, to fulfill all righteousness." What is "righteousness?" David said, all God's commandments are righteousness. Then it becomes us to fulfill all God's commandments." Jesus was not baptized for the remission of his sins, since he had none, but to fulfilll God's commandments. It was after his baptism that God said, "This is my beloved Son, in whom I am well pleased."

Again. he says, "If I declare that spiritual gifts have not ceased, it is my work to show you some evidence." Well, sir, the proposition says, "The Scriptures teach." It is your work to show the evidence in God's Book; but you have not done it.

Then he comes to the church in the days of the "fathers" and was going to tell us about some miracles there. Note the definition of the proposition. I told you in the beginning that, with the death of the Apostles these gifts ceased to be bestowed; and with the death of the last one on whom the Apostles had bestowed this power through the imposition of their hands, the miracles had ceased. Hence, it would bring us down to the life of the "fathers." I am not denying that there were miracles down even among the fathers, because the Scriptures teach that they would continue to that place.

Then he makes reference to "this especial denomination coming up." What were you talking about? The denomination I belong to? I do not belong to a denomination, unless you use "denomination" in the sense of "name." Then I belong to the name Christ—Christian.

Then he reads a ghost story and tells us about some ghosts that were seen, and a man's spirit, and so and so.

That men may see ghosts I do not deny. But I gave you the law the other day. If a man continues in the thought that he is going to be killed; just as sure as he goes down en rapport with that thought he will see himself killed. If he goes into this passive condition, or subjective condition, en rapport with the thought that he is to be killed at a given time, and the thought too, of another man who had been killed, he will think he sees the spirit of the other man.

But to a review, in first Cor. 14:22 Paul says that tongues are for a sign to them that believe not, or to the unbeliever, and I have repeatedly asked the gentleman to give us a tongue, as it is a sign for the unbeliever, and, according to his teaching, if he is right I am an unbeliever. Why has he not presented the sign; just because he can not.

But he made a statement the other day about "God wrestling with Jacob.' 'I called your attention to the fact that the Book says it was a man, not God. Again he asserted that, "Jehovah came down off the mountain with Moses," and that, "Jehovah got mad." I called your attention to the fact that it was Joshua, not Jehovah. This has never yet been questioned. He again asserted that, "Jehovah was not aware of what was taking place in the camp while he was giving the law." I showed you from Exodus 32:5-8 that he was, and that he told Moses what was being done in the camp, immediately after it happened. These were the things to which I desired to call your especial attention—his incorrect assertions.

Now in conclusion, you have the proposition before you; and I ask you to study it carefully in the light of revealed truth—the Book—the Bible. The proposition reads that, "The Scriptures teach that spiritual gifts ceased with the end of the apostolic age." I showed you the language of Jesus Christ, conferring these gifts on the Apostles, and why they were given. I have shown you that the reason ceased; that since there was no more need to confirm the word, and that since they were given to unify "the faith;" that when this was done the spiritual gifts had served their purpose, and that Jesus had given the power to the Apostles to loose these gifts, and that the Apostles had loosed them. And I showed you that that was done when the church was completed. When it was completed, left with a "perfect law of liberty" to guide it into the perfect truth; that henceforth (from that time onward) we need not be children tossed to and fro by every wind of doctrine. I showed you that these miracles, through which it is attempted to deceive the people, that Jesus said that men would come and do these wonders and deceive by them; and he said, If they say he is in the secret chamber, believe it not. That is, if they say he is in the cabinet, if you please, do not you believe it. So I conclude that my proposition is proven.

TIME EXPIRED.

Thank you, ladies and gentlemen.

J. W. RING—NEGATIVE.

Gentlemen Moderators, Beloved Friends:

There now lies before me just thirty minutes to proclaim to you my denial that, according to the Scriptures, the spiritual gifts, such as are recorded in the Bible, ceased with the apostolic age. It is for you to determine whether or not I have closely followed each scriptural passage as presented, and I ask you, as individuals, to determine as to its significance relative to this position. It lies within your hands to determine for yourself individually upon this proposition, and your decision will influence yourself and those to whom you may impart your education. In the vastness of the development of the human family there is no indication that your conclusion about this Bible or any other Bible is going to influence the final judgment of any individual. It remains for you to determine concerning the evidence which I have presented to you since denying this proposition and carefully following each scriptural passage to which reference was made by the opposition, and presenting along with it my reasoning and inviting the same on your part. I feel confident that not an individual member of this jury will say that I have failed to try and conceive wherein appeared this "unity of faith" to which we have been repeatedly referred. I trust that some of you have some concept concerning this matter. I must say, as far as I am personally concerned, if the "unity of faith" indicates the organization of the church and the establishment of its officers, as several times intimated, it is beyond my power to comprehend or to discover such organization anywhere in the history of the world, save in this book; and realizing the small percentage of the human family who accept this Book as foundation for doctrine (and realizing that among these numbers there is a vast difference of conception as to this unity of faith) it would most certainly be unbecoming of me to come in the full spirit of a religion that has manifested in all nations, and attempt to determine whether the conception of this declaration made in this Book must be fulfilled, or followed, according to the Catholic faith (which is the oldest, and there are thousands and thousands of Catholics that deny all other interpretation) or whether I am to come along with Martin Luther and his followers, and accept his interpretation, or whether I am to believe John Wesley (God bless him—he brought a new light to the world, a broader concept of truth, and he has many respected followers in the world to-day). I do not presume to especially follow Wesley, nor the Quakers, nor Emanual Swedenborg, nor the Christian Scientists; but permit each the privilege of his interpretation as the spirit of investigation compels. In the vastness of the human family there is such a diversity of conception concerning our origin, the journey which we are making (called life) and its continuation. I can but proclaim unto you the continuation of all the spiritual gifts that ever blessed the children of men as recorded in this Scripture, as recorded in other scriptures, received by equally intelligent people as scriptures, and followed as though it were the mandate of a God, leading down and through all of these to the present phenomena; a record of which would fill the books of all the libraries of the world were they recorded; and beg of you, as intelligent jurors, to use your reason, your judgment, your God-given faculties, and pursue an investigation of these. You know, my fellow jurors, that I have not dodged during these days; you know I have stood before you in a gentlemanly manner and given you such interpretation as my education, environment and God-given purpose of soul has prompted. Recognizing that you vary in your personal belief I have endeavored to refrain from any personal attack. Realizing, furthermore, that the majority of you stand in wonder, not knowing which way to turn, I have endeavored to multiply the evidence for your consideration until your horizon be extended, and you seek amid the literature of the world and of the Gods of the nations to find the evidence of the presence of spiritual gifts in your midst to-day, whereby you might open the door to the world, and no longer "see through a glass darkly."

Yesterday afternoon a minister came to me and said "brother." (I appreciated it.) "I believe there are points of agreement between you and me." It impressed me as being the spirit of Christ. We want the points of agreement; we want to find as much "unity of spirit" as possible; hence, in reviewing any statement which has been made you know, respected jurors, that I have at all times refrained from personal attack; I have refrained from widening the gulf between man and man because we are all children of one spirit, and that one spirit will, Jesus has said in this Book, is to bring all men to a perfect understanding, to bring us into the "unity of faith" whereby we may seek, find the truth and be made free. We have agreed that these spiritual gifts did exist. Repeated Scripture has been read here (I have not re-read it, but have loudly said amen). I could understand these phenomena, the fruits of these spiritual gifts, because I have seen similar ones. That these were the result of natural law, I have declared unto you, was not understood in those days; but do you suppose that it was any less the result of a known law? At one time the children of earth believed it to be flat. Do you suppose it was any less round because they didn't believe it? Do you suppose that the law by which these phenomena were produced, through the mediumship of Moses, Jesus or Paul, was any less fixed when it operated through them than it is to-day, when it operates through this self-same spiritual gifts in these phenomena of Modern Spiritualism? With utter confidence in your intelligence I believe that you feel certain that if it is a natural law it was a natural law; if it was a natural law it is a natural law. Since these spiritual gifts existed in those days, since God knows the human race has need of some sign to bring them into a "unity of faith," more than ever before, I beg you to try the spirits and find all possible evidence to assure us that the spirit of God abounds in the midst of the human race at the present time. The purpose in those days, we have been told, was to prove that they were from God—that they possessed credentials. The purpose is self-evident, as well that they were given to prove, to convince, to lead the people to a comprehension of the teachings given. To-day there is certainly a great need of some signs by which man may know the truth. In conversation among those whom I have met in the last few days, who declare themselves to be members of respective denominations, I find a vast difference of conception and interpretation. If there was the presence of the spiritual gifts it would be evidence to draw them in the "unity of faith," into the unity of purpose, into the unity of spirit. That these spiritual gifts should exist, that they do exist in the world to-day is indicated by their necessity. The demand of nature, the demand of the world has at all times been the prophecy of fulfillment, and that intelligent people are banding themselves together, into societies of research, not to find out if these phenomena be true, but to understand the laws by which they may be perfected, indicates that the world is aroused to-day with the desire of denying with me that these spiritual gifts have been discontinued. There is as marked similarity between the phenomena of to-day and that of Jesus as there is between the phenomena of Jesus and that attending the prophets, as written in the Old Testament. The development of the people, their change of concept relative to duty, their

associations with each other, socially, politically and religiously, indicate a similarity and striking comparison. A
striking evidence of similarity might be sarcastically referred to in the fact that we are accused, as was Jesus,
of being possessed of devils. That these phenomena are
similar is because they are in the world for the self-same
purpose—to convince people. There is an attempt on the
part of the religion existing, to destroy those who purport
to possess these spiritual gifts, as there was an attempt
to destroy the prophets, the Apostles, and those who
claimed to possess these spiritual gifts. They went on
and proclaimed their gospel and declared that it was for
all the earth, and that all people would come to an understanding. They have never yet come to an understanding. They seem to be getting farther from each other
with each passing year, growing farther apart because
of doctrinal points.   Why should all of these spiritual
gifts have been withdrawn? They were sent to convince.
Did they convince all? They evidently did not impress
the Jews very much. They have never yet, as a people,
accepted an intimation of the teachings of Jesus. They
evidently have not completed their mission in the way of
convincing people. Were they simply given to the Apostles for the perfecting of the faith? Where is the perfected faith? Certain Scriptures have been read to you
and declared to indicate the perfecting of the faith. That
does not make them so; but it places them in your hands
to determine whether they are or no. The self-same passages have been re-read and your interpretation has been
solicited as to whether or not they are indications of the
perfecting of the faith. I do not presume to stand before
you as denying this proposition, and tell you what shall
be your decision. I depend upon your individual intelli-

gence. I do not ask you to follow me in your careful search of these Scriptures, upon which we have agreed to base our reasoning, but I do insist that you search them carefully. Continue, even before them, into such records and scriptures as preceded them, not limiting the field in which you shall search for your evidence; but the broad field of human research. Look carefully to the history of various religions and note how they have grown up to the principles of Modern Spiritualism, an organization which it is my pleasure, aye, my delight, to represent, and watch its growth and its unfoldment. Through its influence I deny that these spiritual gifts have been discontinued. In the declaration of principles made by these Spiritualists I want you to carefully note that one of the six declarations refers to spiritual phenomena. I want to disabuse your minds, if you may have heretofore concluded that spiritualism is naught but phenomena, that it deals with the broad principles of life. It defines itself on the idea of Deity, and I have placed paralled with our declaration ("We believe in infinite intelligence") that beautiful oration, that classical discourse of Paul, when, on Mars Hill, he said, "That Unknown God which ye worship ignorantly declare I unto you." We have declared ourselves firmly as to our position concerning religion, based upon the highest concepts of man's duty to man, and thereby his worship of God in all nations. Surely, you cannot fail, my intelligent and respected jurors, living in a land the government of which is made of, by and for the people (strictly man made, recognizing no God), to appreciate a universal religion that denies the withdrawal of these spiritual gifts, that have come down through the history of all religions of the world as credentials of the presence of Almighty God; as evidences of the presence of the spirit of the Most High, through these spiritual gifts, endowing the children of men with the power to discern spirits, to receive from the spiritual world messages of comfort and strength, that will increase the usefulness of his efforts. Confident that you will rejoice in the existence of a religion that is an echo of the Golden Rule, that has sounded for time immemorial down through the ages; confident that you will rejoice at a religion that emphatically denies that these spiritual gifts have been withdrawn from among the children of men, that they might partake of the manna of heaven, the waters of eternal life, and drink and be athirst no more, I leave this proposition before you. Your attention is invited to carefully read the vast amount of evidence of the existence of these phenomena that we declare unto you in honesty are the continuation of these self-same spiritual gifts. Inform yourselves concerning them and endeavor to so develop your individual powers with which you are endowed that you can prove these to yourself by trying the spirits, as Paul admonished his followers. Realizing that the unfoldment, development, to perfection, of the human race, depends upon the conception of truth in each individual, I do not presume to declare that unless you accept my denial of the cessation of these spiritual gifts, there is going to be any especial visitation of God's displeasure upon you, but rather that since in all of his revealed word he has declared that we could prove our love to him only by our love to each other, we must love one another.

I thank you.

TIME.

Reported and transcribed by H. B. Hopps, Reporter from 410 B. Avenue, Lawton, Okla.

AUTOBIOGRAPHIES

J. W. RING.

In Bradford county, Pennsylvania, on September seventh, eighteen hundred and seventy-six, John Willis Ring was born to Reuben French and Helen Mynet (nee Nickerson) Ring. In September, 1884, the family moved to Kingman County, Kansas. Upon starting, the mother took John with her to see a Medium, who, while in the superior state, stated that John would be a public speaker for Spiritualism before he was twenty-one years of age. One day during the summer of 1885, in Kansas, while playing alone on the prairie, grandpa Nickerson (who passed to spirit life in Pennsylvania) appeared to John and gave a message for Helen, promising to "Always" be a spirit attendant to John. In 1886 the family moved to Jasper County, Missouri. In Avilla, on December 1, 1889, mother passed to spirit-life. Although John's religious teaching had been in orthodox Sunday-schools, where modern spiritual gifts were denied or declared to be of the devil, he saw his mother's spirit born into the "World Beautiful." She became his constant attendant, as she had been in physical life. Clairvoyance was followed by trance, when Sunrise, an Indian who had been commissioned to guard him from birth, manifested. Soon a "band of spirit guides" was formed; by their advice father and son sojourned to Paris, Texas, where, with Capt. S. J. Wright, Col. E. L. Dohoney and Mrs. Stella Pollard, "circles" were held regularly for more than two years.   Father insisted that John be conscious of the words which fell from his lips while entranced, and inspiration followed.   In September, 1896, the "guides" directed their Medium to Galveston, Texas. In the family of George A. Wilson his powers were discovered, and he was engaged as Speaker of The Spiritualist Society of Galveston, Texas, which position he held for nearly ten years, leaving only when the broader lecture field claimed him.

August 1, 1897, John W. Ring was ordained a minister of the gospel of Spiritualism.   During his ministrations as Speaker of the Galveston Society (which owns a magnificent temple at the corner of 14th and Post Office streets), he served as Secretary and President, at different times, of the Texas State Association of Spiritualists, also National Superintendent of Lyceum Work, appointed by the National Spiritualist Association, with headquarters at 600 Pennsylvania Ave., S. E., Washington, D. C.

"Upon visiting my mother's grave some months after her transition, a feeling of loneliness possessed me.   Later, through the mediumship of John Disler (no one present possibly knowing that I had visited my mother's grave), my mother said, 'John, promise that you will never visit my grave.   I want no slab of stone to mark the resting place of my 'deserted house,' but a living monument.   You, my boy, shall take the 'glad tidings of great joy' which comes through this Spiritual Philosophy to the children of earth.   Each life you cheer will be a stone in the monument which I desire.'   How sweet and inspiring such words from the lips of mother as she stands on the shores of LIFE!   So all who pass from physical life unfold into USEFUL 'ministering spirits' to guard and guide the children of earth.

"The world to which my earthly friends have journeyed is the real world, and amid the scenes of experience and discipline through which I am passing, their spiritual presence, to guide and assist, is as the brightest sunshine.

"Just to make men happy, healthy and prosperous, that they may discover the Kingdom of Heaven (that PEACE that passeth understanding) and live USEFUL lives; thus by service to each other unfolding the innate love, which through activity brings each and every child of the infinite into complete and perfect at-one-ment with the POWER OF GOOD."

J. W. CHISM.

The subject of this sketch was born in Comanche Co., Texas, in 1865, April 1.

Comanche county, at that time, was in the "far west," and the red men often made raids into the neighborhood to kill, plunder and steal.

At the age of 27 his father, Jehu M. Chism, was married to Sallie Hackworth, who was at the time 17 years old. To this marriage were born six children— five boys and one girl.

Jehu M. Chism, father of J. W., moved to Texas, from Mississippi, in 1853. He settled first in Washington county, but in 1856 he moved to Comanche, then known as "Mercer's Colony." In this county he served nine years in the frontier service against the Indians. The subject of this sketch was born during the last year of his stay in the west.

Jehu M. Chism and Sallie, his wife, became Christians in early life, and all of their six children obeyed the gospel in youth, save Geo. W., who was about 23 when he obeyed the gospel.

My mother taught school in her own house from the time that I was two years old until I was about five, and I have often heard her say that when I was four years old I could spell nearly every word in the old "blue-back" speller; yet I did not know one letter from another when I would see it.

My first memories are of this school. But in my growing up I was cut off from school privileges, my only schooling being about fifteen months, scattered along from the time I was five until I was about sixteen.

Of the things which made a lasting impression on me in my early life, are the following: My father's strict honesty and devotion to God, and my mother's devotion and godly life. Mother always taught her children that the Bible was true, and was man's sole guide, and urged them to read it for themselves. She was a well educated woman for her time, which gave me an advantage in home study. During the whole of my youth, up to the time of my mother's death, when I was nineteen, I spent my leisure time in study. My hours for sleep and rest were often encroached upon in this way.

In January, 1877, father moved to Stephens county, locating in the valley of the Clear Fork of the Brazos. The first death in my father's house had just occurred. My sister, who was the wife of B. D. Williams, died on December 26, 1876. She left two children, C. B. and Docia A., who are both still living. This death was a great shock to me. but as the months passed I became reconciled to the bereavement.

We erected a log house in the Miller valley, where we remained until November, 1883. During this period I attended three schools. The first was taught by John Simpson, and was held in an old style picket house, made of split poles, one end of each pole being stuck in the ground to make it stand upright. It was covered with clapboard roofing. My next school was when I was about fourteen or fifteen. Miss Annie Love (now Mrs. Add Sloan) was my teacher. I went 35 days to her, during a three months' term. I was very much devoted

to her, and have always attributed what success I have
made in life partly to her influence. Her last words to
me, the evening that school closed, have been a stimulus
to me in the hard trials of life. I can see her earnest,
shining, smiling face now, as it was then, when she
clasped me by the hand to bid me goodbye. Holding
my hand firmly, and looking me squarely in the face,
she said, "Willborn, my boy, do not let your studies
cease. You will never, perhaps, have the privilege of
much schooling, but you can study at home. Never say
fail; never give up. Do not spend your hours idly, but
put in every hour you can in study. You will yet make
a man. I see it in you, and I count on you becoming a
man of worth." It was there that I resolved, under the
influence of that sweet face, to be worthy of her confidence. Ever since then, in the hour of trial, her words
have re-echoed in my ears. My last school was the
next year, when I attended a five months' school taught
by Tyler Crawford. I attended but 51 days, being kept
from more regular attendance by work at home.

After this, until 1884, there was nothing in my life
more eventful than throwing a lasso, catching cat-fish,
killing wild turkeys and riding bronchos. In the fall
of 1883 my father moved again to Comanche county, and
we settled on Rush Creek, about three miles below the
McGuire old Gin, where Downing now stands. In
April, 1884, my mother died of pneumonia. Our crop
was overflowed and lost, and this completely broke us up.

In 1888, I think it was, I went to my brother's, in
Young county. He persuaded me to study photography,
which I did, under him. That same fall I opened a
gallery, taking my youngest brother as partner. At
this profession I worked until 1890. In April of that

year I met Miss Fannie L. Campbell, and on the 4th day of May we were married—on the twentieth day from the day we first met. Soon after we were married we moved to Wichita county. But a drought cut the crops short, and this move broke me up. In April, 1891, I took my wife back to her father's home. On the fourth Sunday in that month, her father persuaded me to preach my first sermon.

For about eight months my wife remained at her father's house, and I worked out from there, making photos from house to house, and thus raising enough money to open a nice gallery again. Accordingly, I opened up at Pilot Point, and as soon as I was in working shape, sent for my wife. When she arrived, I had half a loaf of bread, one pound of bacon and ten cents. While my wife was at her father's home our first child was born, and was at this time six months old. But the next day I did some work, for which I collected $5.00. That encouraged me; but that night fire destroyed all that I owned. Some one stole the $5.00, and I was left among strangers, with myself, wife and child to care for, and with but ten cents!

It was in the summer of 1893 that I held my first protracted meeting. I preached ten sermons (all I knew), and baptized ten people. For this I was paid $8.00. My next meeting, the same summer, I baptized two, and received $35.00, which seemed like a fortune to me.

In the autumn of this same year I held my third meeting. I baptized one, and they gave me $45.00. At this place I so stirred up the Primitive Baptists that I had to meet J. G. Webb in debate in February of the following year. At this debate I arranged to hold three meetings in Collins county the following summer, at

Blue Ridge, at Fayburg and at Bloomdale, and also one near Trenton. It was at the Blue Ridge meeting that the sectarian people became so incensed at me that in September they set a trap and caught me, causing me to pay a fine of $25.00 for disturbing public worship. The fine, with costs, lawyers' fees, etc., amounted to $271.30. This, with my burn-out of the previous year, put me in debt about $600.00. In the autumn of this year I bought a photo gallery at Lewisville, and went to work, preaching as I could. In this way I succeeded in paying about $300 of what I owed. The next year the brethren assured me that if I would drop all else, and give myself entirely to preaching, they would support me.

I moved to Dublin, where I lived for one year and three months. It was there that my finances again fell short, and I began to write life insurance. I moved to Thorp Spring, where I remained a little more than four years. Then I took a contract, covering Oklahoma and Indian Territory, with the Wisconsin Life, for which I worked for two years. This work making it necessary for me to live in Oklahoma, I settled at Norman. But my wife's health failed in Oklahoma, and she contracted consumption. Therefore I resigned my contract with the insurance company and returned to Texas, locating at Gorman, where we remained a little over a year. I quit writing insurance, and determined to devote myself wholly to the work of my Master. This was the desire of my wife. In spite of the return to Texas, she continued to fail until August 21, 1906, when, at 6 A. M., at the home of Brother H. W. Lock in De Leon, Texas, my beloved "brown eyes" passed from the trials of this world into that sweet rest that remains for the people of God. Thank God for the Christian's hope!

A purer woman, I am sure, never lived; a more devoted wife, mother and Christian could not be found. She was always in her place in the house of God, and always ready to make any sacrifice. She sleeps in the cemetery at De Leon, where I hope to be laid to rest, by her side, when the Master calls me.

The death of my wife was a hard blow. I was left with six children. As my wife's last request had been that they should not be separated, I took them with me for a time. Then my sister's daughter, Docia A. Payne, wrote for me to bring them to her, and for some months she cared for them. Desiring to place them in school, I arranged to remove to Denton. But shortly after we moved, our second boy, Jack, was stricken with rheumatism, and the lady with whom he was staying, fearing he had consumption, was unwilling to keep him longer. So, for a time, I scattered the children, taking Jack with me, until I saw that traveling was doing him no good.

In the meantime, I had met Miss Burts Kemper, of Angelina county, Texas, and had decided to make her my wife at a later date. But when the lady was unwilling to keep the children longer, I wrote Burts, telling her of my condition, and she agreed to marry me at once. March 2, 1907, we were married in the Christian chapel at Homer, Brother T. W. Phillips officiating. Burts has proven to be a companion indeed, and a mother to my motherless little ones.

Shortly after we returned home, I placed Jack under the care of an Osteopath. We thought he was improving, so I went to Anson for a meeting. But on the night of April 11, 1907, the Angel of Death called my little one to the home of the blest. His body rests beside that of his mother. He was always a "mama boy," and he did not long survive her.

In all, my life has been a stormy one, but I have been blessed in many ways. Especially was I blessed with a pure, true and devoted wife, who was willing to make sacrifices for her Master. If any glory is due to me for my work in the Master's kingdom, may He give it all to her. And if any glory shall accrue to me, henceforth, I lay it all at the feet of my present wife, who has so nobly stepped into this sacrifice of a preacher's wife, to care for my babies and help me raise them for God and for glory. And when it comes ours to be laid to rest, I hope I may be laid beside my "brown-eyed Fannie," and that my Burts, my faithful and devoted wife, may in her time be laid beside me, that our bodies may rest together until the summons to "come forth." And that we may all be re-united in the glory land, without the loss of one, is my prayer to God. J. W. CHISM.